ALIGN & EXECUTE

IT'S ALL ABOUT THE MONEY...
BUT IT'S NOT!

BY
RICHARD H. TYSON

Align & Execute
It's All About the Money…But it's Not!

TYSON, RICHARD H., Author
ALIGN & EXECUTE
RICHARD H. TYSON

Published by:
CEObuilder Publishing
Orem, UT 84097
CEObuilder.com

In Association With:
Elite Online Publishing
63 East 11400 South
Suite #230
Sandy, UT 84070
EliteOnlinePublishing.com

ISBN: 978-1-961801-63-9 (eBook)
ISBN: 978-1-961801-76-9 (Paperback)

Library of Congress Control Number: 2025900330

BUS025000
BUS075000
BUS020000

QUANTITY PURCHASES: Schools, companies, professional groups, clubs, and other organizations may qualify for special terms when ordering quantities of this title. For information, email rich@ceobuilder.com.

Table of Contents

Preface: How I Made an Ash of Myself—and The Sad Saga
of the Stinky Fish v

Introduction to *Align & Execute*. xix

Chapter 1: Therefore, What?. 1

Chapter 2: Building a Compelling Cause. 25

Chapter 3: Moving from your WHY to WHAT YOU DO. 53

Chapter 4: The Principles that Govern Your Life, Your Work,
and Your Company. 65

Chapter 5: We Know We Need a Compelling Vision, So What is
Keeping Us from Creating and Pursuing One? 105

Chapter 6: A Compelling Purpose Begins With a Person–
One Person: YOU!. 133

Chapter 7: Peeling Your Onion–The Model. 143

Chapter 7A: Your PATHOS 149

Chapter 7B: AUTHENTICITY: A Focus on Yourself. 173

Chapter 7C: Your Personal CAUSE–And the Logic That Provides
Its Credibility. 183

Chapter 7D: ETHOS–The Beliefs & Values That Set Forth How
 You Will Behave in Pursuit of Your Purpose
 and Mission 237

Chapter 7E: RESOLVE–With Your Purpose, Mission, and
 Values Articulated, It is Time to Define & Commit
 to WHAT YOU WILL DO! 263

Chapter 8: Transforming Your Personal Vision into A Vision
 for Your Enterprise. 291

Chapter 9: *It's Time to Open Your Kimono*–Sharing Your Vision
 and Your Emerging Strategies with Your Advocates—
 and Your Adversaries 319

Afterword 343

Acknowledgments. 345

Appendix #1 347

Appendix #2 353

Appendix #3 379

Appendix #4: 381

How I Made an Ash of Myself–and The Sad Saga of the Stinky Fish

In the spring of 1972, I received a letter from the Harvard Graduate School of Business accepting me into their MBA program. I had worked diligently on my undergraduate studies to get accepted and I was *very proud* that I had achieved my goal. *Please note the extra emphasis on the words: very proud.*

I told my bride of two years that once I finished my studies at Harvard we would never again worry about money (having lived in the relative poverty of being undergraduate college students). I felt I had won the "golden ticket" and that the gate to great wealth was about to open. Someday, in the not too distant future, I would be a millionaire. **To summarize my motives at the time,** *it was all about the money!*

I got a bit of a rude awakening at my graduation from Harvard. It was a turbulent time in U.S. history; mortgage rates were over 20%, and my starting salary at a Fortune 100 company was not the big paycheck I had anticipated. My wife, a toddler, and a newborn baby, and I moved to Southern California where we unloaded ourselves into a tiny apartment and greeted more days of belt-tightening and careful budgeting.

Nonetheless, I was a newly minted Harvard MBA, and I felt sure that I had now entered the world that would lead to wealth. I just needed to stay on the path, right?

I gave my best efforts at my first job and accomplished a number of good outcomes for my employer. I was their "fair-haired boy," but before long I became impatient. An executive recruitment firm contacted me with the opportunity to turn around a failing small town newspaper in Idaho. It paid more money and it would get me and my family out of Los Angeles (not a place my wife and I wanted to raise our children). We could afford to buy a home! Not wealth yet, but we were surely on the path.

I had just settled into this new opportunity when Mother Nature intervened. On May 18, 1980, Mount St. Helens erupted, covering the Pacific Northwest with a thick layer of volcanic ash--and serving up what I thought was an outstanding entrepreneurial opportunity. I had marveled at the guys who had made millions of dollars selling Pet Rocks, and now I was sure that many people would jump at the chance to buy vials of authentic Mount St. Helens ash.

Although my area had a slight dusting of ash, the news reported that Yakima, Washington had tons of the stuff all over town. That led me to take a day off from my work to drive to Yakima. I found that the reports were accurate; the ash was everywhere. I rented a storage unit and literally collected my product from the streets adjacent to the unit, filling 20 large garbage bags. I prepared about a hundred or so plastic bottles, then locked up the remaining "raw inventory" in the storage unit and headed for home.

It took a few days to get labels printed for the bottles, print some informative brochures describing the eruption, and run an ad in the National Enquirer tabloid. My total investment at this point was only a couple of thousand dollars, and I was sure that there would be an incredible demand for my product.

Well, incredible was a mite overstated. I did get some orders, but fortunately, not many. I say *fortunately* because in shipping the product, the Postal Service was a bit rough in handling the padded pouches in which I shipped them. The recipients of my product opened the pouches to find a mixture of ash and broken plastic. Of course, I had to make this error right, so my investment increased. I had to replace the plastic containers with heavier glass and pack them in sturdier shipping boxes. My costs went up substantially.

By the time I had corrected my errors, I was now in the hole over $4,000. I kept my ads running in the Enquirer, hoping that demand would grow, but that proved to produce a dwindling return. It seemed that the interest in volcanic ash was a fleeting thing. I finally realized that this was not to be a Pet Rock success story, and wrote the whole thing off as a "learning experience."

The story, however, doesn't end there. After a couple of months, the owner of the Yakima storage unit called me. Having decided to move on, I had forgotten to send a check to him for the rental. He was pretty terse with me, saying that if I didn't immediately make payment, he would confiscate the contents of the unit. In spite of my financial losses, I hadn't lost my sense of humor, so I suggested that it would be best if he took possession of the things stored in the unit, telling him that if he was not satisfied with that, I would send him a check. He agreed to inspect the unit, and decide.

My phone rang again within the hour. The storage unit owner was not amused, to say the least. "That unit is full of the same damn stuff that is still on the ground everywhere here!," he said. "What were you going to do with it??"

I then shared my entrepreneurial journey with him, ending with my commitment to send him a check for the past due amount plus an extra month, if he would save me a trip back to Yakima by disposing of the ash. At this point, he regained his sense of humor and chuckled, "Well," he said, "this is a story I can tell my grandkids...you certainly made an ash of yourself!"

By the late 1980's, my entrepreneurial confidence had rebounded, and my track record as a young businessman was, what I thought to be, impeccable. I had successfully directed two turn-around situations, and had worked in corporate finance, marketing, manufacturing, and general management positions. Once again, I felt *I was destined to succeed!*.

However, I was impatient, still anxious to make my fortune, and I didn't feel like just working for someone else would get it done. So, I started actively looking, once again, for what today we would call a "side hustle." I really had no focus in this pursuit; I just put my ear to the ground, hoping that I would find a great, profitable venture.

Somehow, some friends and I discovered that the Japanese fishing industry had largely overlooked the rich fisheries of Micronesia. As I studied more about this, it became clear that if an American company wanted to import fresh fish from the Pacific, Micronesia represented a great opportunity. I had connections throughout the South Pacific, as well as some interested potential customers for seafood--restaurants in the Western United States.

In researching my opportunity, I contacted several of the fine seafood restaurants in Salt Lake City, Utah. They assured me that if I could deliver fresh sushi-grade tuna, along with snapper, and other high-demand seafood from the South Pacific, they would be interested. I consulted with other contacts who assured me that letter-of-credit financing could be easily obtained. Further, I chatted with just about anyone who would listen, telling them of my exciting enterprise. My enthusiasm was over-the-top—and no one suggested that I might not have asked all the important questions. They all told me what I wanted to hear… *I was destined to succeed!*

I had supreme confidence in my ability to launch this business. However, to do so, I needed an experiment to show that the supply chain could be successfully managed. That experiment, I determined, would be a first shipment from Micronesia to Utah. If that worked, I could surely expand that supply chain to other cities throughout the western United States.

Although I was willing to put my savings on the line, I knew I had to have additional financial backing. I had two business partners, but they had even less money than I. However, one of their fathers expressed interest in helping us. His money made it possible for me to travel to Micronesia to develop the connections I needed there. I was excited, but now I wasn't just risking my money, I had an investor to please. While that made me a bit nervous, I felt that my probabilities of success were very high!

As the day to depart for Micronesia got close, I became a bit apprehensive. Was my enthusiasm for this opportunity overwhelming my better judgment on how to make sure that this worked out? I had done all of the Harvard MBA stuff (I thought) that I needed to; I had developed pro forma financial projections based on feedback I had gotten from a handful of high-end seafood restaurants in Salt Lake. They had assured me that the price I could command for prime cuts of tuna, snapper, and sea bass would bring me a handsome profit. Of course, I would have to prove that I could deliver…

So…I soon found myself in Micronesia. The trip was truly epic! I met with fishermen, who assured me that they would be able to deliver sushi-grade Ahi tuna in significant quantities, along with the other types of fish my restaurateurs would demand.

Then, as if by chance, something amazing happened… I visited a banker at the Bank of Guam on the island of Pohnpei who had served many years ago in the military with my father. That seemed to be just the contact I needed! He introduced me to the governor of Micronesia, who made it clear that they were very anxious to do business with me. After that, I met with the folks at the Continental Airlines office who assured me that they could handle the logistics of getting fresh fish, on ice, from Micronesia to Honolulu and Los Angeles, and on to Salt Lake City without thawing out. My confidence was at an all-time high!

There was a bit of a hiccup when the fishing companies with whom I was negotiating let me know that Japanese seafood importers also wanted their catch. If I wanted their commitment, I needed to act quickly—or the fish would go to the Japanese. Adding to the urgency, the flights out of Micronesia were only scheduled for twice a week—and my flight home needed to be the next day.

Nevertheless, I had the assurances I felt I needed—but no contracts as yet. Even so, I liked the people I had met with—and they all seemed trustworthy. As for financing, while the contacts were all arranged, I had yet to finalize those arrangements. The Micronesian bankers assured me that we could get everything completed remotely, but for my initial transaction, it was clear that I was "on my own dime." So… with a bit of trepidation, but great faith that my initial shipment would be the success I needed to move forward, I put the initial investment on my credit card, shook hands with those whom I assumed were to be my partners—and jumped on a flight home.

The first shipment of "fine fish" was scheduled for three weeks after I arrived home in Utah, on a hot, sunny day in July. As the day approached, my nervousness mounted. I placed a call to Micronesia; they assured me that my seafood would indeed leave the island of Chuuk on the agreed upon date. I relaxed...right up to the time I was contacted by the airline to inform me that the Continental flight from Honolulu to Los Angeles had missed its connection to the Salt Lake leg. My crate of "fish on ice" would be a day late! I stressed to the airline people that the folks in LA needed to find a cool (preferably cold) place for my shipment to spend the next 24 hours. Having arranged for the "grand opening" of my shipment at the Salt Lake airport that day, I called the seafood restaurateurs to reschedule for the next day.

The following day, my crate of fish sat alongside the tarmac at Salt Lake City, profusely dripping a fluid that had an obnoxious fishy odor. It would have been bad enough if I was the only one to witness this, but I was joined by my prospective customers. Well, I thought, maybe once we opened the package, it wouldn't be so bad...

What we witnessed with the grand opening was not sushi-grade tuna. Indeed, none of what we discovered was what I had ordered. At best, it was a fine grade of cat food! In those few moments, I realized that my seafood enterprise was done! One of the restaurateurs summed it up: "Nice try, young man; we won't be buying anything from you today—and probably never."

I loaded my crate onto a truck and brought it home. Not knowing what to do with it, my wife and I emptied our large freezer and crammed it to the gills with stinky fish. I then went to work trying to get someone to take responsibility for my disaster. The airline shrugged it off. *You should have insured it,* they said. They were right. I contacted the fishery on Chuuk. Their response was even more useless. They said that they had been abused in a prior relationship with an American businessman, so this made us even. It didn't matter to them that I was not the one who had abused them. But they were now more than willing to send what I had ordered on the next shipment. *Just send more money!* I contacted the governor of Micronesia. He expressed regret, but said, *without a contract, there's nothing we can do!*

I realized that my destiny on this deal was not success, it was abject failure. The last thing I wanted to do was visit the freezer in my basement to be reminded of my folly. Which was the last mistake I made on this ill-fated venture. Within a few weeks, my freezer died. It took a while, but the odor that began to rise into our living area finally alerted me that the fish nightmare had re-asserted itself. Now, it was threatening my marriage! Fortunately, my wife just sentenced me to several awful days scooping fish slime out of the freezer into the garbage. Although our outdoor trash cans attracted tons of flies for the rest of the summer, my seafood saga had mercifully ended.

So...what were the lessons I learned from these two high-tuition entrepreneurial failures? And, why in the world would I share these two stories at the beginning of a book on the keys to business success?

There are five lessons and primary reasons for starting with these stories:

First, the danger of hubris. These experiences provided me with a deep understanding that I needed to cultivate a balance between self-confidence and humility. Some years after the stinky fish saga, I was privileged to meet and work with Daniel K. Judd, a PhD psychologist and Brigham Young University professor, who introduced me to what he called *counterfeit analyses.*

Counterfeit Analyses show that what often appear to be opposite principles are, in fact, complementary and should coexist. Over the years since working closely with Dan, I have often asked CEOs and other leaders if they felt it was more important to be confident or humble. Most answered very much as I did in the early days of my career: *clearly, confidence was the more important attribute.* A few recognized a need for some humility to provide a counterweight to their confidence, but even fewer felt that humility was the more important virtue.

With a myopic emphasis on confidence, the likelihood of failures in my early entrepreneurial experiences was quite high. Why? Because my confidence became counterfeited into pride, arrogance, and hubris. It created blindspots for me that a more humble, open-minded, eager-to-learn attitude might have allowed me to discern. It led me to seek out only the answers that I wanted to hear from people who would feed my *confirmation bias*. I bought into the counterfeit of confidence—a total lack of humility. Of course, there is also a counterfeit to humility. Too much humility counterfeits into fear, trepidation, self-deprecation, and a total lack of confidence.

It is important to note that the counterfeits of confidence and humility are, indeed, opposites. However, the combination of confidence and humility is a powerful mindset that increases the probability of success. This was a hard and painful lesson that I needed to learn, but I am grateful to have learned it.

The following graphic illustrates the use of Counterfeit Analysis portraying this important insight:

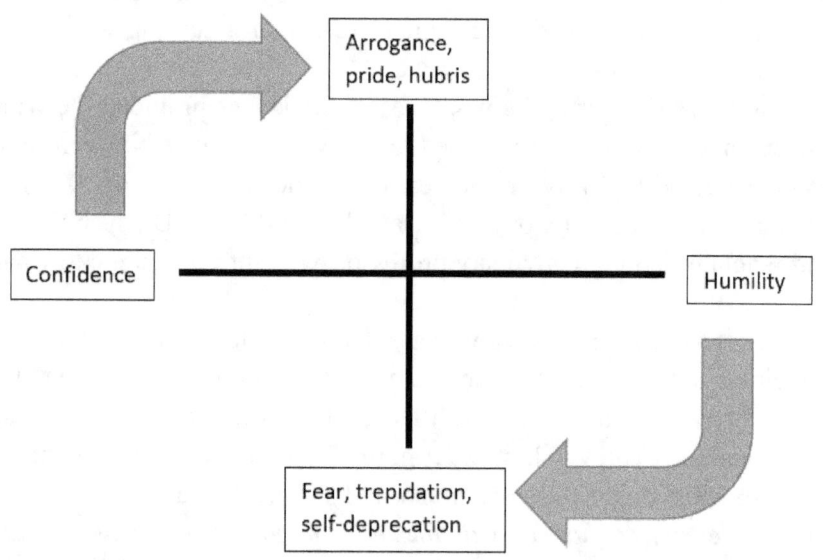

Lesson One: *It is important for a leader to exhibit both confidence AND humility and maintain an appropriate balance in this dichotomy.*

I also learned a second important lesson: business is an extreme sport. One of my favorite avocations is canyoneering. I love getting deep into a slot canyon surrounded by thousand foot vertical walls and hiking into wilderness areas where few people go. To get into such places often requires rappelling, sometimes even multiple rappels. These experiences have provided great adventures that have been a joy in my life. That said, canyoneering is an extreme sport. Every year, people die doing it. Fortunately, the fatality rate isn't terribly high, but the risks of injury or death are always part of it.

The key to being a successful participant in this sport is preparation. And preparation always includes careful consideration of the gear required including such things as ropes, harnesses, helmets, and hardware--as well as wetsuits and special footwear. It involves testing the equipment to ensure it is in good condition. It includes budgeting for new or replacement gear. It requires that each participant be tested on the fundamentals of canyoneering, including the rigging required for safe rappels, even if they've done it many times before. Further, it should include study of the best information about the given canyon from others who have done it. This means reading guidebook information, and seeking the most recent first-hand guidance available from rangers and other adventurers. It also requires accurate current weather information. Inclement weather in many sports is an inconvenience; in canyoneering, it can be deadly. Most importantly, preparation should include making sure that you are part of a team of fellow adventurers who have the skills and the mindset you can trust.

With this type of preparation, I have always come back alive (a bit obvious, since I am writing this). More importantly, my partners and I have guided others on such adventures, and *they* have always come back alive.

So, back to the extreme sport of business. First, I will acknowledge that participating in this sport rarely has the risk of dying--at least not immediately. However, in one respect it is more dangerous than canyoneering. The odds of business failure are staggeringly high. Most experts agree that, at best, only one or two out of five startups make it to their second birthday. My own early entrepreneurial experiences, of course, corroborated that! However, the story doesn't get much better for the 20% or so that made it to age 2. Over the life of their businesses, only about one out of those five achieve consistent profitability. And of that small group (around 4-8% of original startups), only about one out of five were ultimately able to harvest their business in the form of a wealth-creating buyer. That comes to less than 1 percent of the original startups!

My notable failures were certainly significant for me, but not so much for anyone else. I am simply part of a very large fraternity of those who started a new venture and saw it fail. The tuition I paid to become a member of that fraternity was high, but tuition is wasted only when you don't learn new things that will bless you with greater success in the future. I learned the absolute necessity of preparation, and I have applied what I've learned consistently since those early failures. My preparation became the basis for another use of Counterfeit Analysis:

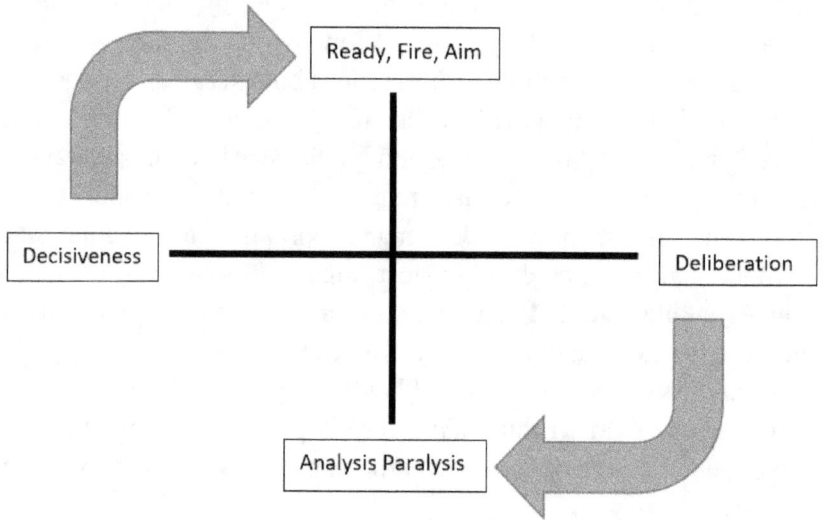

I learned that my preparation needed to be *deliberate*, even plodding. I needed to ask myself the same types of questions that I employ in preparing to rappel into a canyon. What kind of equipment do I need? What investment is needed? What are the inherent risks in this venture? Is there a strong market for what I want to sell? What skills are necessary for success? What research is needed? Who are the experts in this industry that I should talk to? Who might coach me? Who will question my answers? Who is on my team today? Who will I need in the future? Do my strengths align with this opportunity? If not, how will I bridge the gap? What weaknesses do I need to overcome? And, most importantly, am I truly motivated to do this? Does it align with my personal life purpose, mission, and values?

Obviously, deliberation has lots of questions to be answered, and as you can see, it can disintegrate into the counterfeit of Analysis Paralysis. This is why it is important to balance your deliberation with decisiveness. That said, don't make the mistake of defining your decision as "a go" before finishing the deliberative preparation. That very often leads to the counterfeit of Ready, Fire, Aim--or even Fire, Fire, Fire! The key is to *be decisive in your deliberations*. Carefully set your agenda for preparation; then work that agenda decisively.

Had I been more deliberate in my volcanic ash venture, I likely would not have pursued it. I was definitely in Ready, Fire, Aim mode. Had I been more deliberate in my seafood importing business, I might have built a viable and successful company.

Lesson Two: *Being decisive is critical to getting a venture moving, however, deliberate planning is critical to lasting success.*

The third lesson is what Harvard Business School professor, Bill George, has called Crucible Experiences. In his book, *Discover Your True North,* he states that most leaders are shaped by severe trials in their lives, which he calls *crucibles.* He goes on to say, "Psychologist Abraham Maslow found that tragedy and trauma were the most important human learning experiences leading to self-actualization. Crucibles enable people to learn life is uncertain, and they have limited control. This new reality empowers individuals to challenge old assumptions and understand they must demonstrate personal agency to deal with their world. Crucibles often launch leaders into despair, crisis, and doubt. In the midst of a crucible, pain and suffering may overwhelm leaders. With sufficient resilience, leaders emerge from despair and become open to introspection that can catalyze major breakthroughs in their development."[1]

---

[1] *Discover Your True North,* Bill George, page 57.

In retrospect, I don't see my entrepreneurial misfires as severe trials, but they did cost me a lot of money--and more importantly, they significantly undermined my self-confidence for a while. I was certainly traumatized, but the trauma was ultimately a blessing; it led to introspection. It brought me to understand the lessons that I am sharing here, and it also led me to a deep desire to build those lessons into a career of helping other business leaders avoid the landmines that I had so energetically stepped on. In many ways, these disasters set in motion my company, CEObuilder®, and my mission to help good leaders become great, and great leaders become exceptional.

Lesson Three: *We often learn the most from failure... but only if we are willing to learn the lessons it can teach us. We should see failure as a gift of knowledge and wisdom.*

The fourth lesson I learned is the critical need for the guidance of others who have "been there and done that." I needed someone to coach me, to provide a listening ear and the willingness to challenge my assumptions. You see, *I didn't know what I didn't know.* I had many blindspots that needed to be exposed, but in my youthful naivete, I didn't recognize that flaw--and it proved to be a *fatal flaw* to both of my early entrepreneurial ventures. I desperately needed a coach – I just didn't realize it. In the years since, I have learned that all of us need a coach, someone who will "question our answers."

One of my most important introspective insights was the following:

Your best friend will tell you when your fly is down.

On neither of my ventures, did I seek the input of those who would challenge me with hard questions. Instead, I sought those who would look past any flaws in my thinking. I wanted congratulations on my brilliance rather than constructive criticism. As mentioned above, I was guilty of *confirmation bias,* of seeking only the answers I wanted to hear. My fly was definitely down, but I really didn't want anyone to tell me.

This lesson led me to a mindset that has governed me ever since: I need to consistently seek—and empower—those who will challenge my thinking. Most importantly, I need to balance my confidence with humility—and my decisiveness with deliberation. Had I done these things, I would have built a better strategy for success. Indeed, I might even be importing seafood today!

<u>Lesson Four</u>: *Just asking a friend or family for advice often creates a false sense of security, as they are the ones who typically encourage us regardless of our weaknesses. A coach, however, is a knowledgeable person who will guide us in ways that will increase our performance and lead to success.*

The fifth and last lesson I learned focuses on the <u>central role of aligning and executing</u> for success.

Over the years I have dedicated intensive study regarding what successful business leaders do. I have come to understand that while every business is different, *all* business owners, CEOs and entrepreneurs need to have a "core doctrine" to follow. Their job is, by far, the most complex and challenging of any role in business. However, even most who emerge from the world's best business schools generally don't seem to understand that core doctrine. *And, it constitutes the real job description for CEOs.*

That core doctrine is the essence of what I will share with you in this book: *Align & Execute.* In chapter 1, I will introduce you to the CEObuilder® Business Success Pyramid, along with a variety of business models that help CEOs to clearly understand what to do— and when to do it. Our team at CEObuilder® believes that if we create content that gives a clear path for CEO success—and get it out to as many CEOs, business owners, and entrepreneurs as possible, we will ultimately achieve our own Vision of significantly improving the success of CEOs, business owners, and entrepreneurs like you!.

My focus for the past 35 years has been to "build successful CEOs." That includes entrepreneurs, business owners, general managers, and other enterprise leaders. The CEObuilder® *value proposition* (a term to which we will give greater attention in Chapter 3) is to facilitate your success by illuminating your path, such that untested newcomers will clear the early hurdles of leading their businesses, that leaders who pass those initial tests will achieve ongoing success, and that these leaders will become truly exceptional.

Lesson Five: *I not only need a clear view of what my business is all about, but I need to be able to communicate that vision to all the stakeholders of my endeavor. Then, we need to embrace it and make it happen.*

In concluding this preface, I return to where I began. With my education and the opportunities ahead of me, I was destined to be wealthy. It was "all about the money." That was to be the measure of my success. Fortunately, however, a couple of crucible experiences created an epiphany that changed my career path and my life: *I found a higher purpose, one that brought my WHY into focus.*

While financial outcomes are important, they are a result of what we do for others. Put in the proper perspective, they are not the purpose of business, they are a natural consequence of whatever our purpose is. So, the subtitle of Align & Execute is appropriately **"It's All About the Money...BUT IT'S NOT!"**

Welcome to the extreme sport of business!

Introduction to *Align & Execute*

The central premise of this book is that the roles, actions, and behaviors of key stakeholders within your business enterprise must align with your company vision, goals, and strategies. Strong alignment serves as the bridge between your strategy and execution--and alignment is inexorably a function of a series of well-defined, but often overlooked leadership processes, activities, and mindsets. When you understand and effectively utilize them, they will provide you with a proven pathway to alignment, execution, and your desired performance and financial outcomes.

Recent surveys we have conducted with C-level executives have presented us with three major themes addressed in the pages that follow:

1. A pervasive need in most businesses for significant improvement in *aligning* the roles, actions, and behaviors of key stakeholders with the vision, goals, and strategies of their companies.
2. A need for a culture that delivers continuous high *execution* by stakeholders in achieving desired business outcomes.
3. A need for continuous and consistent *financial outcomes*, including return on investment (ROI), cash flow, and growth in the value of the business.

Each chapter of this book will provide a roadmap for you, the business leader, to address these themes.

Consider for a moment the most effective performers in any area of endeavor. What makes them so successful? Observation generally leads to two important insights. First, they display an unmistakable sense of their goal. The winning track athlete knows where the finish line is, and she recognizes that to win, she must get to that finish line before her competitors. Second, she understands the key elements of preparation and execution that are required to win. Simply put, *she knows what to do--and she does it!* This is the basic definition of align and execute.

Sounds simple, doesn't it? Unfortunately, it isn't! The reality is that neither alignment nor execution is easy. The good news, however, is that with the wisdom and experience of others who have successfully navigated the path, it also isn't as hard as it might sometimes seem. That said, many who undertake the process of leading in pursuit of alignment and execution make the mistake of treating it as a one-and-done, check-it-off their To Do List item. To be successful in this endeavor, you must recognize that alignment and execution are essentially an "eternal" quest. There are certainly key elements and standard processes to be considered, but in our dynamic and ever-changing world, you must recognize the importance of being adaptable, and be ready to make mid-course corrections.

Consider the recent coronavirus pandemic. Has this unforeseen and unprecedented situation created any need for reconsideration of your company's purpose, vision, values, strategies, structure, and/or tactics? For some enterprises, the pandemic literally spelled the end of their business. For others, it was inconsequential--and for some, it ushered in a whole new set of opportunities. You may have hunkered down, choosing to cut all nonessential spending just to survive. Or, you may have used the time to increase your efficiencies in anticipation of a profitable return to normal. And you might have even shut down your main venture with an eye to a more appropriate and profitable side-hustle. The point is that a whole new set of strategic and operating assumptions have likely emerged--and no matter how well you've carried out the tasks of alignment and execution in the past, you need to continually work the processes that will deliver results in the days to come.

The first step on this path to alignment and execution is to define your key stakeholders:

- **Leadership--** The role of the CEO, founder, or owner is the single most important element. It is where vision, goals, and strategy begin. If you, the leader, don't have a clear articulation of your purpose, mission, and values, your enterprise will be adrift like a rudderless ship. Execution will be chaotic as your team tries to decipher what to do and why to do it.

  And, if you are the CEO, general manager, or enterprise leader, but not the owner or founder, take heart. This book is also for you. While you likely did not set the original direction of the business, you are responsible to deal with and overcome changes in your market, respond to competitive pressures, technological advances, and even changes in the political climate that were not addressed in the founder's original vision. Your influence and impact on the vision, goals, and strategies of your company are essential!

- **Your Team--** While you, the leader, provide the essential rudder for your enterprise, your team provides the power and locomotion to operationalize your vision. To do this both effectively and efficiently, they must have complete clarity and buy-in regarding your purpose, mission, and values. Further, they must possess the competencies and requisite engagement to fulfill those key foundational goals. Only then will strong alignment and execution take place.

- **Your Organization--** Your organization must provide a highly aligned structure, as well as the processes, roles, and responsibilities that will effectively and efficiently execute your strategies.

- **Your Owners--** While often the CEO is the owner of the enterprise, the leader may not be, or he/she may have only fractional equity. In that case, it is essential that at least a majority of owners support the vision as developed by the CEO and his/her executive team.

As we move forward, it's important that we share a common definition of the Terms used throughout the book:

- *Alignment*

    Alignment is a wonderful, but nebulous concept. We must ask, "With what do we desire to align?

    A typical MBA catch-all generic answer emerged from our surveys: *"You must align your stakeholders with the vision, goals, and strategies of your business."*

    As articulate as this answer is, it leaves a number of unanswered questions:

    ○   What is your vision for your enterprise?
    ○   What are your goals?
    ○   What are your strategies?

    Alignment will remain a nebulous and an impossibly perplexing concept without clear answers to each of these questions.

    As mentioned above, our recent surveys have presented us with three major themes:

    1. A pervasive need in most businesses for significant improvement in *aligning* the roles, actions, and behaviors of key stakeholders with the vision, goals, and strategies of their companies.
    2. A need for a culture that delivers continuous high *execution* by stakeholders in achieving desired business outcomes.
    3. A need for continuous and consistent *financial outcomes*, including return on investment (ROI), cash flow, and growth in the value of the business.

However, the first two responses were actually second and third in their prevalence. The response we received most often was the third: *A need for continuous and consistent financial outcomes, including return on investment (ROI), cash flow, and growth in the value of the business.*

The fact that this was the most critical need expressed by CEOs and business owners is not a surprise, but it is a concern in regard to *cause and effect*. When alignment is defined as simply working to create desired financial outcomes, we fail to recognize that financial outcomes always reside as the ultimate lagging indicators of success. While they represent a critical metric of alignment, a focus on these alone is an oversight that fails to understand the necessity of aligning the other critical elements that will render those financial outcomes. Alignment must clearly define the vision, goals, strategies, and tactics that will ultimately produce consistent and continuous financial results.

- *Execution*

  Without clarity regarding your answers to the alignment questions, execution is also nebulous and perplexing. Even highly motivated executives and other employees tend to be unclear on what they need to do to bring about worthwhile results for their enterprise. While virtually all want to get things done, in many businesses there is often much activity without much results. Again, key questions emerge:

  o Execute what? Does each stakeholder understand what they are to do on a day-to-day basis?

  o What are the leadership functions that must be executed to assure that alignment occurs?

  o What are you--and your leadership team--doing to execute your vision?

- o How have you defined the metrics of both success and the specific actions which enliven the goals that must be achieved by each stakeholder to accomplish that vision?

- o What strategies and tactics must be executed to achieve your goals?

- o What critical actions must be executed to assure financial survival--and ultimately financial success?

In the following chapters I will share ways to answer all the daunting questions listed above–and many more. Be prepared to think deeply, making notes on the thoughts that come to your mind as you craft and implement a future for you and your business that you have only dreamt about until now.

If you're ready, let's get started!

CHAPTER 1

Therefore, What?

A Leader is One who knows the way, goes the way, and shows the way.

John Maxwell

So, what is the path to strong, effective, and efficient alignment and execution?

Alignment & Execution is "All is about the Money," right?

Well, it is...and it isn't.

Let's explore the answer to the critical question for every business leader:

HOW DO WE MAKE MONEY? HOW DO CONTINUOUSLY SUCCESSFUL COMPANIES CREATE PROFITS, CASH FLOW, AND R.O.I.?

Let's start with an absolute truth: *Every enterprise must be financially sound.*

Envision a pyramid, one that I define as *The Business Success Pyramid.* At the apex of the pyramid is the following:

Every enterprise
must be
financially sound

The world of mountaineering provides an appropriate metaphor for those of us who lead businesses. To those who have not climbed mountains, one might simply observe that intrepid climbers achieve the feat of climbing to the summits of peaks like Mount Everest. A bit more investigation, however, reveals that virtually every successful climber is part of a team led by one or more experienced mountain guides. Even a deeper review shows that while the long view is achieving the summit, there are a number of near-term requirements that raise the probability of success. Those include the selection and physical preparations of each team member, arranging for equipment, funding efforts, weather conditions and scheduling. Looking even deeper, we would discover the intensive and continuous preparation of the mountain guides, the team leaders. With the best of these experts, they are the visionaries, those who not only enthusiastically promote the vision of the summit, but also illuminate the path that will bring about that success. They effectively align all of the actions that must be executed to achieve the desired outcomes.

As enterprise leaders, you are the metaphorical mountain guides. You are expected to know the path to the apex of *The Business Success Pyramid,* to the financial success of your company.[2] This is a huge responsibility, one that I refer to as "mission critical." While you

---

[2] My *Business Success Pyramid* is based in part on "The Balanced Scorecard", a concept created by Kaplan and Norton, professors at the Harvard Graduate School of Business.

likely don't have the life-or-death responsibility of a mountain guide on Everest, your stakeholders similarly rely on your leadership. It is essential, then, that you describe exactly the path to success for your enterprise.

As you consider the mountaineering metaphor, you should recognize that setting one's feet on the top of a mountain peak is the result of all the detailed effort that was aligned with that goal. The photograph of the successful climber on top of Everest is a "lagging indicator" of all the "leading indicators" that brought about that snapshot.

In that regard, financial outcomes are LAGGING INDICATORS of business success. Indeed, they are the ultimate lagging indicator for enterprises of all kinds. This understanding leads us to explore a key question for business leaders: *What are the LEADING INDICATORS that create your desired lagging indicator, financial outcomes?*

The generic answer to this question is that the cash register only rings when you provide DESIRABLE OUTCOMES FOR YOUR CUSTOMERS. Thus the path to the apex of business success is through your customer.

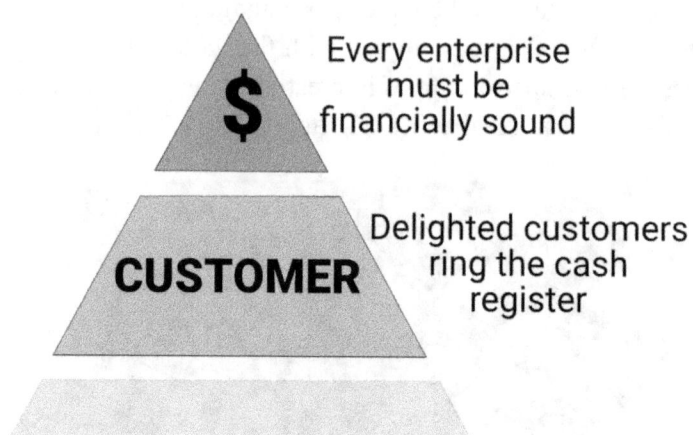

Desirable customer outcomes reflect your Value Proposition. Your Value Proposition may be delivered in the form of a Product, a Service, or some mix of the two. If you delight your customers on a consistent and continual basis, you can demand a fair and profitable price, set mutually agreeable terms to assure cash flow, and watch your economic engine crank out money. A failure to delight your customers consistently and continuously removes the CAUSE that brings about the EFFECT you want.

A simple story illustrates this principle very effectively:

> A young city-dwelling man decided that it would be a good experience to visit Alaska. He wanted to really "rough it," so he arranged to backpack to a remote cabin. The weather in the area he visited started out comfortably warm, but by the time he reached the cabin, it had become quite cold. With great anticipation, he entered the cabin.

It was nearly as cold inside as it was out. Frustrated, the man stood shivering. He yelled at the cold, empty stove: "Give me heat!"

The stove brazenly remained both cold and silent. This wasn't what the young man had anticipated. Unlike his warm home back in civilization, he quickly came to realize that no heat would be forthcoming until he learned that he needed to provide kindling, firewood, and ignition.

So it is with you as the leader of your enterprise. You must provide your customers with the kindling, firewood, and ignition of a compelling Value Proposition to get the financial "heat" you desire. Money, you see, is a function of what you do for your customers!

Your Customer Outcomes that are created by your Value Proposition, are a LEADING INDICATOR for the Financial Outcomes of your business. That said, while Customer Outcomes are LEADING INDICATORS, they are also LAGGING INDICATORS. They are a function of what you do in the day-to-day Operations of your company.

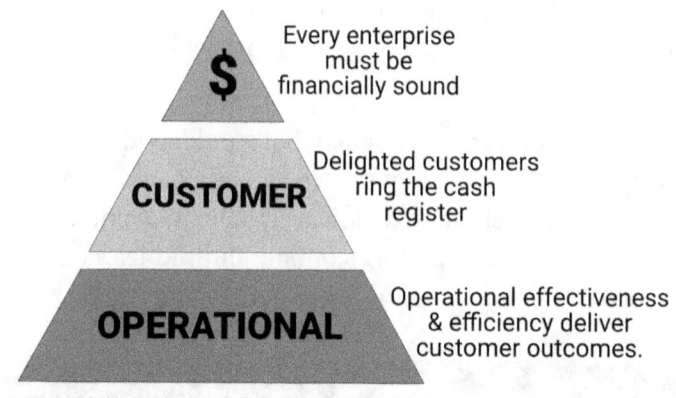

Operations consist of every part of the Value Chain that ultimately delivers your Value Proposition including:

- Design & Testing
- Production
- Delivery
- Marketing & Sales Processes
- Customer Support
- Customer Billing
- Vendor Relations
- Logistics
- Internal Operations, including Human Resources (HR), Accounting, Payroll, etc.

If you are a manufacturer, it includes all of the processes that are critical to the creation and delivery of your products. If you provide your customer with a service, it is all the processes that create that service. If you run a restaurant, it is the operating processes by which you prepare and serve the food, and interact with your customers. If you are a retailer or wholesaler, it is the process by which you purchase stock for your shelves--and market and sell your products.

Operations, then, are the LEADING INDICATOR that drives Customer Outcomes. An effective and efficient Operation creates the Value Proposition you desire to deliver. But...Operational Outcomes are also a LAGGING INDICATOR. This, of course, raises the question of what brings about the Operational Outcomes you require to create the Customer Outcomes that lead to your desired Financial Outcomes.

The simple answer here is that you create operational success through People. Whether your business employs thousands, or you're a sole proprietor, operational outcomes are a result of the actions and behaviors of *people*. People are the *WHO* of alignment and execution. This starts with you, the enterprise leader, but it relies on every person within your organization, as well as those outside your company who, in any way, contribute to the creation of your value proposition and the operations that deliver it.

Alignment and execution demand that every stakeholder performs his or her respective role in an exemplary way. The effectiveness and efficiency of your operation depends on this!

Two essential components bring about the achievement of the People Performance you require; they are the Competency and Engagement of all stakeholders.

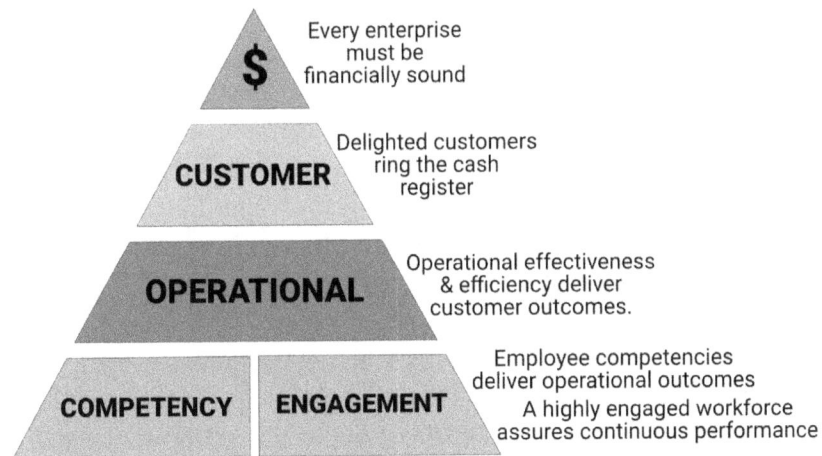

Strong consistent Competency and Engagement of all stakeholders are the LEADING INDICATORS that drive Operational Outcomes. These need to align with those Outcomes, as they align with Customer and Financial Outcomes.

It is critical that business leaders understand that competency without engagement is insufficient. A highly competent team that is not fully engaged is like the young man's cold stove: perfectly capable of providing heat, but without the fuel of strong commitment and engagement, it is cold as a stone.

It is also important that leaders recognize that engagement without competency is also woefully inadequate. High engagement without competency to perform the essential aspects of your operation is at best inefficient; at worst, it is almost always a prescription for disaster.

Most leaders recognize that the competency of their people relies on the effectiveness and efficiency of the experience and training they bring to their jobs, as well as the training they receive at work. Unfortunately, this recognition often does not correlate with a high degree of competence development, especially in small to medium size businesses.

Too many businesses train their employees "by osmosis," meaning that they onboard people into important roles with a minimum of effective instruction. This is often excused as OJT, or "On-the-Job Training." But...if it was described accurately, it would be OJA, "On-the-Job Abdication."

When new employees are expected to become competent by observing others or by simply listening to verbal instructions, we find the process generally fails to render the desired results. Too often, the new employee indicates that they "get it" regarding their required competencies, but unfortunately, this is almost always inaccurate. No one wants to admit that they don't "get it;" that they still have much to learn.

If company leadership recognizes this natural human tendency, they will not assume that newcomers rapidly gain competency, nor will they abandon them until they capably demonstrate the competency required. Otherwise, new employees are set up to fail as they commit operational errors. This inevitably leads to pointing the finger of blame at them, when in fact, the greatest responsibility for competency shortfalls must rest with leadership.

A Tale of Two Newcomers

The company was a niche health care company serving handicapped children, as they described it: an applied behavioral analysis, occupational therapy, speech therapy, and mental health clinic. Their revenue was highly dependent on pre-authorized insurance payments. Like many small businesses, their owners were far more focused on providing their important client service than the details of getting paid. And that led to significant cash flow problems. When pre-authorizations were not done, reimbursable charges were denied by insurance companies. Without insurance offsets, parents of the children served were technically responsible to cover the costs of services, but quite often they were unaware that this was the consequence of failing to get pre-authorization. The problem was one of both attentiveness to proper procedures and communication with parents.

The owner of the company determined to resolve the problem by hiring a highly experienced analyst to make necessary changes. Because of the huge potential financial impact of his work, she offered him a substantial starting salary. He was introduced to the problem, and given a two-day orientation to the industry, the company, and their existing procedures. While it was a rapid introduction, he readily indicated that he understood the problem and knew what needed to be done. With that assurance, the company owner turned him loose to make the necessary changes.

Over the next month, the owner periodically checked in with the analyst. Each time, he assured her that he was making progress, even showing her a detailed spreadsheet that he had developed. While this seemed appropriate, the owner began to worry... when would the newcomer begin to deliver a solution to their problems that rendered an improvement in cash flow? She verbalized this in a meeting with the analyst. Once again, he assured her. *Please give me a little more time,* he implored. The owner suggested that maybe they should hire an assistant who could help with the project. The analyst reluctantly agreed.

Within a few days, the new assistant joined the company. This young lady also received the two-day orientation and training. However, one thing was markedly different about her onboarding. She asked an incredible number of questions, showing a clear intention to understand existing procedures and why things had failed. She readily expressed her concerns when something didn't make sense to her, and wouldn't cease her questioning until she could articulate what she understood to be both the things that were working and those that were not. She met with everyone who had any interface with the financial procedures of the company, including insurance company representatives and some of the parents of the handicapped children who engaged with the company services. In short, she was something of a gadfly, striving to understand the problems and opportunities the company faced in solving their cash flow problems. Her approach to learning her job was solely a function of her own initiative and her sense that she simply didn't know what she didn't know, and would not assume that her past experience made her competent to solve the company's problems.

It took just under three weeks for this new assistant to figure out what needed to be done to resolve the pre-authorization problems, establish effective new procedures, and collect a substantial percentage of the unbilled invoices. During this time, the analyst continued to develop his spreadsheets. The owner finally met with him and asked if he felt that he had earned his paychecks. He adamantly defended himself, assuring her that he had. When the owner called his attention to the work of the assistant, he had to admit that she had been the real producer. It was a few days later that he resigned his position. The assistant moved into his role. The spreadsheets were never used in the new systems she developed. Cash flow continued to improve under her direction.

So, what are the lessons here?

First, as leaders of our various enterprises, we need to realize that newcomers are not fully trained to competence until they can show that they understand your desired outcomes for their jobs, exhibit mastery of the essential actions that will likely produce those outcomes, and feel empowered to ask for--and receive--answers to their questions regarding the work expected. This means that you must not accept the easy answer that they "get it," but rather anticipate that, at least initially, they do not.

Second, no amount of independent diligence will replace intense interpersonal communication with key stakeholders in learning one's job. The assistant in this case study came into the situation with an inherent understanding of this principle, but most newcomers will not. Leadership must take the initiative to expose them to each of those stakeholders, providing both the newcomer and the various stakeholders with the right questions that will uncover what the newcomer needs to know to succeed. This requires some deep preparatory thought on the part of leaders, as well as some interaction with stakeholders as well, but this investment will bear fruit in creating both competency and engagement.

Third, newcomers must be given adequate time to learn their jobs, but leaders must not allow this to drift into an extended period of unaccountability. We must not lose sight of desired outcomes. In this case study, the way the assistant earned her paycheck was by developing and initiating new effective operating procedures that rendered significant cash flow improvement. Every job requires not only actions, but outcomes as well.

It is easy to point the finger of blame at the analyst in this case study. One might even suggest that he deceived the owner by implying that he could solve the problem, and then compounded that deceit by misrepresenting his work as leading to a solution. While there is some accuracy in that assessment, the owner needed to take the lion's share of responsibility for the analyst's failure. She naively accepted his assurance that he understood what needed to be done. Instead, she needed to ask him the tough questions that would truly reveal that he understood what to do. The assistant demanded those questions of herself, as well as everyone with which she interacted, but again, the owner was naive to expect her to do so. She was lucky that the assistant brought that questioning behavior with her.

The last lesson is a summary statement regarding the development of competent employees: *The responsibility for developing necessary competencies rests squarely on the shoulders of enterprise leaders: owners, CEOs, and general managers. It cannot be dodged or delegated!*

So...how well are you doing? Consider your team...what percentage of your stakeholders are Highly Competent, Somewhat Competent, or Inadequate in their Competence? Where are the shortfalls? Effective alignment and execution depends on the strong competency development of your people.

A word of caution here. The challenges identified in the preceding case study also apply when you promote someone or give them new responsibilities. It is easy to assume that because someone is a long-time team member that they know what to do in a new or broadened assignment.

But, do they? For example, if someone is promoted to be a supervisor over a project, they may face a variety of transition and competency issues. They may be required to move from being a user of project software to having an in-depth understanding of the software features required to lead with it. They may be required to interact with new stakeholders who rely on project actions and outcomes. They may be required to have a detailed understanding of financial reports and key performance indicators that were not part of the supervisor's job prior to the promotion.

Recognize that if it is hard to get a new employee or an outside expert to admit that they don't "get it," it is even harder for long-time team members to admit they lack the understanding to be successful in a new assignment. As leaders, we need to take care to not assume competencies are fully developed when promotions and new responsibilities are given to team members. We must not set them up to fail by failing to identify where they require training and support in their new assignments.

To achieve the alignment and execution that leads to the success of your business, you must also create a culture of high engagement wherein your people love the work required to deliver your desired Operational Outcomes. While no one loves every aspect or every moment of their job, your people must be continuously motivated to achieve the desired outcomes of your enterprise.

Statistically, on a national basis, barely 30% of employees are fully engaged in their work.

The implications of this problem are significant:

- Three out of ten employees consistently carry the majority of company responsibilities.
- While they "get a little help from their friends" (the 5 semi-engaged folks), the three top performers are straining against the 20% who routinely fail to engage.
- Your MVPs, the "ever-toiling threesome," while deserving of your adulation, are "burning out!" They are the ones you are

most likely to lose, as they recognize that their engagement is unrewarded with the reciprocal efforts of their teammates.

- If you lose them, you are left with those who cannot, or will not, create the operational success you require!

In the 4th Quarter of 2021, we experienced the Great Resignation. The Great Resignation, also called the Big Quit, refers to the incredible number of American workers who left their jobs voluntarily. In August of 2021, a record 4.3 million employees quit their jobs. Much of the apparent rationale for this out-migration of workers is that the COVID-19 pandemic made people reevaluate what they are getting out of their jobs.

"What they are getting out of their jobs," is a phrase to which leaders should give deeper thought. At the surface, this may appear to be primarily about financial incentives. However, notable organizations like Gallup have found that there are two major causes that are non-financial. The first is that most people who quit their jobs do so because of their boss. They are unhappy with how they are treated, how their ideas are not given merit, and the fact that they often feel that their personal lives don't matter to their boss. The second is that they have discovered that there is no vision or enterprise purpose with which they can align. **Many want to be a part of something bigger than themselves, something that is personally fulfilling**.

If you are finding that your enterprise is experiencing something like the Great Resignation, please don't assume that all the lemmings are running to the sea, or that your lemmings are simply participants in a societal trend. Be more introspective! How do you, and the leaders within your company, treat your people? Have you given them a vision that encompasses a great purpose, mission, and values to which they can believe and want to play a role in achieving? (Much more on that later…)

At this stage of the Alignment and Execution process, you may not be surprised to discover that Competency and Engagement, while being the LEADING INDICATORS for Operational Outcomes, are also LAGGING INDICATORS for Recruitment. Highly targeted

Recruitment is the foundation for both Competency and Engagement. As best-selling author of *Good to Great,* Jim Collins puts it, *"You must get the right people on the bus!"*

Too often, the failure to effectively align and execute starts right here. Your Recruitment processes should clearly define the roles required for operational success and how they will contribute to the consistent and continuous delivery of the value proposition of your enterprise. This should include an understanding of the personality and culture fit required for people to thrive in your organization. While it is important to attract those candidates who meet your experience and education requirements, it is even more essential to find those who will fit in and enjoy being part of your company.

Business Success Pyramid

It is important to understand that Recruitment is not simply hiring. Effective recruitment always begins with a careful assessment of your needs. What are the functions, roles, activities, and behaviors that you need to deliver your desired Operational Outcomes and your Value Proposition to your customers?

With that answer in mind, ask yourself: To what extent does your organization possess the people who can perform those functions right now? Where are the gaps and shortfalls? What do the ideal candidates look like to fill those functions?

With those insights in front of you, what should your vetting process look like to assure that you hire the right people?

Broaden your perspective on hiring to include people and organizations outside your company, including:

- Suppliers
- Bankers
- Accountants
- Attorneys
- Tax Professionals
- Insurance Providers
- Fractional C-Suite Executives
- Advisors
- And maybe others, as your situation requires

Recognize that Recruitment applies to you as well! Ask yourself these questions:

- What are the functions, roles, activities, and behaviors that I need to lead my company?
- To what extent do I possess the skills we need right now?
- Where are my gaps and shortfalls?
- How might I best develop myself to overcome those gaps and shortfalls?
- Where might I turn for clarity regarding growth and development as a leader?

Understand that as important as it is to "get the right people on the bus," it is even more essential to have "the right driver on the bus."

As you frankly answer these questions, don't underestimate the value of a competent and engaged business coach. No business leader possesses every attribute, quality, or skill that he or she will need to succeed. One of the most dangerous leadership challenges is that "we don't know what we don't know." The perspective of a seasoned, highly observant and discerning coach or mentor is often invaluable, even critical, to the success of the man or woman who leads. Seeking competent engaged counsel is not a sign of weakness; it is a sign of leadership intelligence. The old axiom, "It's lonely at the top," is a self-fulfilling prophecy if we allow it to be. But it doesn't have to be that way!

To summarize, Recruitment is the leading indicator for the Competency & Engagement of your people, which in turn leads to your desired Operational Outcomes, which creates your desired Customer Outcomes, which will render the Financial Outcomes you want--and must have!

The CEObuilder® Business Success Pyramid represents the HOW of Alignment & Execution.

As important as each component of the Business Success Pyramid is, it is still an inadequate model to substantially increase the probability that your business will succeed. Consistent and continuous success requires that you--and your people--understand not only the HOW of alignment and execution, but the WHY of your enterprise as well.

Your WHY is, in fact, the essential--even critical--element, without which, the Business Success Pyramid will, in all probability, fall apart.

Your WHY is encompassed in a *Clear & Compelling Company Vision,* consisting of:

- **Your PURPOSE**
- **Your MISSION including Your Value Proposition**
- **Your VALUES**

With this understanding, it is clear that your Vision encircles, undergirds, and holds all the components of the Business Success Pyramid together. It is the mortar that binds–and aligns–each brick of that pyramid.

Business Success Pyramid

VISION

$ Every enterprise must be financially sound

Delighted customers ring the cash register **CUSTOMER**

OPERATIONAL Operational effectiveness & efficiency deliver customer outcomes.

Employee competencies deliver operational outcomes **COMPETENCY** **ENGAGEMENT** A highly engaged workforce assures continuous performance

RECRUITMENT

Competence & Engagement begin with targeted recruitment

Your Company Vision provides...

- An overarching "True North" to direct and motivate your team, and
- The mortar that binds each building block within the Business Success Pyramid, thereby providing strategic and operating continuity over time.

Revisiting the mountaineering metaphor, each level of The Business Success Pyramid is like one of the "camps" that are always established in the climb to the top of major peaks. As the stories of climbs like Everest are told, these camps are always shared as critical components of summit success. What's more, climbers often find themselves moving back and forth between the higher and lower camps. This is done to acclimatize themselves to the lower oxygen levels of high camps. This is again appropriately metaphorical; as business leaders we need to move back and forth between each element of the pyramid. And much like all of the pre-climb preparation, we must take the time to set the Vision (the Purpose, Mission, and Values) to assure our shared readiness to climb.

An Unremarkable Picture that Inspired
Extraordinary Leadership

The company was a manufacturer of what I called "explosive trucks." They took heavy duty truck chassis to which they mounted sheet metal tanks. An auger was affixed below a spigot at the back of each tank. The trucks were sold primarily to the mining industry, which employed them in carrying an explosive slurry to the outback areas of Australia and Africa. The auger provided the drilling needed to create the hole to receive the slurry; this slurry was then ignited by a blasting cap (after the truck rolled a long way away, of course).

I had worked with Don Allred, the company's CEO, as his business coach for some time when I noticed a large picture across his office from his desk. It was a photograph of a high mountain peak in the background, with many rolling hills in the foreground. I asked him where the mountain was located, assuming that it might have been somewhere he had visited or hiked.

His response surprised me; he said he didn't know where it was. I then asked him why he had it mounted so prominently in his office, noting that he had other smaller photographs of family, as well as pictures relevant to the company around his office. He smiled and said, "That picture is the most important image in my business career."

I was stunned--and very curious to know why he would say this about a picture of somewhere he had never been, and didn't even know where it was. He then explained that the mountain peak was symbolic of his vision for the company.

He noted the beauty of the snow-covered summit of the mountain. It represented his vision of what his company was becoming, and why it existed. He said that the climb to that summit represented the company mission, and the value they needed to create for his customers and employees along the way. And then he called my attention to the foothills in the foreground, suggesting that I should pay attention to the darkness of the valleys between each hill. He reminded me that to get to the summit of the mountain, he and his team had to traverse both the hills and the valleys. And, he said, "When we're in the valleys, it's very easy to lose sight of our goal, of the summit of the mountain. The trail becomes dark and tough and we can easily lose our vision of our ultimate goal. As a leader, I have to remember that when we are in those inevitable valleys, my people are prone to lose sight of our vision. My job is to keep it alive in the darkness of the valleys, until we can crest each hill and realize that we are still on the path to success. That is why this is the most important picture in my office and the most important image in my business career."

Sometimes, the business coach receives more coaching than he gives!

A Few Cautions: Avoiding Typical Alignment and Execution Pitfalls

1. **Developing your vision—and then throwing it over the wall for implementation.** There is too often a tendency to think that once the vision is developed, the only requirement for

implementation is one of communication. Implementation is the "real work"—the "doing," and this is the key to the continuous alignment and monitoring of key business stakeholders.

2. **Heads-down focus.** Performance at an individual level is based on executing a series of critical tasks. However, without the bigger picture—a strong sense and commitment to the enterprise purpose, mission, and values—it is difficult, if not impossible, to understand how each stakeholder's actions impact other elements in the system. A heads-down perspective also limits the extent to which an individual will offer to improve a process since there is little appreciation beyond "just doing my job."

3. **Blaming the hired help.** It is easy to blame people for poor execution. After all, they are the ones doing the work. Sometimes there are clear situations in which an individual is not a fit for the job or in which individuals need more training and development to be effective. However, often we find situations where there are dedicated, hard working people working with inefficient, bloated, or cumbersome processes. This is a process problem, not a people problem. Similarly, we sometimes find situations where multiple individuals are responsible for the same task or where key tasks are poorly performed because it is not clear who is responsible for what. This is a job definition issue, not a people issue.

4. **Perpetuating the silo perspective.** All too often leadership teams at both functional and business levels tend to represent their own interests as opposed to unifying the purposes of the whole company. In high performance organizations, the role of the leadership team is defined with clear accountabilities for overall enterprise execution and profitability, not just each person's piece.

5. **Micromanagement.** When the spotlight is on improving performance, many managers have a natural tendency to helicopter in to "tell" their people how things are to be done.

Their hearts may be in the right place, and they generally have the hierarchical authority to jump in—but their tendency to *direct* rather than *engage* their people carries some very negative consequences. Their reports learn to wait for the boss's approval rather than taking appropriate risks in improving their performance or solving problems. And, the best and brightest team members often become so resentful of being micromanaged that they begin to seek "better" personal empowerment opportunities elsewhere.

Having shared the Business Success Pyramid and its inherent leading and lagging indicators, we now face the essential question facing each leader: *Where do I start?*

The answer is that you must start where you are, right now, today!

If you are an entrepreneur, a Start-up Leader just launching your new business, this is absolutely a great time to focus on your WHY, your vision…before launching into the HOWs of the Business Success Pyramid. However, if you are an Incoming Leader (meaning that you have been promoted into or inherited your leadership opportunity), you are likely faced with very specific urgent and important challenges that demand your attention. If you are an Ongoing Leader (meaning that you've occupied your position for some time), such challenges likely fill your daily to-do lists as well.

My advice to clients over the years has been to simultaneously adopt both a short and long range perspective. What I mean by this is that you must not ignore the current problems and/or opportunities which you face. They must be addressed. With that in mind, the Business Success Pyramid provides a useful template for zeroing in on what is most important and urgent right now. That is the short-range perspective that must be addressed, and it gives rise to one key element of our business philosophy at CEObuilder®: *LEARNING IN THE MOMENT OF NEED.* You likely have current needs that cannot be ignored, and an important part of our job is to help facilitate your learning how best to address these.

The inherent challenge with having a strong short-range perspective, however, is that it can become so compelling and overwhelming that it completely drives out your long-range perspective. This is extremely dangerous; it can lead not only to suboptimal achievement of your WHY, but unfortunately has often led to moral and ethical lapses that have brought about business failure and even prison sentences. (More on that in subsequent chapters.)

Make no mistake, as a leader it is one of your most essential roles to establish a solid long-range perspective based on your vision: the purpose, mission, and values of your enterprise. While short-range problems and opportunities must be addressed (your day-to-day HOWs), they should always be measured against your long-range WHY. For that to happen, we assert without equivocation that YOU, as the leader of your organization must build a compelling cause for your business!

Chapter 2 will provide you with insights in that important challenge.

Building a Compelling Cause

Where there is no vision, the people
(and companies) perish...

Amended version of Proverbs 29:18

Make no mistake, leaders of *every* enterprise of *every* type and *every* industry must manage *all* 7 elements of the Business Success Pyramid:

1. Such owners, entrepreneurs, CEOs and general managers must assure that financial systems are in place to measure performance in terms of profit, cash flow, and the value of the business--and as those metrics are reported, they carry the responsibility to interpret, manage, and hopefully deliver those essential outcomes.

2. They are responsible to see that the value proposition of their enterprise is delivered to their customers on a consistent and continual basis; that customer needs and/or wants are fulfilled to the satisfaction of those who spend their hard-earned cash for company products or services.

3. They carry the responsibility to assure that every operating process required to effectively and efficiently deliver customer outcomes are in place, and that those processes function consistently and continuously.

4. They must assure that the team, both internal and external, competently delivers operational outcomes.

5. They must oversee the development of a highly engaging culture where stakeholders can grow and thrive in their important roles and careers.

6. They must recruit the right people, i.e., the talent required to provide a highly competent and engaged team.

7. And, they must develop and implement an overarching vision that inspires a collective enterprise passion for delivering all of these outcomes!

When viewed through the perspective of the Business Success Pyramid, it's not hard to see why successfully leading a business is so inherently difficult.
Given this incredible array of executive leadership responsibilities, leading a business often feels like a giant game of whack-a-mole. Everytime an issue, challenge, or opportunity is resolved, a new one pops up!
As mentioned in concluding Chapter 1, we at CEObuilder® recognize the importance of "learning in the moment of need." That means that we help our clients identify their most pressing concern, issue, or opportunity--and put a laser focus on that challenge. If you are facing a crisis in any one of the seven elements of the Business Success Pyramid, you need to "go to the pain," and work on that issue first. An example might be a flaw in your cash collection processes like the pre-authorization case study regarding the child services company shared in Chapter 1. When that business was leaking cash, leadership needed to concentrate their attention on that concern within the financial element of the pyramid. Another business experiencing lost customers due to slippage in the delivery of their value proposition needs to immediately focus on the operations of their production and delivery system. If, like many businesses today in the post-pandemic era, your business is struggling to find and retain employees, you must address that recruitment issue now. And if such issues reflect

a lack of competence or engagement of current employees, those challenges must also be addressed with immediate action.

The urgency of such current issues, however, often obscures the real root cause of problems. For instance, in the child services company case study, the cash flow issue was symptomatic of a failure to have consistent communication with clients (parents of handicapped children) regarding required pre-authorizations. From the inception of the business, the owner surely recognized the need for a steady stream of cash, but her focus was myopically concentrated on the core purpose of her operation, that of providing care and treatment for handicapped children. Both her words and behavior strongly channeled this focus to her team. While in many respects this was laudable, it also served as a distraction from the creation of solid administrative policies and procedures, including those that ensured that payments for services rendered were consistently and continuously employed.

That core purpose of her business, that of providing the healing and optimal development of handicapped children, represents the essential WHY of her company. The WHY, for her--and for all enterprises-- when well articulated and evangelized inevitably enlivens the HOW. That said, if key elements of the HOW are not addressed, they may well be overlooked or underdeveloped, as were the billing and collection functions for the child services clinic.

It is critical that both the WHY and the HOW be understood for the success of any enterprise, and the primary role and responsibility for that is yours, as the leader of your company. The Business Success Pyramid provides a strong template for your work here, as well as a guide for assuring that your stakeholders understand their roles and responsibilities.

When a leader strongly articulates and evangelizes his or her vision (the WHY) in its proper context within the Business Success Pyramid, stakeholders come to understand the key elements of the HOW, which *aligns* strategy and tactics with the WHY. These include:

- The critical need to attract and engage the right talent for the team

- The importance of developing that talent into a highly competent group of individual and collective contributors

- The need to work together to build a high engagement culture

- The necessity of key operations that will deliver desired organizational outcomes, and their corresponding key performance indicators (KPIs)

- The essential elements of the organization's value proposition that must be delivered continuously to the customer

- How the organization creates revenue, profits, cash, and enterprise value'

If, in the early days of her business, the owner of the clinic for handicapped children had shared her vision for the operation with her team within the broader context of the entire Business Success Pyramid, her team would likely have recognized the critical need for having a systematic approach for billing and collections, among other key company functions and operations.They would have developed those systems before the problem became life-threatening to the business.

I am among the first to congratulate both the owner and the new assistant on solving the cash flow problem. But I will always assert that a problem prevented is better than one that emerges as a crisis demanding a solution. It was surely not obvious to the owner that the root cause of her problem was the failure to share with all stakeholders both her inspiring vision of serving handicapped children (her WHY), as well as the essential elements of the HOW, as set forth in the Business Success Pyramid. And, lest I sound too critical, she is not unusual. Many business owners, CEOs, and general managers make this mistake. The good news is that this is very correctable!

Ultimately the clinic owner recognized her need to articulate and evangelize the company vision in ways that inspire her team and assure that each team member is empowered to independently respond when anything arises to threaten that vision. The owner's challenge going forward is to share the company vision regularly, thereby expanding the perspective of her stakeholders (executives, practitioners, and administrative employees) through helping them understand their respective roles in contributing to the achievement of the vision within the context of the Business Success Pyramid. By making this a part of her everyday interactions with those stakeholders, they are learning to observe where the company is succeeding and where it needs improvement to stay *aligned* with the vision. They are gaining a better understanding of HOW to *execute*, to make the contributions that help the company achieve its purpose, mission and values. Those contributions lighten the leadership load of the owner, as each stakeholder "buys in" to both the company WHY and HOW.

Once past the "duct-tape and bailing wire" phase of dealing with your current pain or crisis, it is essential that you recognize the critical need to *align and execute* with an eye on True North, providing the shared purpose and passion needed to fully engage your key stakeholders in achieving your desired enterprise outcomes. This is the difference between patching the hole in your boat, and reconstructing it into a sleek racing vessel. One of the most essential parts of your job is to focus on the articulation and evangelism of your enterprise vision. *This is especially critical if you have never done it before.* But, even if you lead one of the rare companies that already have a vision statement, we generally find that the align and execute process in this book will help you energize and strengthen your successful implementation of that statement.

Sharing the "big picture" vision of your enterprise offers the unique purpose to which your stakeholders gain a sense of belonging, of strong emotional attachment, and even ownership. They form a psychic allegiance and loyalty to your company, as you build that sense of True North. Over time, stakeholder buy-in is enhanced, and the willingness to sacrifice for the cause increases. Trust and mutual respect are reinforced by the sense that everyone (owners, executives, and all employees) are united in achieving the company vision. While financial rewards, including some forms of incentive compensation, should not be ignored, visionary leadership recognizes that a strong sense of purpose, mission, and values provides the kindling and fuel for the desired blaze of strong financial outcomes for all stakeholders.

Your vision should include your company purpose, as well as your mission (what you do, for whom, and how), and clarity in terms of *what you will* and *will not do* to accomplish your purpose and mission (your shared values), With proper articulation and energetic evangelism over time, you will find that your vision is the centerpiece of a high performance culture of competent and highly engaged stakeholders.

Author Michael Gerber, in his book, *The E-Myth Revisited,* shared the leadership distinction between working *in* your business and working *on* your business.[3] A certain amount of any business owner's or CEO's time will necessarily be *IN-the-business activities* in the first six areas of the Business Success Pyramid. Developing a clearly articulated and compelling vision, however, is distinctly an *ON-the-business activity.*

The late General Colin Powell, noted that "in the military the problem is posed this way: 'Where should the commander be on the battlefield?' The answer: 'Where he can exercise the greatest influence and be close to the point of decision' — the place where personal presence can make the difference between success and failure. A battalion commander leading a charge up a hill with seven hundred troops behind him may be a courageous and inspirational figure, but he is at that moment just another infantryman trying to stay alive. He can't see the whole battlefield; he is not in a position to move forces; he can't communicate with all his subordinates, arrange more support, or keep higher headquarters informed. Because it is important for followers to see and hear from their leader, corporate executives should often visit the plant floor to see what is going on. But then get out of the way so workers, foremen, and line leaders can get on with their jobs."[4]

The point here is both subtle and challenging: your people need to hear from you; they need to know that the captain is fully engaged. But in most cases, they don't want or need you to charge

---

[3] *The E-Myth Revisited: Why Most Small Businesses Don't Work and What to Do About It,* Michael E. Gerber, pages 97-98.
[4] *It Worked For Me: In Life and Leadership,* Colin Powell, pages 56-57.

up the hill with them, to do their jobs or micromanage their efforts. What they need is your continuous articulation and reinforcement of the enterprise vision, and your commitment to listen with an ear of understanding regarding their challenges, providing support for their "in the business" *execution* that *align*s with the vision.

When done properly and evangelized with energy and passion, articulating and evangelizing your vision is a high leverage tool that delivers incredible outcomes throughout the rest of the Business Success Pyramid. Most importantly, it is a tool that multiplies your leadership influence, as it inspires your team to give their very best efforts in pursuit of that vision.

Not all Business Owners, CEOs, and Entrepreneurs are the same...

Developing a powerful vision that aligns your organization and inspires focused execution is not just for those who are about to launch a new venture. If you are a *start-up leader* of a brand new business, what you will learn here will, of course, apply.

However, you may be an *incoming leader* to an existing business. Or, you may be an *ongoing leader* of an existing business. In that regard, you may have already articulated a vision. My experience, having coached CEOs for many years, is that even companies with vision statements posted on their walls will gain substantial benefits by following the processes I will share here.

If you are a **Start-up Leader**, the founder of a new entrepreneurial venture, your company vision will begin with YOU, with your personal Purpose, Mission, and Values. This is the critical foundation of alignment for your enterprise. If YOU are not aligned with the vision of your company, the foundation will be so flawed that it will be virtually impossible to align your team and other stakeholders with it.

If you are an **Incoming Leader**, a CEO or general manager who has been promoted into his or her leadership role--or has been brought into an organization from the outside, it is essential that you discover and understand the vision (or lack thereof) of the business before you begin the process of aligning your personal vision with it. My experience, having served as an Incoming Leader myself, is that inviting the team you inherit to share their existing vision is extremely important. It makes it clear that your style is to listen and learn before issuing marching orders. It also allows you to triangulate the responses you receive and develop an understanding of what your team sees as their purpose, mission, and values.

This is not to say that your personal vision is unimportant. In fact, it is essential. But the process of alignment here is somewhat different than for enterprise founders, what we call Start-up Leaders.

If you are an *Ongoing Leader*, you may have already served many years in the top job of your company. You may have been promoted to that CEO or general manager position, or you may have founded the business. You may, as some of our clients, be soon to transition out of the business, to sell or hand the reins to someone else. You might ask, "Is setting or revisiting our vision really necessary at this juncture?"

The answer is that the processes in Align & Execute will benefit your organization, regardless of where you are as an Ongoing Leader. If your plans are to remain in your leadership role for the foreseeable future, our processes will help you clarify how to manage and lead your enterprise. If you are shifting your focus to handing off the business to a successor, sharing the Align & Execute process with that person or persons can assure that the transition goes smoothly and that agreement regarding future operations is achieved. And, if you are looking to sell your business or merge with another organization, the process will enhance the marketability of your company.

As we address what constitutes a strong, effective company vision, we will share both the similarities and differences in the visioning process for Start-up, Incoming, and Ongoing Leaders.

So...what is a Company Vision, and why do you need one?

A compelling vision provides the following beneficial outcomes:

- It unifies the company, creating a common language and focus that drives both team and individual engagement
- It guides decision-making, both "what to do," and what "not to do"

- It engenders customer loyalty by matching customer needs and desires to your purpose
- It provides a strong guide to your legacy, as it provides direction beyond yourself

What a company vision is not:

- Contrary to the opinion of some, the development of your company vision is not an academic exercise. It is not an esoteric "touchy feely" exercise pursued only by naïve, newly-minted MBAs.

- A compelling corporate vision is not disconnected or unrelated to the other key components of business success. Indeed, it is the foundation for all the other elements of the Business Success Pyramid. It is what overarches, binds, unifies, and directs them. It motivates alignment, execution, and engagement.

- While wordsmithing your vision is a necessity, the words should not simply be a series of superlatives like "becoming the best..." These types of statements rarely resonate on a personal level with the key audiences for them: ownership, executives, employees, customers, suppliers, and the community within which you serve. Furthermore, your vision need not be a multi-page or even multi-paragraph manifesto. Often, the best and most meaningful articulation of a vision are best expressed in just a few powerful words.

- The development and execution of your vision is not a "one-and-done" exercise, nor is it something that you compose, post on the walls of your company, and forget about. Rather, you must assure that it is a powerful dynamic that has a guiding impact on everyday conversation, debate, and decisions.

What then, should your company vision include?

- It should reflect the compelling reason for your enterprise's existence, its "raison d'etre," its purpose. This is typically a statement of what you want your company to become, even what legacy you want to leave. It is what author Simon Sinek calls a "Just Cause, a reason to come to work that is bigger than any particular win, (where your) days take on more meaning and feel more fulfilling. Feelings that carry on week after week, month after month, year after year. If we work for an organization with a Just Cause, we may like our jobs some days, but we will always love our jobs."[5]

- Your company vision provides a significant sense of stretch. It defines where you are going, what you are becoming, and as acclaimed business author Clayton M. Christensen has said, it is "how you will measure your life."[6] It may never be fully achieved, but it will provide the driving force to outcomes far greater than the desires of any one person, including you as the leader of your business.

- This purpose is your company's WHY that provides the passion which propels your collective energy, actions, and decisions. It should be intensely personal to the enterprise leader, who will use it to invite that same intensity of purpose on the part of his or her key audiences. The Gallup organization recently published an article that stated, "leaders must build a purpose-driven culture where purpose drives 'how we do things around here.' Culture matters because perception is reality: You're only as 'good' as stakeholders believe you are — as your culture behaves. No matter what you tell the world, your employees' behavior will speak louder."[7]

The article goes on to say that the following descriptors characterize purpose-driven enterprises:

- ○ "The purpose of our company makes every employee feel their job is important.

---

[5] *The Infinite Game,* Simon Sinek, page 33.

[6] *How Will You Measure Your Life?,* Clayton M. Christensen, James Allworth & Karen Dillon, page 8.

[7] Gallup, *Just How Purpose-Driven is Your Organizational Culture,* Jake Herway, October 22, 2021.

- o   Our employees believe leadership is fully aligned on brand and culture priorities.

- o   Our employees understand what makes us different from our competitors.

- o   Our employees are held accountable for living our purpose and values.

- o   Our purpose and culture attract the best talent in the industry.

- o   Our purpose and values are priority inputs in every leader's decision-making.

- o   Leadership communication is consistently focused on purpose and values.

- o   Our managers are the best in the industry.

- o   Managers are held accountable for coaching their team's performance.

- o   Purpose, brand and culture measures are infused in performance scorecards."[8]

Companies with compelling visions have a strong sense of purpose, mission, value proposition, and core values. Stakeholders have a "heartfelt sense of ownership" for both the organization purpose as well as their own role in the pursuit of that purpose. Gallup asserts that "purpose energizes teams, informs their decisions and guides their day-to-day behavior. Employees know *who* they serve, *what* they serve, and *how* to embody brand promises. A purpose-driven culture walks the talk -- proving to customers, employees, suppliers and communities that you really are who you say you are. It earns brand credibility and stakeholder loyalty." Further, they note that "a purpose-driven culture makes money *through* its purpose."[9]

This is a reminder that the ultimate lagging indicators of business success are financial, and that financial outcomes are a function of

---

[8] Ibid
[9] Ibid

how well you meet the needs and desires of your customers. Author Mark Schaefer in his book, *Marketing Rebellion*, notes that customers increasingly want to do business with companies whose stated purpose aligns with their own beliefs and values.

Schaefer's research shows that "People (customers) want to:

- Feel loved.
- Belong.
- Protect their self-interests.
- Find meaning.
- Be respected."[10]

Schaefer asserts that when a company's overarching purpose is clearly reflected in their brand and marketing messages--and is aligned with their customers' WHY, they will find both Customer and Financial success. He reflects two other insights from the Gallup organization regarding strong purpose-driven enterprises:

- Customers know them for what they want to be known for.
- Customers and employees would use the same words to describe what the purpose of the company is.[11]

Bernadette Jiwa, in her book, *Story Driven,* sums it up this way:

"Great companies have something in common: They don't
try to matter by winning. They win by mattering."[12]

And mattering is a function of their purpose and how that purpose is delivered to both stakeholders within the enterprise, and their customers.

---

[10] *Marketing Rebellion: The Most Human Company Wins*, Mark Schaefer, page 51.
[11] Gallup, *Just How Purpose-Driven is Your Organizational Culture,* Jake Herway, October 22, 2021.
[12] *Story Driven: You Don't Need to Compete When You Know Who You Are,* Bernadette Jiwa, page 13.

Vision setting as a *Start-Up Leader...*

- Your initial focus should be on yourself. What is your *personal purpose* that compels you to pursue this new venture? What is *YOUR WHY*?

- To miss, skip, or overlook this critical step is a huge mistake. Too often entrepreneurs get "shiny object syndrome." They are distracted by the allure of exciting financial possibilities—and fail to define the WHY that will sustain them in the dog-days of their venture. With no foundational purpose, they often cannot sustain their own alignment and execution, much less that of others.

Consider Southwest Airlines' Start-Up Leader, Herb Kelleher

Under Herb's leadership, Southwest formed the following compelling purpose:

"We will become the world's most loved, most flown, and most profitable airline."

This company purpose extended from **Herb's personal WHY:** *He loved people.* He often said, "The business of business is People." Herb was undoubtedly an airline man, but his reason for running his airline was to serve the people he loved–and that included his customers, every Southwest employee, supplier, vendor, and virtually everyone else–including competitors. Author Jody Hoffer Gittell in her book, *The Southwest Airlines Way* describes how Herb's personal purpose translated into his everyday persona, but also literally transformed the airline industry by intensively focusing on the interactions between his team and the flying public. Gittell calls this "using the power of relationships to achieve high performance."

The "how" that is encompassed in the "why" (becoming the world's most loved, most flown, and most profitable airline) is through relationships. Through hundreds of hours of observation and interviews, Gittell identifies Ten Southwest Practices for Building High Performance Relationships:[13]

- Lead with credibility and caring
- Invest in frontline leadership
- Hire and train for relational competence
- Use conflicts to build relationships rather than disrupt them
- Bridge the work/family divide
- Create boundary spanners
- Measure performance broadly
- Keep jobs flexible at the boundaries
- Make unions your partners
- Build relationships with suppliers

These practices are undergirded with *relational coordination,* built on the values of Shared Goals, Shared Knowledge, and Mutual Respect. To make sure that those values are followed, Southwest emphasizes Frequent, Timely, Problem-Solving Communication. The resulting outcomes have proven to be highly effective and efficient performance.

Although Judy Gittell has identified many of the reasons that Southwest has succeeded over the years, that's not the whole story. Professor Michael Porter at the Harvard Graduate School of Business notes that Southwest deliberately chose a set of strategies to deliver "a unique mix of value"[14] for their target customers. They do this by offering short-haul, low-cost, point-to-point service between midsize cities and secondary airports in large cities. They have avoided large airports and long distances between destinations. Through fast turnarounds at gates of only 15 minutes, they are able to keep their planes flying longer hours than their competitors and provide frequent departures with fewer aircraft. Automated ticketing at the gate encourages customers

---

[13] *The Southwest Airlines Way,* Judy Hoffer Gittell, page 55.
[14] *Harvard Business Review, "What is Strategy?",* Michael E. Porter, November-December 1996

to bypass travel agents, eliminating the expense of commissions. And a standardized fleet of Boeing 737 aircraft boosts the efficiency of maintenance.[15] (As of this writing, Southwest also did not offer meals, assigned seats or premium classes of service. However, in response to recent customer feedback, they are rethinking these policies. It will remain to be seen how changes to their strategic model affect customers and financial outcomes.)

Southwest's target customers are business travelers, families, and students. Their frequent departures and low fares attract price-sensitive customers who often would otherwise travel by car or bus. As Professor Porter says, "...the essence of (their) strategy is in the activities–choosing to perform activities differently or to perform different activities than rivals"[16] — and perform those activities in consistent exemplary ways. And for Southwest, that demands that they stay focused on relationships with their customers, their employees, unions, suppliers, and everyone else with whom they interact. They have done this remarkably well over the past 50 plus years!

This is not to say that Southwest has avoided major problems over the decades. But the legacy left by Herb Kelleher was that problems were to be expected–and they represented opportunities to be problem-solvers and strengthen Southwest's relationships with customers, employees, and even adversaries. Here are some of those "problem opportunities"[17] they've faced over the years:

1. Legal and Regulatory Hurdles

- **Initial Legal Battle:** When Southwest Airlines was founded in 1967, it faced significant legal challenges from established airlines. Competitors like Braniff, Trans Texas, and Continental attempted to prevent Southwest from operating by lobbying for legal and regulatory roadblocks. This litigation spanned a period of four years, multiple appeals, and finally a decision

---

[15] Ibid.
[16] Ibid.
[17] https://chatgpt.com/c/aa14071c-8371-4672-9699-3d3743a2e9d0

by the Texas Supreme Court which ultimately found in favor of Southwest's right to operate as an "intrastate carrier" in the limited Texas Triangle: Dallas, Houston, and San Antonio.[18] Herb Kelleher was the lead and primary attorney for Southwest in all of these cases.

- **Wright Amendment:** In 1978, the federal Airline Deregulation Act was passed, allowing Southwest to quickly become an "interstate carrier."[19] However, in 1979, U.S Congressman from Fort Worth, Jim Wright, proposed and passed an amendment that restricted flights from Dallas Love Field, Southwest's home airport, to only within Texas and the neighboring states of Louisiana, Arkansas, Oklahoma, and New Mexico. The amendment further prohibited Southwest from advertising, publishing schedules, checking baggage, or publishing through fares regarding travel from Dallas Love Field and any city it serves outside Texas and the four bordering states.[20] This severely limited Southwest's ability to expand. The amendment was eventually repealed in 2014, but it posed a significant challenge for decades.

2. Economic Crises

- **Oil Crises and Fuel Prices:** Like all airlines, Southwest has been vulnerable to fluctuations in fuel prices. The oil crises of the 1970s and subsequent spikes in fuel costs have been major challenges. However, Southwest has often mitigated this through strategic fuel hedging.

- **Recession Impacts:** Economic downturns, such as the recessions in the early 1980s, post-9/11 period, and the Great Recession of 2008, led to reduced travel demand, impacting

---

[18] *Nuts! Southwest Airlines' Crazy Recipe for Business and Personal Success,* Kevin & Jackie Freiberg, page 18.

[19] Ibid, page 25.

[20] Ibid, page 26.

revenue. Southwest responded with cost-cutting measures and a focus on maintaining customer loyalty.

3. Operational Challenges

- **Rapid Expansion:** Managing rapid growth posed significant operational challenges. Expanding routes, integrating new technologies, and maintaining consistent service quality across a growing network required meticulous planning and execution.
- **Pilot and Crew Shortages:** At various points, Southwest has faced challenges related to pilot and crew shortages. These shortages have been exacerbated by industry-wide issues such as aging workforce and training bottlenecks.
- **Boeing 737 Max Quality and Safety Concerns:** Major aircraft manufacturer Boeing continues to face the music over numerous safety incidents on its planes. While virtually all U.S. carriers rely heavily on Boeing, Southwest operates their entire fleet of 815 aircraft made by Boeing. The temporary grounding of all its Boeing 737 MAX 9 airliners has been particularly onerous. "This reliance on one company is unparalleled and is exposing incredible vulnerability across the industry that will likely continue to create challenges as we head into peak travel season.[21]

4. Competition

- **Low-Cost Carrier Competition:** As a pioneer in the low-cost carrier (LCC) model, Southwest faced increasing competition from other LCCs like JetBlue, Spirit Airlines, and Frontier Airlines, which have adopted similar business models.
- **Legacy Carriers:** Competing with established legacy carriers, which often had more extensive route networks and international flights, was a continual challenge. Southwest's

---

[21] https://www.newsweek.com/southwest-airlines-problems-worrying-other-companies-1896950

strategy focused on maintaining low costs and high efficiency to compete effectively.

5. Labor Relations

- **Union Negotiations:** Southwest, with its highly unionized workforce, has faced numerous labor disputes and contract negotiations. Ensuring good relations with unions while controlling costs has been a delicate balance.

- **Strikes and Threats of Strikes:** At times, the threat of strikes has posed significant operational risks. Negotiating fair contracts while ensuring operational continuity has been a recurring challenge.

6. Technological Upgrades

- **Reservations System:** Southwest faced a significant challenge when upgrading its outdated reservation system. The transition to a new system in the 2010s was critical for improving efficiency but required substantial investment and careful implementation to avoid disruptions.

- **IT System Failures:** There have been instances of IT system failures that led to flight delays and cancellations, highlighting the importance of reliable and robust technology infrastructure. Most critically, this occurred between December 21 and December 31, 2022, when Southwest was forced to cancel more than 16,700 flights, stranding millions of travelers in airports around the United States.

7. Crisis Management

- **9/11 Attacks:** The terrorist attacks on September 11, 2001, had a profound impact on the airline industry, leading to a dramatic drop in passenger demand and increased security costs. Southwest managed to remain profitable by maintaining a strong balance sheet and cost control.

- **COVID-19 Pandemic:** The COVID-19 pandemic presented unprecedented challenges, with travel demand plummeting and new health regulations emerging. Southwest navigated this crisis through cost-cutting measures, government aid, and a focus on employee and passenger safety.

8. Environmental and Regulatory Pressures

- **Environmental Regulations:** Increasing environmental regulations and the push for sustainable practices have posed challenges. Southwest has had to invest in more fuel-efficient aircraft and sustainable practices to meet regulatory requirements and consumer expectations.

- **FAA Regulations:** Compliance with Federal Aviation Administration (FAA) regulations, including those related to safety, has required continuous investment in training and technology.

While Herb Kelleher was at the forefront of meeting and solving many of these challenges, the airline industry is dynamic; problems can–and will–keep emerging. Herb's successors know this only too well. But Kelleher set the standard for how to deal with such challenges that continues to pervade the attitude and behaviors of Southwest's leadership today. As Colleen Barrett, who served as President and Chief Operating Officer of Southwest from 2001 to 2008 put it, the tougher the opposition, "the more determined Herb got that this airline was going to go into the air—and stay there."[22]

Southwest Airlines' ability to overcome these diverse challenges has been a testament to its continuous focus on creating and maintaining strong relationships with every stakeholder–and while some of their

---

[22] *Nuts! Southwest Airlines' Crazy Recipe for Business and Personal Success,* Kevin & Jackie Freiberg, page 26.

current challenges are significant, their track record and consistency in staying true to their purpose, mission and values gives investors and the flying public confidence in a bright future for the company. Their past successes, their ability to resiliently solve their problems, and enduring company culture all grew out of Herb Kelleher's love of people! By focusing on serving people in exceptional ways, he anticipated that they would love to fly Southwest, fly it often, and be happy to pay for the experience.

One of Herb's successors as CEO of Southwest, Gary Kelly, described Herb this way:

> "Many of you likely knew Herb personally. He knew more people than anyone I ever met. …Everywhere we went, he knew somebody—if not everybody. Herb meant so much to so many people. Several people have asked me what I think his legacy will be, and it's hard to narrow it down to just one thing. But if pressed, I would say Herb's legacy is love. Herb loved people—all people. He loved Southwest. He loved his friends and family. And he loved life."[23]

---

[23] *Southwest Airlines In-Flight Magazine,* March 2019, page 12.

Herb's love of people–and love of life–has led many to describe Southwest as a "nutty company." While they have made many important strategic decisions over the years, the personality of the company didn't grow out of strategy; it grew out of the personality of its founders–most particularly Herb Kelleher. His maverick personality became the corporate persona: what authors Kevin and Jackie Freiberg have described as "determination, a flair for being positively outrageous, the courage to be different, the vulnerability to love, the creativity to be resourceful, and an esprit de corps that bonds people."[24]

Southwest's persona has been at times shocking to some observers. Their early positioning of the airline as the Love Airline, even today, is a classic example of marketing outrageousness. With creative direction from the Bloom Advertising Agency, they set out to define their airline like unto a witty, pert, beautiful, and attentive woman. Kelleher described it as "a hard-hitting, spectacular 'love' campaign." Its theme: "Now there's somebody else up there who loves you."[25]

Based on that theme, Southwest flight attendants were selected for their "special sparkle." "A cute girl without a great personality was not good enough."[26] Cute, however, was also important–and they made the bold and outrageous decision to dress their attendants in hot pants! Authors Kevin and Jackie Freiberg describe them as "outrageously outfitted but thoroughly trained and eager to fly; they were commissioned to make the usual unusual. An ordinary business trip became a love affair. Aboard the *Love Bird,* drinks were Love Potions, peanuts were Love Bites, drink coupons were Love Stamps, and plane tickets came from Love Machines." The women who were selected as flight attendants were extroverts who loved being in the "people business."[27]

As an upstart newcomer to the highly competitive airline industry, such outrageousness garnered invaluable publicity; they were the talk

[24] *Nuts! Southwest Airlines' Crazy Recipe for Business and Personal Success,* Kevin & Jackie Freiberg, page 36.
[25] Ibid, page 38.
[26] Ibid, page 39.
[27] Ibid, page 40.

of the town in Dallas, Houston, and San Antonio–and soon throughout the United States. While this was a marketing coup, it is clear that it also reflected Herb Kelleher's love of life–and his love of people!

That love of people became infectious. Still today, Southwest leaders routinely leave the executive suite to fly on their own aircraft–and to mix and mingle with employees at every level within the company. They encourage their people to be authentic, to use their own personalities and be themselves as they interface with their customers, and to listen and learn from them. And beyond that, they stress that while working hard is expected, having fun is also essential. One of the past Southwest advertisements featured ten of their original flight attendants who shared this message: "We've been telling corny jokes for 25 years, and so far no one has gotten up and left!"[28] Even today, you are likely to hear a corny joke or two on a Southwest flight.

In their book, *Nuts!,* Kevin and Jackie Freiberg point out that "when people work hard for something they believe in, a special bond inevitably develops between them. This is what happened with the original employees. From the start, Southwest has always thought of itself as an airline of people who care about people; the original team at Southwest worked hard to uphold that standard. From the very beginning, Southwest was a family…We had this wonderful blend of people who cared….We've all turned out to be the very best of friends…The esprit de corps the original team felt is still apparent, even to outsiders. Sandra Force, an original flight attendant, says, 'People from outside the company tell us all the time that they cannot believe what we have, compared with other companies.They can just see such a family and closeness that's not apparent in other large companies.'"[29]

So is Herb Kelleher's love of people still manifested in the Southwest Airlines' culture today? As leadership transitions have occurred, each new CEO has endeavored to maintain and grow how the airline manifests its love of people in everything they do. Since Herb stepped down as CEO in 2001, the company has had strong leadership that has

---

[28] Ibid, page 43.
[29] Ibid, page 44 & 45.

moved forward strategically, while remaining dedicated to the purpose, mission, and values of its founders–most notably Herb Kelleher. They include James Parker, who succeeded Herb and served as CEO until 2004, Gary Kelly who served as chief executive from 2004 to 2021, and Bob Jordan, who sits in that chair today. These leaders, along with scores of other managers, supervisors, and frontline employees have played critical roles in staying true to the company's core principles while shaping Southwest's ongoing strategies, operational efficiency.

As a Start-Up Leader of Southwest, Herb Kelleher largely set the foundation for the company's vision with his own WHY:

Herb Kelleher WHY	Southwest Airlines WHY
PEOPLE: "Herb loved People." He often said, "The business of business is People."	To **become** the world's most loved, most flown, and most profitable airline.

Herb manifested his personal love of people through his creation, Southwest Airlines. While he certainly recognized the importance of all components of the Business Success Pyramid, his passion was seeing those who flew his airline having such an enjoyable experience that they would come to love flying Southwest, flying it again and again. He recognized that their experience necessarily had to include being a great value for their traveling dollar, and that by being cost conscious, he could provide them with attractive pricing while securing profitability for the company.

Vision setting as an *Incoming Leader...*

- You must seek to discover the existing vision of the organization you have the opportunity to lead.
- This may be very obvious if the company has set forth their WHY and their stakeholders know—and function well—in pursuit of that purpose.

- Or it may be an intense challenge to unearth the WHY. This is very often the norm. Often, there is a general sense of purpose, but it has not been articulated in a manner to assure a general consensus of key stakeholders.

- Either way, discovery of the existing vision (or even the lack thereof) should precede your moves to align that vision with your own.

- By initially subordinating your personal vision to the vision of the company, you will enhance the likelihood that stakeholders will support you when you do align your values with those of the enterprise.

Consider two of Southwest Airlines' Incoming Leaders after Herb Kelleher.... Gary Kelly and Bob Jordan

Gary Kelly had the advantage of working closely with Herb for over 30 years. He knew Herb's personal purpose, as well as the company's vision. He said, "Herb taught me what it means to care for and love your people. Herb had an unadulterated joy and true love for life and everyone he met, and if you were lucky enough to know him, you know how special he made you feel."[30]

Gary has sought to continue that vision and has aligned himself to it. Even in the face of weather disruptions, COVID-19, and pilot shortages, Gary continued to provide leadership that adhered to Herb's personal and corporate values and purpose. Most importantly, it aligned perfectly with his own purpose as well. Today, he serves as Chairman of the Southwest Board, having handed over the role of CEO to Bob Jordan in February of 2022. Bob continues to carry on the Herb Kelleher legacy of love for people, and a commitment to becoming the world's most loved and flown airline.

More, in Chapter 4, on Bob Jordan and how he, and Southwest, have maintained and built upon the Herb Kelleher vision...while

---

[30] Ibid.

dealing with the unexpected and extraordinary challenges faced by the airline over the Christmas travel challenges of 2022.

But what if you are an Incoming Leader where a compelling vision does not exist? What if you are tasked with turning around a sinking ship?

- Recognize your role: you are a catalyst for change; you must establish the importance of a new vision for the company.

- Caution: Ask questions and listen intently before deciding what the vision should be; seek to understand before being understood.

- Begin to develop the enterprise vision based on what you have learned.

- Make sure the company vision aligns with your own vision; it must fit with your WHY, if you are to successfully lead.

- Collaborate on wordsmithing the company vision with key stakeholders.

Vision setting as an *Ongoing Leader*...

This is generally a hybrid of the Start-up Leader and the Incoming Leader. You should:

- Assess the existing vision of the organization. Are all key stakeholders able to articulate the vision themselves, without any prompting or coaching from you? An absence of that capability generally is a clear sign that the vision has not been developed, evangelized, or even been shared with your team. If key stakeholders can give a reasonably consistent version of the vision, can all employees do so? Is the vision compelling?

- Does the vision reflect your personal purpose; i.e, What do you want to achieve in your life? Are you passionate in the pursuit of your personal purpose? Are you equally passionate about the company vision? Do you continuously evangelize that vision with all company stakeholders?

- Given your introspective answers to these questions, begin to develop (or recharge) the enterprise vision.

- As with the Start-up and Incoming Leaders, make sure that the company vision aligns with your own vision, fitting with your WHY.

- Collaborate on wordsmithing the company vision with key stakeholders.

One incredible story of an Ongoing Leader that I find very relevant here is that of Andy Grove, the late president of Intel. In 1985, the long-time purpose of Intel was to produce computer chips, the memory essential to the function of PCs. That had been the company's bread and butter since 1968.[31] They were deeply invested in pursuing that vision and built a multi-billion dollar business in doing so. However, business slowed down in the fall of 1984. Demand fell rapidly, and

---

[31] *Only the Paranoid Survive,* Andy Grove, page 82.

as Grove shared in his best-selling book, *Only the Paranoid Survive*, they "couldn't wind down fast enough to match the market slide. (They) were still building inventory even as (the) business was heading south."[32]

Intel had been losing money on memories while trying to compete with Japanese producers of high-quality, low-priced, mass-produced parts. For the better part of the year, Intel steadfastly adhered to the original business vision and the strategies that had earlier been successful. However, sometime during mid-1985, the following interchange took place between Andy Grove and Gordon Moore, co-founder of Intel:

> Grove: "If we got kicked out and the board brought in a new CEO, what do you think he would do?"
>
> Moore: *Without hesitation,* "He would get us out of memories."
>
> Grove: *Numbly staring at Moore,* "Why shouldn't you and I walk out the door, come back and do it ourselves?"[33]

With that insight, Grove and Moore started on the difficult journey of resetting Intel's vision. It was a gut-wrenching experience that Andy described as literally giving up their identity as an enterprise- -and then resetting it[34]. It was what he called a *strategic inflection point*, which basically means that the entire Business Success Pyramid (my description, not his) had to change when the foundational vision required transformation. That Intel not only survived and thrived in the years that followed is a tribute to the ongoing leadership of Andy Grove and Gordon Moore.

---

[32] Ibid, page 88.

[33] Ibid, page 89

[34] Ibid, page 90

Intel today is once again facing an existential crisis. Can the current Ongoing Leaders guide them through the current challenges? Time will tell. But like Grove and Moore, they will likely need to reassess and reset their vision as they navigate through this latest strategic inflection point.

CHAPTER 3

Moving from your WHY to WHAT YOU DO

If you have built castles in the air,
your work need not be lost; there is where they should be.
Now put foundations under them.

Henry David Thoreau

Your company purpose sets forth your WHY, but the articulation of your vision requires more than that...

It requires a clear and compelling **MISSION, what your enterprise *does* on a consistent and continuous basis.**

This MISSION should encompass your VALUE PROPOSITION, which is *the value you promise to deliver to your customers*. It is what makes your product or service attractive to your customers. A compelling value proposition meets five criteria:

1. <u>It's specific</u>: It clearly sets forth specific benefits that a specific target customer will receive. It intensely focuses on understanding the most urgent and expensive needs of that customer.

   Clayton Christensen suggests that "many products fail because companies develop them from the wrong perspective. Companies focus too much on what they want to sell their customers, rather than what those customers really need.

What's missing is *empathy:* a deep understanding of what problems customers are trying to solve."[35]

2. <u>It goes to the pain</u>: It demonstrably solves specific customer problems or improves his or her life in significant and specific ways. To zero in on the pain your customers are experiencing, ask the following questions:

- Is the current solution your target customer is employing too costly? What are the cost dimensions of that current solution? Is it simply the dollar cost? Or is it the complexity of the transaction that's creating the pain?

- What is frustrating or annoying for the target customer in their current experience in solving their problem?

- How would you define the value proposition of the current solution that the target customer is buying? (Yours and that of your competitors)

- What are the main difficulties your target customer has with the current solution and its inherent value proposition?

- What negative social consequences do your target customers fear, given the current solutions?

- What risks make your target customer averse to the current or potential solutions?

- What common mistakes does your target customer make that you might solve?

- What barriers do you see that prevent your target customer from adopting current or potential solutions?

- What worries your target customer? What keeps them up at night?

With answers to these questions in hand, strive to define customer pains as concretely as possible. The team at strategyzer.com

---

[35] *How Will You Measure Your Life?*, Clayton M. Christensen, James Allworth & Karen Dillon, page 99.

recommend that you get deeply granular in this regard. "For example, when a customer says 'waiting in line was a waste of time,' ask after how many minutes *exactly* it began to feel like wasted time. That way you can note (that specifically the pain is) 'wasting more than *X* minutes standing in line.' When you understand how exactly customers measure pain severity, you can design better pain relievers in your value proposition."[36]

One of my clients, a roller coaster manufacturer, developed a highly engaging solution for their patrons who waited to board one of their popular water rides. They installed large squirt guns at intervals along the queue that allowed a fun level of participation that caused people who were waiting in line to largely eliminate the frustration of wait-time.

3. It creates customer gains: Often, strong value propositions deliver specific upside benefits rather than simply overcoming downside pain. They address the outcomes desired by customers, sometimes even gains they have not articulated or anticipated. They may include such benefits as cost savings, functional utility, enhanced social status, or even just feeling physically or emotionally better. They might provide enjoyment or fulfillment in unique and special ways. Your challenge is to define the gains your product or service offers--through the eyes and perspective of your target customer, rather than through your own eyes and perspective.

   The strategyzer.com team suggests that in seeking the gains that customers want, you should consider the following categories:

   o **"Required Gains**: These are gains without which a solution wouldn't work. For example, the most basic expectation that we have from a smartphone is that we can make a call with it.

---

[36] *Value Proposition Design: How to Create Products and Services Customers Want,* Alex Osterwalder, Yves Pigneur, Greg Bernarda, Alan Smith, page 14.

○ "**Expected Gains**: These are relatively basic gains that we expect from a solution, even if it could work without them. For example, since Apple launched the iPhone, we expect phones to be well-designed and look good.

○ "**Desired Gains**: These are gains that go beyond what we expect from a solution but would love to have if we could. These are usually gains that customers would come up with if you asked them. For example, we desire smartphones to be seamlessly integrated with our other devices.

○ "**Unexpected Gains**: These are gains that go beyond customer expectations and desires. They wouldn't even come up with them if you asked them. Before Apple brought touch screens and the App Store to the mainstream, nobody thought of them as part of a phone."[37]

Once again, you should strive to define customer gains as concretely as possible. This often requires deep questioning--of both yourself, and your target customers.

4. <u>It provides a job or function that customers cannot easily fulfill for themselves</u>.

This is what Clayton Christensen calls *The Job-To-Be-Done Theory*:

"When a company understands the jobs that arise in people's lives, and then develops products and the accompanying experiences required in purchasing and using the product to do the job perfectly, it causes customers to instinctively 'pull' the product into their lives whenever the job arises. But when a company simply makes a product that other companies can also make--and is a product that can do lots of jobs but none

---

[37] Ibid, page 16.

of them well--it will find that customers are rarely loyal to one product versus another."[38]

The result of an intense focus on understanding the jobs for which your customers hire your product or service is that you become increasingly capable of responding directly to those needs through your value proposition.

5. <u>It is uniquely your own</u>: It stands out as differentiable from the offerings of your competitors. In this regard, there are key considerations:

   A. **What are the current value propositions that *your* customers buy?** Very specifically, why do they buy your value proposition? How successful is your value proposition in doing the job they are hiring you for, in solving their problem, or in providing substantial gains for them?

   B. **What are the current value propositions that the customers of your competition buy?** Very specifically, why do they buy the competitor's value proposition? How successful is the competition's value proposition in doing the job they are hiring them for, in overcoming their pain, or in providing substantial gains for them? As you consider these questions, make sure that you also consider the solutions that they may have "purchased" internally, choosing no available option in the market, but have created for themselves.

   C. **What would increase your customers' and target customers' likelihood of adopting your value proposition?** How might you improve your solutions to better perform the job they are hiring you for, to overcome their pain, or to provide substantial gains for them?

---

[38] *How Will You Measure Your Life?*, Clayton M. Christensen, James Allworth & Karen Dillon,, page 103.

D. How might you make your value proposition unique in the marketplace? Are there ways to be "first to market" with your improved value proposition? Are there natural barriers to entry that will make it difficult for competitors to copy your value proposition?

E. Consider what you might offer that neither you nor your competitors are offering. Are there potential customers that have not purchased any of today's existing value propositions? Often, there is a segment of the population that has not discovered or bought into any existing value proposition. Ask yourself, what might they be looking for and why have they yet to purchase any of the value propositions currently being offered? From the earlier example, consider those with mobile phones that didn't have GPS or a camera. Today those features are expected–and are often even more important than the phone.

Caution: Brand slogans are rarely synonymous with value propositions.

They may be useful marketing messages that provide direction to your value proposition, but they generally fall short of providing a strong value proposition. A value proposition that includes each of the five preceding components is required to construct a compelling mission statement to be used in conjunction with your company purpose.

The development of a strong, compelling and well-targeted value proposition is driven by asking good questions. I strongly recommend the model shared by Warren Berger in his book, *A More Beautiful Question*. He suggests that the process of value proposition creation should begin with three simple questions:

1. *Why are things as they are?*

2. *What if things were different? What might a new reality look like? What changes might be possible that would eliminate pains, add gains, or do jobs that our target customer would value?*

3. **How** *might we create those changes?*[39]

The following case study shares the journey of one successful business leader who effectively asked the questions that Warren Berger suggests in developing a compelling mission and value proposition for his company.

Amputees are Introduced to a New Value Proposition

In the summer of 1976, twenty-one year old Van Phillips was water-skiing on an Arizona lake. The driver of the motorboat pulling him failed to see that a second boat was coming right at Phillips. The ensuing collision resulted in the amputation of Van's left leg, just below the knee.

In the hospital, Phillips quickly recognized that his life had changed. Prior to the accident, he had been full of life, handsome and athletic. Now, he had to deal with all of the pain that came with the loss of his leg and foot. Of course, there was physical pain, both that which was associated with the trauma to his body, as well as the psychological, emotional, and social pain. The latter categories loomed large; indeed, they impacted how Van perceived the future. Visions of being a cripple for the rest of his life were incredibly unsettling.

His caregivers tried to be reassuring, but when they shared the "state of the art" prosthesis with Van, he recoiled at what he saw. They presented him with a "pink foot attached to an aluminum tube,"[40] which would be fitted to what remained of his leg. He tried out the contraption, but found that he tripped easily. Further, it exacerbated the pain in his stump. All of the medical professionals, and virtually all of his

---

[39] *A More Beautiful Question: The Power of Inquiry to Spark Breakthrough Ideas,* Warren Berger, page 7.
[40] Ibid, page 12.

friends, told him that he just had to learn to accept that this was his "new normal." Phillips recalls, "I knew they were right, in a way--I did have to accept that I was an amputee. But I would *not* accept the fact that I had to wear this foot."[41]

If Clayton Christensen was weighing in on Van Phillips' story, he would call our attention to the fact that *the job* of the prosthetic at the time it was fitted to Van's stump was simply to replace the missing leg and allow him to walk again, even if his resulting gait was awkward. Prosthetic manufacturers basically saw their product as introducing amputees to their "new normal."

Van saw the job of the prosthesis much differently. In his mind's eye, he saw *its job* as allowing him to return to the physical activities he loved. *The job* was to allow him to run, jump, and even compete with non-amputee athletes. He hoped for a solution that would not only mitigate the physical pain associated with the prosthetics of that era, but also eliminate the psychological, emotional, and social pain he was experiencing. And, he wondered if he might even be able to turn his injury into an asset. After all, he was sure that he was not the only amputee who was dissatisfied with the "new normal."

With this dissatisfaction, Van Phillips found himself asking the first question Warren Berger suggests in his book. **Why** should I settle for this lousy foot? If they can put a man on the moon, **why** can't they make a decent foot?[42]

When Van asked these questions of prosthetic experts, he was greeted with antipathy. Obviously, he was naive to think that anything could be done better than the products currently being used. He was routinely dismissed as he asked them why they weren't trying to make a better prosthesis. After

---

[41] Ibid.
[42] Ibid. page 14.

several such rejections, Van had an epiphany: he was asking the wrong question! Instead of asking the experts why *they* don't create a better solution, he asked himself: why don't *I* create that solution?

That shift in thinking led him to dive into the world of prosthetic technology. If he was going to create the solution he desired, he concluded that he would have to learn much more about the current state of the art. Van enrolled in one of the top prosthetics study programs in the nation at Northwestern University. This led to a job in a prosthetics lab in Utah, which further allowed him to understand why prosthetic limbs were designed as they were.

As he gained experience in the prosthetics field, Phillips never forgot his personal mission: to develop a better prosthesis for leg amputees, beginning with himself. This ultimately led him to ask a series of "what if" questions.

- **What if,** in other realms, there are ideas that could be applied to prosthetics? He pondered, "**what if** you could replicate a diving board's propulsive effect in a prosthetic foot?"[43]

- **What if** a human leg could be more like that of animals that run with great speed and agility? For instance,"**what if** a human leg could be more like a cheetah's?"[44]

- And as Van explored these ideas, he finally asked "**What if** instead of a traditional L-shaped lower leg and foot, you dispensed with the heel and created a limb that was one continuous curve, from leg to toe?"[45]

Of course, that was not the end of the road. He then faced the third of Warren Berger's questions: **How** can I bring

---

[43] Ibid, page 35.
[44] Ibid.
[45] Ibid..

my discovery into being? Berger notes that while this is the action stage, it is still driven by questions:

- **"How** do I decide which of my ideas to pursue?
- **"How** do I begin to test that idea, to see what works and what doesn't?
- "And, if/when I find that it's not working, **how** do I figure out what's wrong and fix it?"[46]

For Van Phillips, each question led to considerable experimentation and prototyping, including many ideas that failed. He was literally his own test dummy for each iteration that he tried. He "created somewhere between two hundred and three hundred prototypes. A lot of them broke the first time you put your weight down on them."[47] Van learned from each failure. As Warren Berger shares in his book, "he was failing forward, the whole time."[48]

Van's personal mission, to create a better prosthetic solution for leg and foot amputees, led to a value proposition that promised less pain (physical, psychological, emotional, and social), as well as significant gains in mobility, stability, and performance. His products do the job for which they were hired: to assure that amputees are able to run, jump, and enjoy active lives. These were the personal passions that led Van Phillips to found the Flex-Foot corporation in the mid-1980s. His products became disruptive innovations that revolutionized the prosthetics industry. Van's vision of helping amputees live without limitations has been carried on by the company that acquired Flex-Foot in 2000, Ossur Prosthetics, an Iceland-based business.

---

[46] Ibid, pages 36-37.
[47] Ibid, page 37.
[48] Ibid.

Let's return now to Southwest Airlines...

From the prior chapter, you will recall the Purpose or WHY of Southwest Airlines:

Southwest Airlines WHY
To **become** the world's most loved, most flown, and most profitable airline.

How does the WHY of Southwest translate into a Mission & Value Proposition? If they want to show love for people (Herb's, Gary's, and Bob's personal purposes)—and to be loved by them to the extent that they fly their airline often, spending their hard-earned cash to do so— _what must they do as an airline? What is the Value Proposition?_

For Southwest Airlines, their Mission Statement & Value Proposition became...

*"We connect people to what's important in their lives...
through friendly air travel, through reliable air travel,
through low-cost air travel."*

While these words are simple, and easy-to-understand, they carry *significant, intense, and personal meaning* to Southwest's various important audiences who bring that mission and value proposition to life, including:

- Owners & Investors
- Board Members
- Executives
- Employees
- Suppliers
- The Financial Community
- And—most importantly, their Customers

Let's check for Alignment...

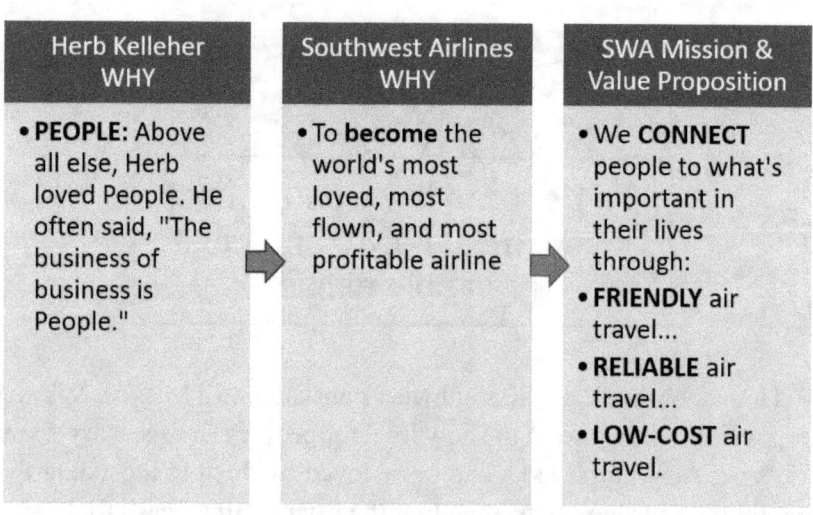

*Whether you are a Start-Up Leader, an Incoming Leader,
or an Ongoing Leader, it is this type
of Alignment that you need to create!*

CHAPTER 4

The Principles that Govern Your Life, Your Work, and Your Company

He who floats with the current, who does not guide himself
according to higher principles, who has no ideal,
no convictions--such a man is a mere article of the world's
furniture--a thing moved, instead of a living and moving
being--an echo, not a voice.

Henri Frederic Amiel

The final essential component of a strong, compelling company vision is...

- A clear statement of company VALUES, those principles by which your company functions and governs itself.

- Your company values set forth what you will, and will not, do in pursuit of your Purpose and Mission.

One of my most enjoyable (and challenging) leadership opportunities was serving as a Scout leader of young men. I did this for over 30 years and had enough incredible experiences to literally fill multiple volumes. Several of these have provided me with valuable insights for leadership at all levels, circumstances, and even for business. One that provides a strong metaphor for the importance of values follows.

Dead Horse Point and the Scouts

The state of Utah is blessed with five national parks. They literally range from A to Z:

- Arches
- Bryce Canyon
- Canyonlands
- Capitol Reef
- Zion

As a Scout leader, I have had the joy of visiting each of these extraordinary parks with boys ranging from age 12 to 18. Beyond the Big 5, I have also taken Scout troops to many of Utah's amazing state parks. Most of them rival the national parks for both beauty and adventure. And adventure is often closely associated with danger. I'm very grateful to say that I never had anyone die on our adventures, but as you might imagine, there were a number of occasions where injuries occurred.

One of the most stunning state parks that we visited over the years was Dead Horse Point State Park, located near Canyonlands National Park. The park is unique in that it is a peninsula in the sky that stands two thousand feet above a gooseneck bend in the Colorado River. Three sides of the peninsula have unforgiving vertical faces that drop into thin air.

The point got its name from the story of 19th century cowboys who rounded up wild mustangs and herded them onto the peninsula. The cowboys recognized that if they blocked off the thirty foot wide entrance, the point would provide a natural corral. The mustangs couldn't retreat, and all other options spelled certain death. Unfortunately, the cowboys overlooked the fact that it wouldn't take long for the horses to succumb to the heat and lack of water on the point. When they returned, all they found was a herd of skeletons. Today, the legend is that the ghosts of the mustangs still haunt the peninsula.

As spooky as that sounds, the real danger of a Dead Horse Point adventure today is the 2000 foot drop. Especially with a group of 20 or so boys, a significant part of my job as a Scout leader was to reinforce the deadly nature of gravity. Prior to our departure to the Point, I stressed the importance of staying away from the edges of the cliffs. While there was not a protective fence at every ledge, I pointed out that where such fences were in place, everyone needed to stay inside those fences.

When we arrived at the park, I reminded the boys of my earlier admonitions. I felt confident that they understood and would obey. With that, I told them to stick together as a group, and to go ahead and explore the area. That was all the permission they needed; they took off for the ledges.

I was one of several adult leaders, and we were not nearly as fast as the boys in heading to the overlook areas. We were absorbed in chatting about the incredible rugged beauty of the area when I heard a shout. "Mr. Tyson, come quick! Travis is hanging over the edge!"

I sprinted in the direction of the shout, arriving at a ledge where our boys were gathered. There, leaning out over the canyon was Travis, with two of his buddies hanging onto the back of his belt. I must admit that he was getting a far more vertical view of the canyon below than anyone else, but he also got my firm hand on his belt as I jerked him back to safety.

This stunt led to a makeshift meeting with the group (well away from the edge of the cliff), where I emphasized that such disobedience wasn't just an affront to my leadership, it could very well result in death. My lecture was pointed, even a bit harsh. I made it clear that any more infractions would result in the end of our outing. It worked...there were no more infractions (at least on that trip!).

Later that evening, as we sat around our campfire, I decided to share a few thoughts with the boys regarding fences and fence posts. I asked them, "Why do you think we have fences?" They responded, "To keep things inside, to protect them from leaving, or protect them from being stolen."

I then asked, "Why didn't the cowboys build a fence around the edges of Dead Horse Point?" The boys laughed. "They didn't need to, the big drop was enough to keep the mustangs inside; it was a natural fence."

"So," I said, "those horses were actually pretty smart. They stayed away from the edge. *Maybe,* they were a bit smarter than a few of you today. Can you imagine a horse hanging out into space to check out what was at the bottom?" Everyone laughed again.

I then asked, "Do you guys know what a metaphor is?" We had a good discussion, and they came to understand that metaphors often provide a physical example that is similar to something else, often a principle. With that understanding, I said, "So, guys, if a fence is designed to keep things inside, to protect those things, what principle might that teach us?"

It took a while for them to wrestle with this, but soon one of the older boys said, "I think it's like being honest. If you know that you shouldn't lie or cheat or take someone else's stuff, then that acts kind of like a fence that you shouldn't climb over or go around."

That led to more discussion about the importance of personal values, and how each value is like a fence post that serves to help us live up to what we believe. I then brought the boys back to Travis's death-defying escapade. I looked over at him and asked him why he had risked his life. He shrugged his shoulders and said, "I just thought it would be fun...

and I was sure my buddies would hang on to me. I knew I wouldn't fall."

I then shifted my focus from Travis to the rest of the troop. "You see, Travis's answer is like that of so many of us when we climb over the fence, when we act against our core values. We think it would be fun, or that it isn't dangerous...just this once, or that a little bit of disobedience will be okay...no one will get hurt. But a little bit of disobedience always has consequences. Today, the consequence was a big lecture from me, and that is an important role of being a leader. Sometimes a leader has to be the 'chief reminder' of core values--and that will require a strong lecture. If the leader is successful, no one dies or gets badly hurt. If not, at the very least, you get another lecture, or maybe you lose your privileges to do the things you love. What the leader always hopes is that he brings everyone home safe and sound."

By the time we were ready for crawling into our sleeping bags, we had together learned a great lesson about the importance of values, of deciding what we each would, and would not do, in order to stay safe on our Scouting adventures, and to be good people and live good lives.

Dead Horse Point will always be a favorite place for me. Its beauty and the adventure inherent in the park are incredible. But I am even more grateful for one evening with a group of Boy Scouts when together we learned the lesson of fences and fence posts.

The Lessons of Dead Horse Point:

- Sometimes horses are, indeed, smarter than people. The horses recognized that a 2000 foot drop was deadly; the forgetful cowboys obviously weren't very smart--and neither were our Scouts who needed a fence to corral them!

- Metaphorically, each fence post represents a core value, a principle that we will not violate. These will keep us safely away from the errors that likely will hurt us strategically, morally, or legally. They will help keep us focused on what really matters.

- Scouts are slow to learn; sometimes they are as forgetful as the cowboys in the Dead Horse Point story. They require multiple tellings and correction--and leaders must recognize that is their responsibility to provide that guidance. Often, adults are similarly balky in learning. The leader's task, that of "chief reminder", is to recognize this human tendency and diligently, but patiently, keep the discussion of core values alive.

- Leaders must "walk their talk;" hypocrisy is a leadership killer!

Moving from Dead Horse Point to the Adventures of Business

There are, unfortunately, too many examples of enterprises that have had a compelling Purpose and Mission without strong governing values. More than a few of those companies are on the ash heap of business history. Since the turn of the century, these include notable enterprises like Enron, Tyco International, WorldCom, and Bernie Madoff, each of whom scandalously stand out in what might be termed the Business Hall of Shame. Recently, Elizabeth Holmes of Theranos and Sam Bankman-Fried of FTX have joined their ranks. Most people recognize these stories as the product of the unbridled greed of a few unethical business leaders.

However, their lack of conscience was not isolated. Indeed, it often became infectious, even to firms that were once known for their adherence to high-integrity practices. Highly esteemed CPA firm Arthur Andersen, for instance, loosened their grip on their guiding principles in order to maintain their multi-million dollar engagement with Enron.

The Rise and Fall of An Accounting Icon

The Arthur Andersen story is a cautionary tale. The man for whom the firm was named, Arthur E. Andersen is in many ways the classic American success story. Born in 1885, he was orphaned at the age of 16. From that time forward, he worked days as a mail boy while attending school at night. In 1908, while working full-time, he graduated from the Kellogg School at Northwestern University in Chicago. That same year, he became the youngest CPA in Illinois. Five years later, he founded his own accounting firm with his partner, Clarence DeLany.

Andersen was a pioneer in the development of accounting as a profession, as well as being a strong voice for accounting standards, serving at one time as the chairman of the board of CPA examiners of Illinois. He believed strongly in developing a team of highly educated and competent accountants, establishing the profession's first centralized training program. His commitment to education extended beyond the accounting profession ultimately leading to his election to the board of trustees of Northwestern University. He served as the president of that board from 1930 to 1932.

Arthur worked as president of his company until his death in 1947. "He never wavered as a zealous supporter of high standards in the accounting industry. A stickler for honesty, he argued that accountants' responsibility was to investors, not to their clients. This gave rise to the uniform look of all the so-called 'Arthur Androids', as employees referred to themselves, the intent being to provide the same service the same way to all customers in all locations.

"For many years, Arthur's motto was "Think straight, talk straight'—an axiom passed on from his mother. During the early years, it is reputed that he was approached by an executive from a local rail utility to sign off on accounts containing flawed accounting, or else face the loss of a major client. Arthur refused in no uncertain terms, replying that there was 'not enough money in the city of Chicago' to make him do it. The railroad fired him, only to go bankrupt a few months later."[49]

Fast forward to June of 2002, when the Arthur Andersen Company was convicted of obstruction of justice for "shredding and doctoring documents related to Enron audits."[50] Andersen's top executives had gradually drifted far from the core values that Arthur E. Andersen had held so dear. They justified this by asserting that "Enron was Andersen's biggest client, paying more than forty-nine million dollars in fees...Clients like that could expect to be kept happy."[51] Investigators later said that "the lines between Enron and Andersen had become so blurred that even senior Andersen management not involved in the day-to-day auditing of Enron were sucked in by it."[52]

Of course, not all of the Andersen executives drank the Kool-Aid. Carl Bass, who worked with the firm's Professional Standards Group, had stood his ground regarding many of the sketchy accounting practices conjured up by the Enron financial team. His voice, however, became too shrill for both Enron and Andersen, and he was forced out of his position. It is fitting that as many of the key players in this story went to prison, Carl was "snapped up by a competing accounting firm, where he works when not being consulted as one of the government's favorite witnesses."[53] Even so, the Arthur Andersen story sadly evolved from a classic American

---

[49] *Final Accounting: Ambition, Greed, and the Fall of Arthur Andersen*, p. 9. Barbara Ley Toffler, Jennifer Reingold, page 9.
[50] *ABC News,* "Arthur Andersen Goes Out of Business", August 31, 2002.
[51] *Conspiracy of Fools,* Kurt Eichenwald, page 406.
[52] *Chicago Tribune,* "Ties to Enron Blinded Andersen", September 3, 2002.
[53] *Conspiracy of Fools,* Kurt Eichenwald, page 667.

success story to an extraordinary American tragedy...all because of a failure to stay true to their core values.

Your Values are Core Beliefs that have enduring meaning, for you personally, and for your enterprise

The author of *StrengthsFinder 2.0,* Don Clifton, has identified one strength that every leader should possess. He calls it **Belief**, having "certain core values that are enduring." He goes on to say:

> "These values vary from one person to another, but ordinarily your Belief theme causes you to be family-oriented, altruistic, even spiritual, and to value responsibility and high ethics--both in yourself and in others. These core values affect your behavior in many ways. They give your life meaning and satisfaction; in your view success is more than money and prestige. They provide you with direction, guiding you through the temptations and distractions of life toward a consistent set of priorities. This consistency is the foundation for all your relationships. Your friends call you dependable. 'I know where you stand," they say. Your Belief makes you easy to trust. It also demands that you find work that meshes with your values. Your work must be meaningful; it must matter to you. And guided by your Belief theme it will matter only if it gives you a chance to live out your values."[54]

The StrengthsFinder assessment is designed to help the user discover his or her personal strengths, and to provide practical tips on how to play to those strengths. Clearly, not everyone will have Belief as a major strength. However, one's personal Belief system and the values that extend from it are critical to strong leadership. You must not only talk the talk, you must walk your talk. And you must articulate what

---

[54] *StrengthsFinder 2.0 from Gallup: Discover Your CliftonStrengths,* Don Clifton, page 45.

you believe and expect of yourself and your stakeholders. Every word that you use to express the values you expect your team to live by is important...and you have the primary responsibility for that definition and communicating it. Failure to do so opens the door to potential disaster. The following story shares a case in point.

Do Whatever It Takes

I met the man at a restaurant well outside of a small rural town. He had been referred to me by a client who said that this fellow had a story I needed to hear. He was trim, well-groomed, and modestly dressed. He was, in my estimation, in his mid-forties. I wasn't sure that he was the guy I was to meet when I walked in, but after a moment or two, he strode toward me. "Hi, I'm Jim, I guess you're here to see me."

We sat down together in the farthest corner of the restaurant. Jim thanked me for meeting him, saying, "I recognized you from your picture on your website. My friend told me about CEObuilder®, and after getting an understanding of what you do, I told him I felt a strong need to share my story with you."

Still unaware of what he had on his mind, I invited him to go on. He bowed his head for a moment, and then said, "I probably should give you a little background before I get to the meat of things. I grew up in a farming community in a western state. I was one of six children, and I was blessed to have wonderful, amazing parents. They raised all of us to be God-fearing Christians. We learned to not lie, cheat, or steal, as well as to be kind to others. I was a straight-A student all the way through school, I was an All-State football player, and an Eagle Scout. And when I graduated from high school, I went on to get both a bachelor's degree and a master's degree. I married my high school sweetheart. I was the epitome of the fair-haired boy."

He went on, "After I finished my education, I was recruited by a number of companies, and I chose a great publicly traded company in California. They offered an incredible salary with more benefits than I had ever imagined. I worked hard for them, and I rose in the ranks rapidly. My wife and I were blessed with two beautiful children along the way. We were even able to afford a beautiful home not far from the beach. I felt that I was among the elite, that nothing could derail me. Soon, I was offered the opportunity to lead a division of the company. I knew I could succeed, and I readily accepted the job."

"My executive responsibilities provided the chance to work closely with the company founder and CEO. We became good friends, and he willingly empowered me to run my division with very little oversight. His direction amounted to this: '*Just do whatever it takes* to get the financial results we need to keep our share price growing.'

"I loved the latitude this counsel gave me, especially since we had several aggressive competitors. I took the CEO's counsel to heart and increased my own aggressiveness. At first, this wasn't anything more than cutthroat pricing and some corporate meanness, but when our competitors responded in kind, I began to do unethical things; things that my parents and my wife would never have agreed with. I justified these actions by rationalizing...I was simply doing what I was told, *doing whatever it takes.*

"For over a year, my actions delivered the results my boss expected. In fact, my performance far exceeded his expectations. Even so, he didn't increase my compensation, and I soon found myself resenting this. That resentment led me to further slippage in my ethics; I started to skim off a portion of division revenue into a private account.

"A few months into this embezzlement tactic, the CEO called me into his office. He was obviously agitated. He shared that a routine audit of recent transactions in my division had revealed that two of my senior managers had been discovered to be embezzling. He asked if I knew anything about this, to which I could honestly say that I did not. He expressed his relief at this, saying that while these managers would be fired and have charges brought against them, he would protect my reputation through all of these necessary actions.

"I'm sure I looked gut-shot, which didn't surprise the CEO. No doubt he felt that I was stunned by the announcement that people I had trusted had betrayed that trust. Of course, what he didn't realize at that moment was that my own actions had betrayed him.

"I trudged back to my office, deeply depressed. Would my own embezzlement be discovered? And if so, would I lose my job and perhaps my freedom, maybe even my home, and my family? My depression occupied the rest of the day, and resulted in a sleepless night. My wife became very concerned. Was I sick?, she asked. *I was...sick of who I had become.*

"By the next day, I had determined what I had to do. I returned to the CEO's office and confessed my errors, my crime. He was stunned; how could I have ever thought that what I had done was okay? His reaction began with shock, then anger, and then progressed to heartbreak. He wept, and I wept. He said that he would do what he could to protect me. Maybe, I would be able to resign and arrange to pay back the money. Maybe, by doing this, I might be able to avoid criminal prosecution.

"In the days that followed, many meetings with attorneys occurred. The hope that criminal charges would not be filed soon faded. As a public company, the fiduciary responsibility of the board of directors would not allow for this. I lost my job and became extremely well acquainted with the legal system. In the end, I was convicted for my crimes and was sentenced to federal prison. As bad as this was, the worst consequence was that, a few months into my incarceration, my wife filed for divorce. In the course of violating the trust of my boss, I had violated her trust as well.

"I sit before you today, having been paroled from prison. I've served my time, and I am hopeful that I can start over. I want to get back to the values that I was taught as a child. I have started a small business here in Podunk, where no one knows me, and I'm committed to doing things right."

As I listened to this man, I felt deep sympathy for him. Although I felt he had paid an appropriate price for his mistakes, I was saddened at how much he had lost. I thanked him for sharing his story, but then asked why he felt a need to share this with me, a stranger. His response: *"You work with business leaders, don't you? If they could hear my story, perhaps they might be ever more careful in staying true to doing things right."*

I then asked him what he had learned from his mistakes. He said that he knew that he had to own his decisions, that he couldn't blame anyone but himself for what he had done. That said, he also shared an insight that I have never forgotten.

He said, "The purpose and mission of our company were both clear. However, the only statement of company values that was ever offered was 'we do whatever it takes.' No elaboration was ever given regarding what this meant. It was left to each executive and employee to define their actions in terms of doing whatever it takes. I'm not saying that everyone interpreted these words as I did. But, as leaders, it's clear to me that doing whatever it takes needs more definition. No one at the company would have suggested that this included illegal activities, but without more definition, it became much easier to do things that weren't ethical or appropriate."

At this point, I agreed that my new acquaintance should address my CEO Forum, which he did shortly thereafter.

Every word within your Vision Statement (your Purpose, Mission & Value Proposition, and your Values) has meaning!

The preceding experience has led me to understand that *all words have meaning--and that an essential role of leaders is to make sure that the desired meaning is understood by all stakeholders.* This includes every word within your Vision Statement (your Purpose, Mission & Value Proposition, and your Values). Especially in the area of Values, leaders must extend their articulation beyond the one or two word descriptors that so often are shown on company values statements.

What Do You Do When Your Values are in Conflict?

As I walked into the corporate offices of my client, I noticed a framed poster in the lobby. It had been added since my last visit, and I was intrigued to read what it said. I was impressed with the fact that it set forth the company's purpose, mission, and values. These had been a regular agenda item for our coaching sessions over the past two years, and I was pleased that the company executives had articulated these important components of their vision.

As I waited for the CEO to usher me into his office, I noted that among the company values were the words INTEGRITY and PROFITABILITY. I certainly couldn't argue with either of these one-word values, but I wondered....might these ever come in conflict with each other? And if employees were faced with a conflict, how would they handle it?

These questions were on my mind, as I sat down with my client. He had his own agenda for our time together, so that is where we focused. However, as the coaching session came to a close, I complimented the CEO on the new poster. I also asked him questions regarding the potential conflict between integrity and profitability. I was a bit surprised at his reaction. He said, "Look, Rich, we've spent months zeroing in on the words for this document. We've had lots of executive meetings and we've discussed every aspect of it. It's time for us to move on. I don't see any conflict between any of our values, and I trust the judgment of my people to work things out if a conflict ever arises. We have more important things to focus on!"

Feeling somewhat reproved, I assured him that we would focus on his agenda, that I only wondered about what might prove to be a conflict. With that, I headed out the door.

During the ensuing months, our coaching sessions focused on the CEO's agenda. He and I were both pleased with the process, as well as the company's performance. I didn't bring up my concerns about the potential conflict between his company values, recognizing this was out of bounds.

In early December of that year, my client invited me to sit in on a year-end meeting of his executive team. I found myself sitting at a conference table with eight executives, including the CEO who sat at the head of the table. The meeting was celebratory. The company had met virtually all of their financial goals, and the upcoming year looked to be even better. Congratulations were expressed among the team, and year-end bonuses were authorized. I was grateful to be recognized for my contributions to company strategies as well.

As our time together came toward an end, the CEO invited me to say a few words. He said, "Rich, you've always been good to help us see around corners. What do you see that we should be thinking about as we move into a new year?"

I could have just added my acclaim for the success of the business, and I did acknowledge that. However, my gut told me that I should raise the issue regarding company values. So I said, "There is something I have been wondering about." Among your company values, you list integrity and profitability. I wonder if these ever come into conflict with each other, and if they do, how do you expect your people to respond?"

The CEO shot me a rather menacing glance, but having opened Pandora's Box, I went on. "Let me pose a scenario for you. It's about this time of year, and you're in the process of signing one-year contracts with your customers. Your top salesman is visiting with your largest customer, with the intention of getting the contract signed. This has been pretty routine for a number of years, but this year, the customer has a new purchasing agent. As the contract is presented for his signature, he slides it back across his desk. 'Your prices are too high,' he says. 'Unless you sharpen your pencil, we'll be going with your competitor next year.'"

"Your salesman is shocked. He tries to negotiate, but in the end, he realizes he will have to decrease the price of your products. He also realizes that he will have to get permission from corporate to do this. Shocked, and a bit discouraged, he throws the unsigned contract into his briefcase, and heads for the door. However, just as he's about to step into the hallway, the purchasing agent calls to him. "Well, wait... Perhaps we can work something out. If you were to have a big-screen television on my porch on Christmas Eve, I think I could be persuaded to sign that contract."

My client CEO quickly responded. He said, "That would never happen. And if it did, my salesman would know how to handle it." He then looked to his V.P. of Sales, and asked, "Isn't that right?"

At this point, the Sales Manager looked down at the table. It took him a few seconds to respond, and when he did, he looked across the table directly at me. He asked, "How did you know?"

Everyone in the room was stunned. The CEO stood up, *"What do you mean, how did you know?,"* he asked, glaring at his V.P.

The Sales Manager then told his own version of the story. It was very similar; the only change was that the big-screen television was a small fishing boat. The question, then, was "How was this handled?" The answer was not a comfortable one for the Sales Manager or the CEO; the boat was acquired and delivered on the basis that retaining this highly profitable customer was more important than the principle of integrity.

The remainder of the executive meeting was not nearly so celebratory, but it turned out to be the most important part thereof. Decisions were made regarding how such issues should be handled in the future, much of which focused on communicating value conflicts with the executive team in order to assure that the right decisions were made.

As I got up to leave the meeting, I was asked again, "How did you know?" My answer was in two parts. First, I certainly did not know. I was posing a hypothetical, but it was one that seemed somewhat probable. And second, I knew first-hand about its probability because early in my career, I was told that the only way I would retain a profitable contract with one of my customers was to have a case of whiskey on his front porch for Christmas. I failed to deliver the desired gift, and I lost the customer. But my integrity was intact. Of course, I had to develop new strategies to attract customers who were both high integrity and highly profitable. That wasn't as easy as becoming a whiskey delivery boy, but it was the right thing to do!

Make Sure You All Speak the Same Language

Author Brene Brown in her best-selling book, *Dare to Lead*, shares that simple value words like Integrity and Profitability must be defined by other terms that set forth desired behaviors. One such word is TRUST, which she has defined in terms of seven key elements, or sub-values. They form the acronym: BRAVING.

- **"Boundaries:** You respect my boundaries, and when you're not clear about what's okay and not okay, you ask. You're willing to say no.

- **"Reliability:** You do what you say you'll do. At work, this means staying aware of your competencies and limitations so you don't overpromise and are able to deliver on commitments and balance competing priorities.

- **"Accountability:** You own your mistakes, you apologize, and make amends.

- **"Vault:** You don't share information or experiences that are not yours to share. We both need to know that confidences are kept, and that neither of us are sharing any information about other people that should be confidential.

- **"Integrity:** You choose courage over comfort. You choose what is right over what is fun, fast, or easy, and you choose to practice your values rather than simply professing them.

- **"Nonjudgment:** I can ask for what I need, and you can ask for what you need. We can talk about how we feel without judgment. We can ask each other for help without judgment.

- **"Generosity:** You extend the most generous interpretation possible to the intentions, words, and actions of others."[55]

---

[55] *Dare to Lead: Daring Greatly and Rising Strong at Work,* Brene Brown, pages 224-226.

Notice that each of these sub-values is defined by other words. The sub-value **Boundaries**, for instance, is defined by the words: respect, asking, willingness to say no. These words bring us much closer to desired behaviors that will render the sub-value, which in turn, is a key component of the overarching value of Trust.

Notice also that Brene Brown has created terms that are unique for the enterprise that pledges allegiance to the value of Trust. While most of us would have a rough idea of what Reliability, Accountability, Integrity, Nonjudgment, and Generosity are, Boundaries and Vault probably don't mean much without elaboration. Even those terms that are more familiar almost always have their own unique meanings in the context of a given enterprise. This demands that we dig deeper as we define and articulate personal and company values.

The late Tony Hsieh, founder of the online shoe store, Zappos, recognized that the best way to build a culture that reflected the values of the company was to compile the stories that clearly presented those values and culture. In his book, *Delivering Happiness,* he shared how this was accomplished:

> "'We….just ask *all* of our employees to write a few paragraphs about what the Zappos culture means to them, and compile it all into a book.' Tony said. And just like that, the idea of a Zappos Culture book was born, and it's been part of Zappos ever since. Every year, a new edition of the Zappos Culture Book is produced, which we give out to prospective employees, vendors, and even customers."[56]

Tony sent the following email to all employees in August 2004:

From: Tony Hsieh
To: All Zappos Employees
Subject: Zappos Culture Book

---

[56] *Delivering Happiness: A Path to Profits, Passion, and Purpose*, Tony Hsieh, pages 134-135.

We will be putting together a mini-book as part of the orientation package for all new hires about the Zappos culture. Our culture is the combination of all of our employees' ideas about the culture, so we would like to include everyone's thoughts in this book.

Please email me 100-500 words about what the Zappos culture means to you. (What is the Zappos culture? What's different about it compared to other company cultures? What do you like about our culture?)

We will compile everyone's contribution into the book. If you wish for your entry to be anonymous, please indicate so in your response. We will be distributing the book to all new hires as well as all existing employees.

Also, please do not talk to anyone about what you will be writing or what anyone else wrote. We want to know what the Zappos culture means to you specifically, as it will be different to different people.[57]

The Zappos Culture Book has become a compendium of stories that define the behaviors that deliver on the company's Ten Core Values. Tony responded to a question that is often asked: *Why does an employee on page 40 sound strangely similar to someone else on page 128 or 340?* His answer: "It's because everyone at Zappos lives by the 10 Core Values. By sharing a common belief system, Zappos employees become the unified brand to the world.[58]

The key to Zappos' success was not just to define their vision in terms of the company's purpose, mission, and values, but to create the culture that delivered on the promises inherent in that vision. Tony Hsieh discovered that the best way to create and evangelize that culture

---

[57] Ibid.
[58] Ibid, page 141.

was through the stories told by his people about the company. Their stories gave life to the company's Ten Core Values:[59]

1. Deliver WOW Through Service
2. Embrace and Drive Change
3. Create Fun and a Little Weirdness
4. Be Adventurous, Creative, and Open-Minded
5. Pursue Growth and Learning
6. Build Open and Honest Relationships with Communication
7. Build a Positive Team and Family Spirit
8. Do More with Less
9. Be Passionate and Determined
10. Be Humble

He gave an important caution for leaders regarding such core values:

> "Many companies have core values, but they don't really commit to them. They usually sound more like something you'd read in a press release. Maybe you learn about them on day 1 of orientation, but after that it's just a meaningless plaque on the wall of the lobby. We believe that it's really important to come up with core values that you can commit to. And by commit, we mean that you're willing to hire and fire based on them. If you're willing to do that, then you're well on your way to building a company culture that is in line with the brand you want to build. You can let all of your employees be your brand ambassadors, not just the marketing or PR department. And they can be brand ambassadors both inside and outside the office."[60]

---

[59] Ibid, page 154.
[60] Ibid.

Key insights:

- Do not expect strong Alignment & Execution if you—and your key stakeholders—do not speak the same language.
- As the leader of your enterprise, it is essential that YOU actively engage in defining the words that comprise your Vision, Mission (including your Value Proposition), and your Values; if you don't actively engage in defining and interpreting those words, others will…
- Your stories, and those of your company, will help give definition to those words.
- You must become a collector and sharer of those stories.
- Documenting your stories—and publishing them—are proven, effective strategies for alignment and execution (as shared in Tony Hsieh's best-selling book, *Delivering Happiness).*
- You must be your company's Chief Evangelist, the person who continuously shares, defines, and promotes the Vision (Purpose, Mission & Value Proposition, and Values).

Let's return again to Southwest Airlines...

The following is the narrative for the video: **Southwest Airlines: Our Purpose and Vision.** It is used to evangelize the company vision, including their purpose, mission, and values. They use it in onboarding new employees, and reinforcing their vision with the thousands of people they employ. It represents one example of a company's approach to setting--and living--their vision. The video can be accessed at:

https://www.youtube.com/watch?v=eGxMf88I5g4

"At Southwest Airlines, we're united by a purpose. A purpose that is at the heart of everything we do. It's the simplest and purest expression of why we exist. Our purpose at Southwest Airlines is clear.

We exist to connect people to what's important in their lives through friendly, reliable and low-cost air travel.

This purpose is why we get up every morning and why we matter to the millions of people who fly with us each year...and if we live this purpose every day, we'll achieve our vision: to become the world's most loved, most flown, and most profitable airline. **But it all starts with you.**"

WE CONNECT PEOPLE TO WHAT'S IMPORTANT IN THEIR LIVES THROUGH FRIENDLY AIR TRAVEL

Story #1

Jessica Chatellier, SWA Customer: We had to go to the airport for my husband to be deployed for six months to Kuwait. So when we got to the airport, we were sure that we wouldn't be able to go past security with him. We would have to say goodbye...

Kelli Evans SWA Customer Service Agent: I saw him walk up in uniform and I saw a whole bunch of family members standing nearby. So I asked him if he was being deployed and he said yes. And I asked him if they all wanted to go to the gate with him, and he said, "Yeah, that would be great."

Jessica Chatellier, SWA Customer: So we were very happy because that bought us about 30 more minutes for us to spend time together, but once it was time for him to go on the plane, we had our moment, we hugged and said goodbye. The kids did really great. I was holding it together, but we wanted to stay and watch his plane take off. One of the Southwest employees came over, and tapped us on the shoulder again, and said, "Can I please do something for you?" The thoughts in the back of my head were...what can you possibly do to make this any better at this point?

Felix Joseph, SWA Operations Agent: I realized we had about three to four extra minutes before the scheduled departure time.

Jessica Chatellier, SWA Customer: He stepped away for a moment, made a quick phone call and came back and asked if the kids and I would mind coming onto the plane. So we were very excited. The kids ran down the tunnel. When we got to the end of the tunnel, they called out on the intercom asking if there was a John Chatellier on the flight. We saw my husband's hand go up in the air. And the kids were able to run to him and give him one last hug. And the amazing part was the whole plane cheered and everybody was really excited for us. So we got one last moment with him before they closed the doors and the plane took off.

Felix Joseph, SWA Operations Agent: It was a touching moment. All the passengers started clapping, and everyone was tearing up.

Jessica Chatellier, SWA Customer: When I talked to him when he had landed in Kuwait, he said that that whole moment, that experience made him realize that people were going to be watching out for us, watching out for him, and just taking care of us overall.

<u>Story #2</u>

ABOVE AND **BEYOND**

Tommy Saugey, SWA Customer: I boarded the plane in Little Rock. I was running late and didn't have time for breakfast. It was a busy and crowded plane. The last two people on the plane were a lady and her daughter. And there were not two seats together, so the little girl started getting upset. So I got up and gave them my seat because there was a seat beside me. I flew into Phoenix and realized that, in the layover there, I couldn't get off the plane. I was pretty hungry, so I asked the attendant, Amy, if there were any turkey sandwiches for sale. She said "No, I'm sorry," but she went and got me some chips and things like that. Then she disappeared and a few minutes later she reappeared with a turkey sandwich. She had gone out on the concourse and bought me a sandwich. And I thought that was above and beyond. And, you know, I tried to pay her, but she said, "No, this is my way of saying thank you for giving up your seat. She saw that I had a problem, I had to wait a while for lunch and I would've never expected that, but she went the extra mile.

Story #3

DAD'S **FLIGHT** HOME

Ronnie Flanigen, SWA Customer: I just feel like Southwest is part of our family.

Patrick Flanigen, SWA Customer: Even with our kids being away from us, it brings us closer. When my father passed away in Buffalo, New York...and Southwest flies to Buffalo. So we land in Buffalo and we do the funeral. My dad had a full honor guard, and part of that ceremony is that the flag is folded up and handed to the family members. An Air Force tradition that we celebrate is to honor the pilot or the military member, we would ask that the flag be flown in the cockpit of an airplane. So when we got on our plane out of Buffalo, I asked the pilots if they would do me the honor of carrying my dad's flag in the cockpit. Both the pilot and the co-pilot looked at me and said, it would be an honor for us to fly that for you.

Jeffrey Fortezzo, SWA Captain: Of course we were thrilled to do something like that to help him. So we had it in the cockpit for the last flight home for his father.

Patrick Flanigen, SWA Customer: The flag up in the cockpit was just perfect for us. They honored dad and he got to fly one final flight home. It's where a pilot belongs, up in the cockpit.

Story #4

WE CONNECT PEOPLE TO WHAT'S IMPORTANT IN THEIR LIVES THROUGH **RELIABLE** AIR TRAVEL: DOING **BUSINESS** WITH SOUTHWEST

SWA Business Customer: I am a pretty regular Southwest business traveler. It's just a different flying experience than any other airline. Everybody just is having fun with their job. They board the fastest, they get your bags off the fastest. They're efficient which is always great. I knew exactly when I would land every week, so I could easily schedule my meetings and the rest of my day around it because I knew they were going to be on time. Leaving home was not my favorite part of the work week, but Southwest made it the best. They made it the easiest to leave and come back home by making an enjoyable experience to come and go every week.

Story #5

THE **ADVENTURES** OF HANOVER BEAR

Lara Shelton, SWA Customer: We were taking Southwest from Jacksonville to Kansas City, with a layover in Nashville. It was just enough time to grab a piece of pizza and accidentally leave a backpack with our most prized possession, Hanover Bear. We didn't discover this until we landed in Kansas City, at which time we all freaked out! We called Southwest's 800 number. They gave us a direct line to someone in the Nashville airport.

Emily Thorne McCarthy, SWA Customer Service Agent: As a mom, I can relate to that because I told her that I had two daughters, so I understood the trauma that the little boy was going through missing his Hanover Bear.

Lara Shelton, SWA Customer: I believe it was around 11 o'clock at night or something and she felt so bad that Will was going to have to sleep a night without Hanover Bear. She said she would do her very best to find him.

Emily Thorne McCarthy, SWA Customer Service Agent: So I went upstairs to our play area, and sure enough, the little blue backpack with the boy's name on it was there.

Lara Shelton, SWA Customer: We couldn't believe; not only did she find it, but that she would really work hard to get it to him. I want to say that it was maybe two days later; not only the bear was in it, but a note from the bear.

> Dear Will,
>
> I had a very funtime at the airport in Nashville! There were lots of people and planes to see. When it was time to go to sleep, I missed you. I asked a nice lady at Southwest to call Mommy so I could come home.
>
> Please give me a big hug!
> Love, Hanover Bear

Story #6

WE CONNECT PEOPLE TO WHAT'S IMPORTANT IN THEIR LIVES THROUGH **LOW-COST** AIR TRAVEL: SOUTHWEST AIRLINES **DELIVERS**

Vicki Iliff, SWA Customer: My story starts May, 2011, when I got a phone call from my only child telling us she was pregnant with my first grandchild. Our excitement ended about two weeks later when my son-in-law called to tell us that she had a very serious condition called hyperemesis. So I went to Birmingham and spent the weekend with her. Then I came back home and figured that I would see her again over the summer because I'm a teacher. Two weeks later, I was in the post office and got a text from her. And the text said, "Mommy, I can't do this."

So I went to my principal and my principal said, "What are you doing here? Go!" I went home and was able to book a flight on Southwest the next morning. And not only book a flight, but use my points. I would have spent any amount of money to get there, but instead I spent $2.50 using my points. That trip lasted until the end of August. I stayed with her all summer and it was probably the hardest thing we've ever done. But when I left to come back to school in August, I knew I could get back there if I needed to--and she was much better by then. She was able to go back to teaching too. So during my daughter's pregnancy and the eventual delivery, I was able to go five round trips from Orlando to Birmingham. I was able to get there within 24 hours of my first grandchild being born. After this all happened, I realized what a significant role Southwest had played in the whole story. Southwest really came through for us.

Story #7

THE **BEST** CHRISTMAS GIFT EVER

Katie Reilly, SWA Customer: Last Christmas was my first Christmas away from my family. I couldn't really afford to go home for Christmas because I could only get four days off at work. One evening in November, my phone went off right before I was going to bed and it was Southwest and their Ding Fare Alerts. It was available to go to Chicago for Christmas for those four days. So I decided to call my friend and tell her that we were going to surprise my parents and that she was going to pick me up from the airport. And we were going to film the whole thing. Since I hadn't been home in six months, my mom was extremely upset that I wasn't going to be there for the holidays. My mom's reaction was priceless. She was crying; she cried for almost two hours. It was the best Christmas gift I could have ever given them and without Southwest, there was no way I was going to be able to go home and give that to them. It was a very very good Christmas.

Lara Shelton, SWA Customer: **Because of you, my son can sleep well at night.**

Vicki Iliff, SWA Customer: **Because of you, I was able to be at my daughter's side throughout her difficult pregnancy.**

Jessica Chatellier, SWA Customer: **Because of you, my family and I have a memory for a lifetime.**

Katie Reilly, SWA Customer: **Because of you, I was able to give my parents the best Christmas gift ever.**

SUMMARY MESSAGES

- You work for a company of people, not a company of products or promises.

- You work alongside the best people in the world, people committed to a common purpose: To connect people to what's important in their lives through friendly, reliable and low-cost air travel. A purpose much bigger than ourselves.

- We can never rest on our laurels, thinking that we've arrived. We must always continue to be hungry and humble, never complacent. Because more than 100 million customers rely on us every year to connect them to important events safely. It's a pretty sacred responsibility.

- Because of you, a business person can close the deal of a lifetime. A child from the heartland can encounter the majesty of the ocean. A father can hold his daughter for the first time. And a daughter can make it home in time to hug her father for the last time. These experiences are irreplaceable. $20 too high, or 20 minutes too late, and those experiences vanish forever.

- **By maintaining our low-cost, we're an airline people can afford to fly.**

- **By reliably delivering on our promise, we are an airline people can trust.**

- By offering friendly customer service, we are an airline people can love.
- This purpose, offering air travel that is friendly, reliable and low-cost enables us to offer customers a better way. And together, they mean the difference between success and failure, between an experience won and a connection lost.
- No one connects people better than we do. You're part of an amazing legacy--and you're the catalyst for an exciting future. And whether you're on the ground or in the air, in an office, or at a gate, what we've created is worth anything and everything to keep. Because hardly anyone else has it. And you do. We do, together.
- Our vision is to become the world's most loved, most flown, and most profitable airline.You inspire and deliver this vision. You are the heart of our purpose. *You are Southwest Airlines.*[61]

THE VALUES OF SOUTHWEST AIRLINES

- Connection
- Friendliness
- Reliability
- Cost Conscious
- People
- Competence
- Commitment
- Unselfishness
- Continuous Improvement
- Initiative

---

[61] *Southwest Airlines: Our Purpose and Vision,* **https://www.youtube.com/watch?v=eGxMf88I5g4**

- Humility
- Safety
- Engagement
- Trust
- Love
- Excellence
- Legacy

Each of these values are manifest in the stories of how Southwest works, day-in and day-out, to achieve their purpose and their mission.

But wait! Beginning on December 21, 2022, and continuing through December 31, Southwest canceled more than 16,700 flights, stranding millions of travelers in airports around the U.S.. A loss of an estimated $425 million in company revenue brought CEO Bob Jordan to an earnings call with investors. He responded contritely, "We really made a mess for our customers and employees," he said. "At the end of the day, that kind of disruption cannot happen again."[62]

Many airlines experienced disruptions during the weekend of Christmas, 2022 as a result of an Arctic air mass that brought huge winter storms across the eastern and central U.S.. Southwest's cancellations, however, stretched well past the weekend.

The Southwest "mess" brought an investigation by the Department of Transportation (DOT). They concluded that the company must provide refunds and reimbursements to disrupted travelers, and indicated that Southwest executives might be charged with engaging in unrealistic flight scheduling, which under federal law is considered an unfair and deceptive practice. Company spokespersons have denied that this was the case.

In response to this potential allegation from the DOT, Southwest issued the following statement: "Our holiday flight schedule was thoughtfully designed and offered to our customers with the backing

---

[62]   https://www.cbsnews.com/news/four-day-workweek-boosts-employee-satisfaction-retention-bernie-sanders/

of a solid plan to operate it, and with ample staffing. Our systems and processes became stressed while working to recover from multiple days of flight cancellations across 50 airports in the wake of an unprecedented storm." They continued: "Southwest is acutely focused on learning from this event….and mitigating the risk of a repeat occurrence and will work with officials on the investigation."[63] The company is fully engaged in updating and improving their systems in that regard.

By mid-January, 2023, the company completed virtually all of the required reimbursements and refunds related to holiday travel cancellations. In doing so, they lost over $800 million in pretax profits, leading to a net loss of $220 million in the fourth quarter of 2022.[64]

In a subsequent statement, the company stated, "Thus far in January 2023, the Company has experienced an increase in flight cancellations and a deceleration in bookings, primarily for January and February 2023 travel, which are assumed to be associated with the operational disruptions in December 2022. As a result, the Company currently estimates a negative revenue impact in the range of $300 million to $350 million in first quarter 2023,"[65]

They went on to say that "25% of those customers caught in the holiday meltdown have future travel booked on Southwest. Some of those trips have been booked with the points offered by the company in the wake of the cancellations — travelers were offered 25,000 points as a gesture of goodwill — and others with cash."[66]

So, how did Southwest perform when evaluated against their clearly stated values, during their 10 day disaster….and in the days that followed? Let's check it, point-by-point:

---

[63] Ibid.
[64] Ibid.
[65] Ibid.
[66] Ibid.

THE VALUES OF SOUTHWEST AIRLINES

- **Connection:** During the 10 days between December 21 and December 31, 2022, SWA travelers went through the worst meltdown in flight connections ever experienced in the airline's history. While some customers have determined to "forgive and forget," many feel that their trust has been violated. Even with refunds and reimbursements, it is likely that it will take months or even years to rebuild that trust.

- **Friendliness:** From virtually all reports, SWA employees kept their cool and treated their customers with respect and kindness. However, the emotions of both travelers and employees were sorely tested. That said, SWA executives and front-line employees are deeply committed to retaining their friendly, helpful, and good-humored approach to their customers.

- **Reliability:** The airline's reputation for reliability took a huge hit. It will take them considerable time to restore the faith of their customers and the industry on this crucial value. But they are diligently working to that end.

- **Cost Conscious:** It has, no doubt, been an extraordinarily tough pill to swallow in addressing the huge financial impact of the December 2022 debacle with SWA shareholders. However, the airline has stepped up their responsibility to take care of customers who were disrupted, and to initiate the investment required to update and improve their systems. And, in the midst of these investments, they have recognized the need to continue to be both cost-conscious and price-competitive.

- **People:** In the midst of the 10 day "mess," virtually all people (SWA travelers and employees) experienced stress unlike anything they had ever experienced with the airline. However, employees never lost sight of the paramount importance of people to Southwest. This starts and ends with customers, but clearly encompasses the SWA family as well. Although the "mess" was stressful, the airline's commitment to people never wavered.

- **Competence:** During the debacle, SWA's competence seemed to be "absent without leave." Clearly, the company must address their competencies to deal with extreme weather events, and provide better contingency processes to deal with them without disruption to the traveling public. Their efforts to do this are underway.

- **Commitment:** The airline's commitment both during and after the 10-day meltdown has never been in question. Even in the midst of this crisis, SWA executives and employees remained committed to their travelers, although their abilities to resolve the problem proved to be beyond them. Today, they are committed to learn from their mistakes and resolve them.

- **Unselfishness:** A failure to solve a crisis in the moment it is happening is not selfish; it simply reflects a lack of effective solutions. The willingness to reach deeply into company coffers for refunds and reimbursements can hardly be considered selfish.

- **Continuous Improvement:** If ever there was an opportunity for improvement, the December debacle is it! In the midst of cancellations and upset customers, it is unlikely that front-line SWA employees were thinking about how their system could be improved. However, after things settled down, it is clear that SWA executives are deeply engaged in that effort.

- **Initiative:** Initiative is best demonstrated by how quickly and well executives and employees respond to problems and opportunities. In the midst of this crisis, SWA employees throughout the country strived to give the best response at their disposal. Unfortunately, the SWA system did not allow them much leeway. Since that time, Bob Jordan and his team have shown great initiative in both owning the problems inherent in SWA systems, and moving to resolve them.

- **Humility:** SWA has been significantly humbled by this experience, both during and after. The greatest evidence of this is that they did not attempt to blame others for their failures. While they acknowledged that the weather was a contributing factor, they recognized that their systems were inadequate.

- **Safety:** Clearly, safety considerations are always paramount, especially in bad weather conditions. While travel disruptions are uncomfortable, SWA customers were not subjected to undue hazards. The airline continues to be 100% committed to the highest safety standards.

- **Engagement:** In the midst of a crisis, it can be tempting to disengage, to try to run away from the tension surrounding you. Surely there were some of these tendencies with SWA employees as they felt impotent to solve their customers' travel needs during the period of massive cancellations. However, since that time, the company has proven their commitment to engage with every traveler to resolve their needs and retain them as SWA customers.

- **Trust:** For travelers facing cancellations with no ready alternative flight, trust clearly was destroyed. And trust that is so visibly decimated is not easily restored. It will take incredible effort over months, and even years, in addressing each of the key values shared here to fully restore trust. SWA executives and employees are pledged to do just that.

- **Love:** A traveler who has just been informed that their flight home for Christmas has been canceled probably doesn't feel very loved by their airline. Love, like trust, is earned…and since it has taken a hard blow at SWA, love will take time to be restored. Employees will need to reflect their love for their customers–and one another–even more than in the past. They are working on it.

- **Excellence:** No one, not even those of us who are fans of Southwest, will give them high marks for the December debacle. They clearly failed in the moment of this crisis. However, their long history of excellence, although a bit scarred, provides the basis for their outstanding team to overcome the challenges that they experienced–and mitigate such problems for the future.

- **Legacy:** Some observers might wonder if Herb Kelleher is "spinning in his grave" over this "mess." My answer: "Probably not." You see, Herb knew that airlines are, by their very nature, subject to significant risks. The reality is that on any given day, or any given flight, hundreds of things can–and will–go wrong. But if you truly love and care about PEOPLE, you do your very best to serve them with meticulous excellence, friendliness and good humor. You step up to your problems–and you solve them. Herb would want to know what the SWA family had learned from all of this–and how they will do better next time. That will make this experience part of the Southwest success story and legacy!

On that note, let's check again for Alignment...

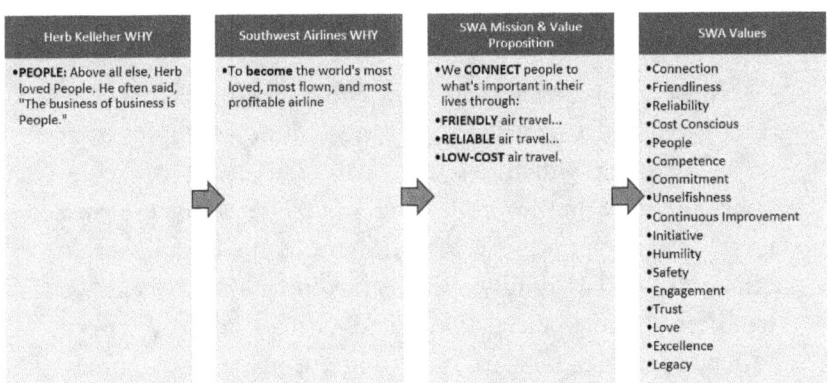

Herb Kelleher WHY	Southwest Airlines WHY	SWA Mission & Value Proposition	SWA Values
•PEOPLE: Above all else, Herb loved People. He often said, "The business of business is People."	•To become the world's most loved, most flown, and most profitable airline	•We CONNECT people to what's important in their lives through: •FRIENDLY air travel... •RELIABLE air travel... •LOW-COST air travel.	•Connection •Friendliness •Reliability •Cost Conscious •People •Competence •Commitment •Unselfishness •Continuous Improvement •Initiative •Humility •Safety •Engagement •Trust •Love •Excellence •Legacy

As discussed earlier in this chapter, the personal values of Herb Kelleher are manifested in the values of the company he founded, Southwest Airlines. Gary Kelly and Bob Jordan have continued with full and energetic commitment to those values. They align well with the Southwest WHY (their purpose), as well as their mission & value proposition. Those values set the standard for what their executives and employees will and will not do to assure that their purpose, mission, and value proposition are achieved. Their stories reflect those values and set the foundation for their corporate culture.

At this point, one might appropriately ask, how well does the Southwest Vision (purpose, mission, and values) translate into performance and financial outcomes? One of the key performance indicators (KPIs) within their Southwest value of Continuous Improvement is *gate turnaround times.* In the airline industry, turnaround time equates directly to money. Herb Kelleher put it this way, "Planes make money in the air, not sitting on the ground." When aircraft are parked, they represent an unproductive cost to the company. Southwest puts a hyper-focus on turnaround time–stressing the importance of consistently surpassing their competitors in this key metric.

Competition, however, didn't fail to notice Southwest's success– and they soon began to adopt similar strategies. It was surprising to many industry observers that the efforts of other airlines were largely unsuccessful. Why? Rasmus Hougaard and Jacqueline Carter in their book, *The Mind of the Leader,* answered this way:

> "Because other airlines lacked Southwest's social cohesion. Southwest had established a strong culture of compassion in its teams , which led to a stronger sense of social cohesion–the bond for collaboration. To get a plane turned around requires up to twelve different teams to collaborate efficiently and willingly. Pilots, ticketing agents, baggage handlers, maintenance teams, and tarmac crews all need to work together to more quickly get a plane in the air. In most airlines, these functions aren't particularly keen to collaborate because of distinct power hierarchies and cross-team disputes. The culture instilled in Southwest Airlines, however, is one of genuine respect and concern. Pilots aren't seen as superior, and maintenance crew members aren't seen as expendable. They're all part of the same organism, with the same purpose of getting their passengers in the air as quickly

as possible–and accomplishing this while experiencing joy and kindness toward one another. Much to the chagrin of other airlines, operational procedures are not the cause of quick turnaround times–compassion and cohesion are."[67]

Since Herb Kelleher founded Southwest Airlines in 1967, they have been one of the most profitable airlines in the world. When asked what he attributed this success to, CEO Gary Kelly responded:

"Herb Kelleher, our founder, said that we are a people business. Technically, we may be an airline, freighting customers around the country, but the foundation of that is our people. Everything we do is done by our people. All problems are solved by our people. All happy customers are made happy by our people. If we did not put people first, they would not be able to do a great job."[68]

The purpose of Southwest Airlines began with Herb Kelleher's personal love of people. He articulated that into his unique personal purpose, mission, and values–and then worked tirelessly to incorporate that vision and philosophy into the Southwest culture.

Although Southwest has not avoided significant challenges over the years (including the December 2022 flight cancellations crisis), this culture has sustained strong performance and financial outcomes in good times and bad. It is especially significant to note that the culture has continued beyond the life of the company's founder. Herb Kelleher not only was the architect of an outstanding business success, he left a legacy that continues to care for and serve people.

[67] *The Mind of the Leader: How to Lead Yourself, Your People, and Your Organization for Extraordinary Results,* Rasmus Hougaard and Jacqueline Carter, page 203.
[68] *Compassionate Leadership: How to Do Hard Things in a Human Way,* Rasmus Hougaard and Jacqueline Carter, page 25.

So, what are your values, both personal as well as those in your business?

Do they align well with your purpose, mission and value proposition?

Might they need more definition?

Might they be bolstered by the stories your stakeholders tell about you and your enterprise?

Do those values need more clarity and articulation to provide the culture you need to succeed?

Your answers to these questions are important, even critical to your success, and perhaps to your survival as the leader of a successful enterprise. Core Values are an essential part of each leader's personal and enterprise vision. Like your Purpose and Mission, they must be thoughtfully defined and articulated. Together, these key elements of your Vision represent the existential foundation for the alignment and execution of your business—and your life.

That said, I have too often found that my encouragement to address these key elements of Vision falls on deaf ears. *My question is WHY???*

It is in pursuit of an answer to this question that I have written the next chapter of Align & Execute.

CHAPTER 5

We Know We Need a Compelling Vision, So What is Keeping Us from Creating and Pursuing One?

Irresolution on the schemes of life which offer themselves to our choice, and inconstancy in pursuing them, are the greatest causes of all our unhappiness.

Joseph Addison

Most of us are very well acquainted with the process of resolution setting at the beginning of each new year. Unfortunately, most of us are also very well acquainted with failing to keep those resolutions.

As the late author and businessman, Arnold Glasgow has said, "Most good resolutions start too late and end too soon." Why is it that human beings recognize the inherent need for great resolutions, for compelling visions for our lives and our enterprises, yet so often fail to have the resolve to create and pursue those visions?

Famed inventor, engineer, and businessman, Charles F. Kettering, cut through all of the many excuses we use for failing to make and keep our resolutions, for failing to develop and pursue compelling visions. He put it this way: "No one would have crossed the ocean if he could have gotten off the ship in the storm."

In other words, we must recognize that any resolve, any commitment, will face the storms of opposing forces. Those forces may be afflicting you right now, as you begin to venture forward. Indeed, they may assault your emerging vision head-on, causing you to question or procrastinate your efforts. And if that is not the case, you surely must anticipate that other unforeseen storms will sooner or later confront you.

A compelling vision will define the distant shore with all of the positive outcomes associated with arriving there. That vision will define who and what you and your enterprise want to become, how to navigate the waters ahead, and what you will—and will not—do to cross the seas. That vision, with its associated outcomes, fuels your resolve to set sail. But the initial resolve is not enough. It is woefully inadequate…. if you treat vision setting as an event. It must be seen as a process that prepares you for the journey—and the storms ahead. And then, when you have won the hearts and heads (your own and those of your key stakeholders), you must unitedly put your hands to the oars and pay the ongoing price required to cross the metaphorical ocean of your vision. *You must not get off the ship when the storms come.*

The costs required to arrive at the distant shores where you'll reap the benefits of a compelling vision begin with dedicating the time and effort required to develop that vision. Subsequent chapters herein will provide you with a path for that time and effort. Even so, I have found that sharing the path is often premature without first helping you clear the way for your journey.

In that regard, it is important to first clearly assess where you are today. Please take a few minutes to thoughtfully and accurately answer the following questions:

1. *Today, right now, do **you** have a compelling Personal Purpose, the WHY for your life?*

   Please note that this question is focused on **you**, not your business, company, or venture. If you have a clear Personal Purpose, please pause from reading and take a few minutes to articulate that purpose in writing, here and now. If you have yet to develop a Personal Purpose, or have not articulated it; don't despair, beginning in Chapter 7, I'll share a proven path that will get you there.

_____

_____

_____

_____

2. *Today, right now, do you have a compelling Company Purpose, the WHY for your enterprise?*

   Note that this question is focused on your business, company, or venture. If you have that Company Purpose, please take the time to articulate it in writing, here and now. If you don't have a clearly articulated Company Purpose, that path will also be defined herein.

_____

_____

_____

_____

3. *Today, right now, do you have a clear Mission and Value Proposition–for yourself and your business?*

   If your answer is "yes,", please take a few minutes here to articulate your Mission and Value Proposition in writing. If you don't have these–or if they are unclear, I'll soon address them as well.

_____

_____

_____

_____

4. Are your Core Values crystal clear, not only to yourself, but to your key stakeholders? Specifically, what are those core values?

If your answer is "yes,", please take a few minutes to write them here. If you don't have these, they will also be addressed in upcoming chapters.

_____

_____

_____

_____

*5. Are **you** fully aligned with your Vision (Purpose, Mission, and Values)? Are each of your key stakeholders fully aligned?*

This is a critical question which generally demands more than a quick answer. If you are unsettled about your Vision, or if any of your key stakeholders are not in tune with it, this must be addressed. Upcoming chapters will provide you with guidance on this important issue.

6. Is there a need to fortify the foundation of your enterprise by strengthening your Vision?

We have yet to find a leader who answers all of the first five of these questions affirmatively—and the answer to the sixth question is virtually always YES. Outstanding leaders recognize that successful alignment and execution of their strategies requires clarity regarding their Purpose, Mission, and Core Values. Even so, we find that for many, the development of a compelling Vision is difficult and elusive.

Over three plus decades of working with CEOs, business owners, and general managers at CEObuilder®, we have found that while the reasons for this vary, they generally fall within the following responses:

- You are experiencing inadequate profitability and cash flow. You are compelled to keep your focus there, and consequently, you feel you have no time for developing your vision; you'll get to it when the money improves.

- As the leader, you have to solve all of the major problems–and there are so many that you can't spend time on anything that doesn't have immediate value.

- Your "To Do List" is endless; you never feel that you get enough done. You simply can't add vision-setting to your list right now.

- You're often undecided as to where to focus your attention. Adding visioning seems to exacerbate your indecisiveness.

- You're lonely...it's indeed lonely at the top, and you don't know where to turn for help on so many things. Setting a compelling vision is just one of them.

- If you could get others to carry some of your load, you might have time for visioning, but you're unable to delegate key aspects of leadership to others. You fear that they will not, or cannot, do the job necessary.

- You're so deeply involved with the details of the business that you struggle to think strategically. Your vision is simply to survive day-to-day.

- You excuse yourself, ignoring the fact that you are caught up in a daily game of whack-a-mole. You say, "We are fine. We're just experiencing the typical ups and downs of every business. We've made it this far without a clearly articulated vision; besides everyone knows what we do and everyone is working hard."

- A vision and mission and all that stuff is just touchy-feely crap!

These "reasons" for failing to develop a compelling vision are not really reasons at all. Michael Gerber, bestselling author of *The E-Myth* and *The E-Myth Revisited* puts it this way:

> "Most entrepreneurs are merely technicians with an entrepreneurial seizure. Most entrepreneurs fail because you are working IN your business rather than ON your business."

Or, as the old business proverb goes, "When you're up to your neck in alligators, it's hard to remember that your initial objective was to drain the swamp!"

If this feels familiar to you, welcome to a very large club! Virtually anyone who has launched into a new venture, or has been promoted into the top leadership role (or has inherited it), has felt this way. When an enterprise is new, or very small, the leader must wear multiple hats, including product/service development, production, sales, marketing, finance, accounting, HR, customer service, etc. YOU do it all…or at least you try.

Let's pause for a moment to consider your job description as CEO, owner, general manager, or leader of your enterprise. You are ultimately responsible for every aspect of your Business Success Pyramid:

Business Success Pyramid
CEO's Job Description

VISION

$ Every enterprise must be financially sound

Delighted customers ring the cash register **CUSTOMER**

OPERATIONAL Operational effectiveness & efficiency deliver customer outcomes.

Employee competencies deliver operational outcomes **COMPETENCY** **ENGAGEMENT** A highly engaged workforce assures continuous performance

RECRUITMENT

Competence & Engagement begin with targeted recruitment

YOUR VISION MUST BE CONTINUOUSLY & ENERGETICALLY EVANGELIZED. IT IS THE MORTAR THAT HOLDS THESE BUILDING BLOCKS TOGETHER.

CEObuilder
We Build Successful CEOs

While the pyramid is a helpful reminder of your job, it doesn't take long for most leaders to find it to be quite daunting. Over our years of coaching CEOs and other leaders, we've noted that these individuals are among the most dedicated and hard-working people on the planet. We've also noted that when you try to do all of these things yourself, you are setting yourself up for failure. This is true for two reinforcing reasons:

1. You are ultimately unable to sustain your extraordinary efforts; in other words, you burn out, and....

2. You fail to build the competencies, engagement, and buy-in of others sufficient to assure that you can delegate much of your load.

Failing to succeed in building a team of committed and competent people, you lack the essential scaffolding to build a successful business.

A simplistic view of this problem would be to simply focus attention on the training and development of your employees. While that is indeed necessary, it skips the essential focus on vision setting, whereby you engage your own heart and mind, and the hearts and minds of your team members. Failure to articulate your personal and enterprise purpose, mission, and core values overlooks the critical importance of establishing a strong, compelling foundation for everyone. When this is accomplished and is thoroughly communicated and understood, you have the cause to which you will rally others, to which they will desire to belong. They will desire to step up and help you carry the heavy load that constitutes your job description.

Vision setting, then, is definitively an *ON The Business* function, perhaps the most important *ON The Business* function for your enterprise, and even for your life. And when leaders focus intensive time and effort on this specific *ON The Business* function, they inevitably find that their IN The Business challenges diminish as their team members increasingly carry the load for those concerns.

Our business and economic environment has recently been shaken to the core by a global pandemic, social unrest, and economic instability. These factors have certainly exacerbated the pain points that were identified in a recent CEObuilder® survey. It is not surprising that anxieties are driving our reactions, and that those reactions tend to make fire-fighters out of us, rather than fire-preventers. But the natural focus on just staying afloat, of short-term survival, too often will consign you to "do what you've always done, only working harder than you ever have." Unfortunately, if you do what you've always done in today's business environment, you don't just get what you've always gotten, *you get less than you ever have.*

What is more needed than ever before is real visionary leadership. It requires you to become a strong *ON The Business* leader. It requires you to become an accomplished visionary leader! You must decide that in spite of your overwhelming To Do List, you will find *On The Business* time to dedicate yourself to the process of developing both your Personal and Enterprise Vision. There is no better time than the present to make this decision. Failing to decide and fully commit shackles you to the grind of all the endless minutiae that keeps you from both business and personal success.

This will stretch you to be sure, since your IN The Business tasks won't miraculously evaporate. While your commitment to move forward with vision-setting is critical, you must, of course, deal with your realities. It's poor counsel to simply say, "Stop doing your IN The Business tasks. You know—and so do I—that if you go cold turkey on those challenges, your business is toast. (A great sandwich, but a lousy business strategy!)

The challenge is that setting a compelling vision is almost always seen as Important, but not Urgent. IN The Business tasks, on the other hand, are often seen as Urgent, with many clearly being both Urgent and Important. ***Urgent and Important* always trumps *Important, but not Urgent*...BUT SHOULD IT?**

Consider Personal Fitness...

Is regular exercise and a healthy diet important? Virtually everyone would say "Yes." But are these practices Urgent? Most would say "No."

But should we wait to eat right and exercise until Personal Fitness becomes both Important and Urgent?

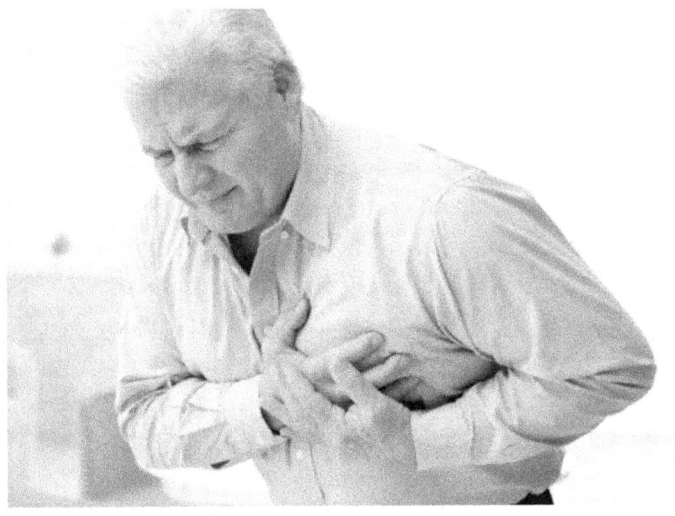

Setting a strong, compelling Vision is as IMPORTANT and URGENT for your enterprise as diet and exercise are for your health!

The prospect of a life-threatening health event should be a sufficient reason to adopt better habits, right? Yet one of the most predictable and pervasive annual societal events, as mentioned above, is that of the New Year's Resolution, wherein hordes of unhealthy folks make a "commitment" to lifestyle changes that will render them sleek and destined to add many years to their lives. Studies have shown that what starts out as an enthusiastic endeavor often deteriorates rapidly. One out of every four resolvers don't stick to their program for even one week. More are gone by week two, and a third have failed by the end of January. By July, over half have lost their resolve. And by year-end, only one of four who were "committed" remains dedicated to their efforts.

Why is failure to keep resolutions so universal? Much has been written about this concern. Some attribute it to a lack of willpower or grit to see things through. Others cynically believe that most resolvers really have no intention to succeed, but simply go through the motions because such goal-setting is expected. Still others believe that most folks fail to fully comprehend the costs required to enjoy the desired benefits. And most behavioral scientists note that failure often comes from the twin errors of not having strong outside support, and failing to have a motivating accountability system that holds their feet to the fire.

Each of these are factors in resolution failure, but what we most often see with CEOs and business owners is not the lack of willpower, nor is it insufficient desire to succeed. And, most recognize that the costs of success are immense. Having strong support from others, including advisors and coaches is certainly important, as is having an accountability system that measures the consistency of effort and results. BUT, the most pervasive and critical disruptor of making and keeping the resolve to articulate and evangelize both a personal and company vision is the overwhelming endless list of IN The Business stuff that leaves no time for the essential *ON The Business* strategic and visionary responsibilities. IN The Business responsibilities are *here and now*, and they demand your attention *here and now!* The *ON The Business* stuff will have to wait until you have time.

Too often, time for that never comes…

But it must, or your work on the endless IN The Business "to dos" will eventually destroy you, or your business–or both!

The fact is that your job description as leader of your enterprise, as mentioned above, includes every aspect of the Business Success Pyramid. The buck stops with you, and whether your company is publicly traded, privately held, or even if you are a sole proprietor, you are responsible for the success or failure of your enterprise. You may be able to manage all of these dimensions on your own…for a while. But this is almost always unsustainable over the long haul.

So, what is the solution? What is the path to business success and your personal success as a leader? By this point, you surely recognize the importance of resolving to articulate and evangelize your vision. But there are still the ominous IN The Business demands that you will face tomorrow morning, and each tomorrow morning on the horizon. They are not going away, and you will continue to feel the intense suction of responsibility for them.

Your sense of commitment is laudable, but it is misapplied. If you allow yourself to be continually distracted by the IN The Business stuff, you will never get to your critical *ON The Business* responsibilities. And you will, in all probability, fail as the leader of your enterprise. You will carry the incredible load of your job until it crushes you. The only solution is to develop a deeply committed team to **execute** the IN The Business tactics, while you **align** their execution with the vision that motivates not only yourself, but each of them.

Fundamentally, it boils down to how you use your time–today and in the future. You have to start where you are; that is, how you spend your time. You will need to very deliberately track your time, using a Time Log, to understand what typically fills your days. And then you will need to analyze and categorize your activities.

Introducing the URGENCY versus IMPORTANCY MATRIX

Q1: Very Urgent, Not Important	Q2: Very Urgent, Very Important
Q3: Not Urgent, Not Important	Q4: Not Urgent, Very Important

The late Stephen R. Covey famously used a version of this matrix to call attention to the dimensions of what we call *The Urgency-Importancy Challenge.* Consider each quadrant of the 2X2 matrix shown above.

The top left quadrant (Q1) is the residence of the ravenous Urgency beasts that devour the critical bottom-right quadrant (Q4), those Importancies that are not yet urgent. You undoubtedly have more than a few Q1 activities in the course of a given day. A classic example of this is spam email. Direct marketers assault us with hundreds of *urgent* messages and offers, some of which have been so well developed as to be almost too attractive to ignore. While these can seem quite compelling, they are very often incredible time-wasters. Your challenge, of course, is to recognize them for what they are, and manage the temptation to get sucked in.

When you allow yourself to spend any significant time in Q1, the beasts that reside there feed on Q4 activities until it is too late, forcing you into a "crisis overlap" of Urgency and Importancy, shown in the upper right quadrant (Q2). While not all Q2 requirements come from a failure to manage Q1, this is very often the case. When it is, you likely experience deep regret that you have allowed this to happen...if you are fortunate enough to survive!

This sense of regret can be a very good thing if it leads you to change your ways. However, too many leaders regress and return to a life dominated by Urgencies. At least, until the next crisis.

It's important to add that the worst error is to allow yourself to spend time in Q3, where activities which are neither urgent nor important reside. While typically these are appropriately labeled time-wasters, a bit of Q3 can be worthwhile, especially if you are a high achiever who is intense and driven. Such Q3 activities might include games, entertainment, and recreation. That said, if they indeed provide a respite from the intensity of your workaday life, these activities might more appropriately be categorized as Q4, not urgent but very important.

So, where do *your* activities fall on the Urgency versus Importancy Matrix? We suggest that you take time to carefully consider that question, with the goal of defining your activities both in terms of the matrix, as well as how much of your time falls into the categories of IN The Business and *ON The Business*. Begin by completing the following two tables. As you do so, don't worry about being precisely correct. At this point, what you are looking for is a general sense of where you are today. Just be as objective as you can. There are no *correct answers*, just honest ones.

ANALYSIS OF YOUR "*IN* THE BUSINESS" ROLES

ROLE	HOURS/ WEEK	URGENCY (High, Medium, Low)	IMPORTANCY (High, Medium, Low)	WHICH QUADRANT?
Product/Service Development				
Production				
Sales				
Marketing				
Customer Service				
Finance				
Accounting				
Taxes				
Human Resources/Hiring & Firing				
Legal				
Other?				

ANALYSIS OF YOUR "*ON* THE BUSINESS" ROLES

ROLE	HOURS/WEEK	URGENCY (High, Medium, Low)	IMPORTANCY (High, Medium, Low)	WHICH QUADRANT?
Vision Development				
Vision Evangelizing				
Strategizing				
Problem-Solving				
Coaching Others				
Team Building				
Competency Building				
Connecting - Internal				
Connecting - External				
Other?				

When you have completed these analyses, you are now prepared to consider some possible changes in your priorities and how you spend your time.

Let's start with the easiest suggestion, the "low hanging fruit." Strong candidates for elimination are any Quadrant 3 activities, those that are neither Urgent nor Important. This is not to say that, on occasion, a bit of mindless vegging might be beneficial, but if it is, you might reclassify it as not Urgent, but still Important because it helps you recharge. For instance, I often find an hour of reading at the end of the day relaxes me and prepares me for sleep. This is obviously not Urgent, nor is it generally Important…except that it serves an important purpose in my routine.

Moving beyond low hanging fruit is, as you might expect, a more difficult challenge. Indeed, we have found that it typically involves some intense focused work. As you consider the critically essential *On The Business* tasks involved in developing a compelling and articulate vision, you will need to find the time for both Vision Development and Evangelizing. While you may already have a well-developed vision, I have rarely found an enterprise that has no need to strengthen either the articulation or the promotion of their vision–or both. And that always demands a shift in your priorities and time management.

In order to find the time required, we have found that a meticulous time audit will help you find chunks of time that you can shift from your current activities to Visioning. So the challenge is this:

Engage Yourself in a One-Week Time Audit, using the format shown below:

DAY	TIME	ACTIVITY	URGENCY (High, Medium, Low)	IMPORTANCY (High, Medium, Low)	WHICH QUADRANT?
1	6:00am				
	6:15am				
	...				
	11:45pm				
	12:00am				
2	6:00am				
	6:15am				
	...				
	11:45pm				
	12:00am				
3 - 7	As Above				

Please note that what you see here is an illustration of the general format for the Time Audit. You will find a downloadable PDF Time Audit form at at www.ceobuilder.com/books.

Recognize that the greater your attention to completing this form, the greater its value will be for you. That said, while the document suggests an activity entry for every 15 minutes, we recognize that some activities will occupy a longer block of time. For instance, a staff meeting might run for an hour or two. In that case, you will simply write STAFF MEETING in the time block when the meeting commences– and draw a line on the form to the time when it ends. If you use a secretary or administrative assistant, you might ask for their help in making sure the Time Log is meticulously completed.

You will also note that the time audit starts and finishes each day during what are probably non-work hours. The intention is to include all of your waking hours, not just work. Remember the goal is for you to find the time for Visioning–and that may come from hours when you are not at work.This is not to suggest that your non-work time isn't Urgent or Important; it simply provides the observation that there may be hours that can be allotted to Visioning, if in-the-office time is scarce.

At the end of each day, take a few minutes to fill in the last three columns on your Time Log. What was Urgent (High, Medium, or Low)? What was Important (High, Medium, or Low)? Based on this, in what Quadrant do these activities reside?

When you have completed the Time Audit for a week, review each day, carefully considering which quadrant each of your activities falls into:

- QUADRANT 1 ACTIVITIES: Those which you define as Very Urgent, but Not Important

- QUADRANT 2 ACTIVITIES: Those that are Very Urgent and Very Important

- QUADRANT 3 ACTIVITIES: Those that are Neither Urgent nor Important

- QUADRANT 4 ACTIVITIES: Those that are Not Urgent, but are Very Important

To facilitate this process, we have provided downloadable Quadrant Categorization Worksheets at at www.ceobuilder.com/books.

The format for these is as follows:

QUADRANT 1 ACTIVITIES: Very Urgent, Not Important			
ACTIVITY	DELEGATE	ELIMINATE	OTHER ACTION

Since Quadrant 1 activities are most often distractors and time disruptors, they are likely candidates for elimination. Assuming they would also be distracting and disrupting to other members of your team, you should probably eliminate them. If on the other hand, their urgency makes it difficult to totally dispose of them, you may want to delegate them, either within your organization or outside of it.

An example of this with one of my clients was a steel fabrication company whose owner found himself constantly assailed by "his buddies" to take on their small low-margin jobs. This happened so often that he found that the company became distracted from larger, higher margin work. Until he made a firm decision to refer his friends to his competitors, these distractions virtually destroyed his profitability. This was not easy for him; indeed, it impacted his friendships. But once done, his business became significantly more profitable.

The removal of Quadrant 1 activities represent an excellent source of opening your busy life to focus time on your *ON the* business work, especially that of setting your Vision.

Let's now consider the next Quadrant Categorization Worksheet, Quadrant 2 Activities: Very Urgent and Very Important:

QUADRANT 2 ACTIVITIES: Very Urgent, Very Important				
ACTIVITY	ME ONLY	ENGAGE OTHERS	FULLY DELEGATE	OTHER ACTION

Quadrant 2 activities often dominate your time as a leader. They include current strategic initiatives, foreseeable problems for which you may have procrastinated addressing (such as the health crisis discussed above), as well as unforeseen new challenges that may emerge. These include what are commonly described as *black swan events.* Such events are defined as rare occurrences having potentially severe consequences that are beyond what is normally expected. Our recent experience with the global COVID-19 pandemic is a classic example of a black swan event that presented all leaders with an unforeseen Quadrant 2 challenge.

Your options with Quadrant 2 are more limited than with any of the other quadrants. Some of these necessarily require your full attention, sometimes without the assistance or inputs of other members of your team. However, you should give some deep thought to the possibility of engaging others. An example of this is my task in writing this book. On the surface, this appears to be a one-person creative effort. However, after challenging myself to find ways to share this load, it is clear that I can better respond to the double-barreled pressures of urgency and importancy by engaging my executive team. We've determined that I will share each chapter after I complete its initial draft, and that they will be responsible for providing a review and critique on a timely basis. This relieves some of the pressure of making sure the book is edited and coherent in its message. This doesn't mean that I have fully delegated my central role, but it does provide immense help.

Quadrant 2, both with clients and on a personal level, has generally not been a source of freeing up much time. However, by focusing on ways to make these activities more productive, you will often find that you will more efficiently complete them than you have in the past.

Let's now consider the next Quadrant Categorization Worksheet, Quadrant 3 Activities: Not Urgent and Not Important:

QUADRANT 3 ACTIVITIES: Not Urgent, Not Important			
ACTIVITY	DELEGATE	ELIMINATE	OTHER ACTION

As mentioned above, these activities provide the best opportunities for freeing up your time. Just be sure that you have categorized them correctly. After completing this worksheet, one CEO with whom I have worked was convinced that his customary morning conversations with employees on his plant floor were Quadrant 3. He confessed that each morning he would walk through his factory, chatting for an hour or so with various workers. These were informal chats that provided him with the opportunity to express his interest in their families and personal activities outside of work. With some sadness, he said that these conversations were neither urgent, nor important.

I asked him a few questions about what he saw as the advantages of his chats, to which he replied that he felt that they had humanized his relationship with his people, but that it was pretty clear that he could free up five or more hours of his time every week if he eliminated them–and that it would also free up time for his people to be more productive.

I suggested that we survey other CEOs to see what they thought. After having done this, it was almost unanimous that he should <u>not</u> eliminate his morning conversations, as his peers perceived that his interactions were contributing to the high level of engagement he enjoyed from his people. Indeed, most of his fellow CEOs expressed their interest in beginning to implement this as a very worthwhile *ON The Business* activity, one that was not Urgent, but Very Important (Quadrant 4).

That brings us to Quadrant 4 Activities: Not Urgent, Very Important:

QUADRANT 4 ACTIVITIES: Not Urgent, Very Important				
ACTIVITY	ME ONLY	ENGAGE OTHERS	FULLY DELEGATE	OTHER ACTION
Setting a clear, compelling Vision for my enterprise	Initially	Soon	Never!	

Quadrant 4 includes your *ON the* Business Activities which provide the compelling Purpose for your enterprise, your Mission and Value Proposition, and the Core Values that govern your behavior, decisions, and strategies. While not urgent, they are extremely important for every business. These are the initiatives that will facilitate your long-term success, both personally and as an organization. Of all the work you will do as a leader, these are ultimately the most essential tasks for which you are responsible!

As you can see on this worksheet, I have placed setting a clear, compelling Vision for your enterprise at the top of the list. I recognize that you may have already endeavored to do this, perhaps articulating your

Vision and even posting it prominently, or publishing and distributing it throughout your organization. While this is commendable, when I have surveyed client employees regarding what the Vision is for their company, hardly any were able to give an answer that was close to the published version. This has led me to understand that developing a clear compelling Vision does not end with the wordsmithing process. Indeed, that is only the proverbial "tip of the iceberg."

If you have articulated your Vision, the greater task is one that never ends. You must evangelize it every day in both your words and deeds. Further, you must recognize that your Vision must begin to manifest itself not in just what you do and say, but in what your employees do and say. As they work to live the Purpose, Mission, and Values of your enterprise, they will create the stories that transform your Vision into reality. Those stories need to be journalized, published, read, and regularly discussed to provide the latticework that will support and sustain your culture over the years. Some of our clients have even memorialized these stories into what they call their "Wall of Fame." They post in a prominent location brief accounts of outstanding vision-supporting stories along with the photographs of the employees who were the heroes in each story. They honor and celebrate those who live their vision, thereby increasing the focus on the behaviors that reinforce and sustain that vision.

Returning to the Quadrant 4 Very Important, but not Urgent Activities, what items currently populate your worksheet? We have discovered that although these activities constitute the very initiatives that will lead to personal and enterprise success, they often get very little day-to-day attention. It is very much like our procrastination of adopting a healthy diet, adequate rest and exercise that will give us a long, robust and productive life. The key question for you regarding your Quadrant 4 items, especially those that have to do with your Vision (your Purpose, Mission, and Values) is "If not now, when?"

The challenge here is to make a firm commitment to getting started.

Recognize that you will experience resistance to Visioning.

The first resistance you will face is from the person you see in the mirror. Even when you have freed up time from your Urgencies, and even when you fully acknowledge the importance of a compelling vision, it is human nature to relegate it to "if and when I get around to it."

Your executive team and employees will also likely resist. With their regular responsibilities and their own Urgencies, adding visioning may seem to be an unwarranted and unnecessary burden.

And then there are the spoken and unspoken excuses for procrastinating. Among the many we have heard over the years, the following have been prevalent:

> *"When we are as profitable as I want us to be, then we'll think about our vision for the company. Our focus must be on ROI above all else!"*

> *"Look, we are losing customers to our competitors. What we need are better competitive strategies, not a vision statement to hang on the wall."*

> *"Our main focus has to be on operating efficiencies. My vision is to get leaner and more efficient. End of story!"*

> *"I can't worry about our vision right now. I have to keep an eagle eye on my people to make sure they get things right!"*

> *"My people simply won't engage at a level I can count on; riding herd on them leaves no time for visioning."*

> *"Recruitment of the talent we need is harder than ever. Talk to me about visioning when we're staffed properly!"*

> *"We're just too busy to take time to work on our vision right now."*

It is critical that you realize that each of these are excuses, not legitimate reasons to procrastinate engaging in visioning. The health analogy fits perfectly here. Why don't we eat right, get enough sleep, and exercise regularly? Our reasons for not doing so are actually the blatant excuses that set us up for short-term health problems–and long-term heart attacks. Even so, most often we casually dismiss the needed changes in behavior as the things we'll do when we finally get the time and perfect circumstances. Too often, the time runs out and the circumstances get worse.

So, how should you deal with your excuses? First, you must accept them as rationalizations that are, at most, only partly rational. With that acknowledgement, you must then step outside of yourself and confront each excuse. *They demand an objective response from you!*

Let's consider each excuse that I've shared with you. As an objective observer who sincerely desires to help another leader who gives the excuse, how might you respond?

EXCUSE	RESPONSE
Inadequate financial outcomes: profit, cash flow, ROI	
Loss of customers, declining market share, failure to compete	
Inefficient operating processes	
Can't rely on the competencies of my people	
Too many of my people are disengaged	
We can't find or attract the talent we need	
We're just too busy!	

Please understand that this is significantly more than an academic exercise. If you are to successfully lead the journey to a clear and compelling Vision for your enterprise, you must be prepared to deal with all of the excuses, distractions, disruptors, and detours that you will face along the way. And, as mentioned above, you may be the greatest excuse-offerer in your organization. You may require a significant dose of self-talk to keep yourself accountable and on track for the processes shared in the coming chapters. And, you will undoubtedly need to be ready to respond to both the spoken and unspoken excuses your people are likely to employ to justify their own procrastination.

To jump-start your thinking regarding the excuses presented here, consider my responses:

EXCUSE	RESPONSE
Inadequate financial outcomes: profit, cash flow, ROI	How might a strong sense of shared Purpose, Mission, and Values impact our financial outcomes? Might we be able to focus on our near-term financial situation while also carving out some time to create a clear and compelling long-term Vision? What if we dedicated one morning each week to work on our Visioning process?
Loss of customers, declining market share, failure to compete	As we more fully zero in on our shared Purpose, Mission, and Values–and consider their impact on our customers, how might our Vision improve our customer relationships, marketing, and sales? Specifically, how might we improve our Mission by carefully readdressing our Value Proposition? What if we were to make Visioning an essential element of how we serve our customers?
Inefficient operating processes	How might we build both efficiency and effectiveness into the core Values of our business? By incorporating those essentials into our Vision, how might we engage our people in a *kaizen* (continuous improvement) mindset and culture? How might we focus on our current operating inefficiencies while also carving out time to create a long-term Vision that creates world-class operating systems and processes?
Can't rely on the competencies of my people	How might creating a strong sense of shared Purpose, Mission, and Values impact the motivation of our people to become increasingly competent? How might we build individual and team competency into the core values of our company? How might this develop into essential strategies and tactics for training and development? How might Visioning provide long-term solutions for the competency challenges we presently face?
Too many of my people are disengaged	How might a proven Visioning process act as a catalyst for engaging our people? How might that process contribute to a sense of buy-in that will provide the foundation for a high engagement culture? Is it worth a try?

We can't find or attract the talent we need	How might a clear and compelling Vision be attractive to the talent we require? What if you offered more than a job? Instead, what if we offered the opportunity to participate in a Vision that truly makes a difference in the world–and that will facilitate the career growth and development of new people? Might this become a magnetic force, drawing talent to our doorstep?
We're just too busy!	Might being too busy keep us from doing what is most important? If we can find a smidgen of time each week, we could begin the process of Visioning. What if we just take the first step or two of a proven Visioning process? Could we dedicate an hour or two on Friday mornings to get started?

You have probably noticed that my responses are nearly all questions directed to the person giving the excuse. That is by design; I want that person to think deeply about their excuse and the high probability that it will become calcified procrastination!

Please recognize that my responses here represent how I have responded to the excuses given to me by CEOs, company presidents, and owners. You may utilize similar responses with your people in influencing them to move forward with visioning, but it has been my experience that the most important person to convince is YOU!

So...start by challenging your own excuses. The Time Log and Quadrant experiences, when done meticulously, always serve to identify chunks of time that you may use to get started. Cast off your excuses and procrastination and get busy!

A clear and compelling Vision, including your Purpose, Mission, and Values, will set the stage for both near-term and long-term success.

But don't just take my word for it...

Consider the counsel of these notable leaders and business gurus:

- *Bill George, Harvard Business School Professor & former Chairman and CEO of Medtronic:* "Have you discovered your

True North? Do you know what your life and leadership are all about? True North is your orienting point—your fixed point in a spinning world—that helps you stay on track as a leader. It is derived from your most deeply held beliefs, your values, and the principles you lead by. It is your internal compass, unique to you, that represents who you are at your deepest level."

- *Simon Sinek, best-selling business author:* "Great leaders are able to inspire others to act." Their goal "is not to give you a course of action, but to offer you a *cause* of action. Every leader—and every company—needs a *Just Cause*, a specific vision of a future state that does not exist."

- *Liz Wiseman, best-selling author of "Multipliers: How the Best Leaders Make Everyone Smarter":* Leaders need two essential strategies…(1) To show the big picture, and (2) To explain the "why." People need to understand the overall picture before they can do their piece well. Good leaders tell people what needs to be done and let them figure out how to do it. Great leaders explain "the why," so people understand both the what and the how. "The Why" lets people know why their contribution matters.

- *Warren Bennis, University of Southern California Professor & Founding Chairman of The Leadership Institute at USC:* "Leadership is the capacity to translate vision into reality. The manager asks how and when; the leader asks what and why. The manager accepts the status quo; the leader challenges it. Too many bosses are driven and driving, but going nowhere. Leaders talk journey; an inclusive, learning-filled, rollicking journey."

- *Clayton Christensen, Harvard Business School Professor:* In his best-selling book, *How Will You Measure Your Life?,* Christensen asks three pivotal vision questions every leader should consider: "How can I be sure that I will find satisfaction in my career? How can I be sure that my personal relationships become enduring sources of happiness? How can I avoid compromising my integrity—and stay out of jail?"

- **Robert F. Kennedy, former U.S. Attorney General:** "Few will have the greatness to bend history itself, but each of us can work to change a small portion of events. It is from numberless diverse acts of courage that human history is shaped."

- **Victor Frankl, author, psychiatrist, and holocaust survivor of Auschwitz:** "Man's search for meaning is the primary motivation in his life and not a 'secondary rationalization' of instinctual drives. This meaning is unique and specific in that it must and can be fulfilled by him alone: only then does it achieve a significance which will satisfy his own *will to meaning.*"

It is this definition of your "unique and specific meaning," Your Personal Vision, that is our target in the next chapter!

CHAPTER 6

A Compelling Purpose Begins With a Person–One Person: YOU!

*What our deepest self craves is not mere enjoyment, but
some supreme purpose that will enlist all our powers and
will give unity and direction to our life. We can never know
the profoundest joy without a conviction that our life is
significant—not a meaningless episode.*

Henry J. Golding

*The two most important days in your life are the day you
are born—and the day you find out why.*

Mark Twain

Having objectively evaluated your IN The Business roles, you should now be able to recognize which of those have dominated your time. The question that now confronts you is which, if any, of these roles can you eliminate, delegate, or subordinate in order to give adequate focus and concentration to setting your personal and enterprise vision.

You should begin by weeding out Quadrant 3 activities (Not Urgent, Not Important) and Quadrant 1 activities (Very Urgent, Not Important). These activities are the "low hanging fruit" that need to be picked, pruned, and discarded with a view to freeing up time for Quadrant

2 (Very Urgent, Very Important) and Quadrant 4 (Not Urgent, Very Important) activities. However, you should not neglect the possibility that even these may represent opportunities to engage others in helping you accomplish them. Delegation is a viable alternative even in many of these Very Important areas.

Take the time to brainstorm your options for freeing yourself from a significant portion of your IN The Business roles, thereby gaining the essential bandwidth to address your *ON The Business* roles. Strive for laserlike clarity regarding your *ON The Business* responsibilities (Quadrant 4). Expand your brainstorming to consider ways to establish these responsibilities as your highest priorities, to which you will dedicate specific blocks of time…ideally every day. It is essential, in considering your *On The Business* roles, that you block out time specifically to address your personal and enterprise vision.

A few key principles must be understood regarding the Visioning Process:

- Visioning necessarily must begin as a "very personal" exercise.

- It's about you as a leader, not only of your people, but of yourself.

- It's about articulating *your* passion and purpose.

- It's about being fresh and aligned with your current circumstances, including the marketplace, the economy, and those you serve.

- Zeroing in on this is generally more difficult for most of us than we anticipate–even if we have spent time on it in the past.

- Too often we default to simple answers like, "I just got involved with this business (or my career) because… it's a good way to make money, or because it fits with my education, or because I inherited my opportunity from my father." *These are not visionary statements; they do not reflect the compelling purpose, mission, and values that drive consistent excellence over time!*

- Our goal in Visioning is not to define the reasons for your career choice; rather it is to set forth statements of passion and purpose that act as strong motivators for your key constituents–owners, partners, employees, associates, and family. And most importantly, YOU!

Whether you are a Start-Up, Incoming, or Ongoing Leader, your Personal Vision is critically important. Clarity of your personal passion and purpose will provide the driving force that will sustain you through both the challenges and opportunities that you will encounter in your career, in your present venture—and in your life. Even if your present leadership role is one in which you have engaged for many years, bringing your Personal Vision into a tighter focus will enhance your own alignment and execution—and that of your people.

Consider the insights of these notable leaders:

Reatha Clark King, Chair of the National Association of Corporate Directors & former VP of General Mills: "If you're aiming to be like somebody else, you're a copycat because that's what people want you to do. You'll never be a star with that kind of thinking. But you might be a star–unreplicable–by following your passion."

Steve Jobs, Co-founder and former CEO of Apple Inc.: "The only way to be truly satisfied is to do what you believe is great work. And the only way to do great work is to love what you do. If you haven't found it yet, keep looking. Don't settle. As with all matters of the heart, you'll know when you've found it."

Todd Rose, Director of the Mind, Brain, and Education Program at the Harvard Graduate School of Education: "The first step of the journey (to success) is always the same: the decision to prioritize fulfillment. ...do not focus on the potential wealth to be had or how masterful you might one day become. Instead, recognize an opportunity that fits your individuality–and seize it. From that point forward, you make your decisions based upon who you are, rather than who others say you should be. By continuing to make decisions in this manner, you inexorably develop excellence."

Warren Bennis, University of Southern California, Professor & Founding Chairman of The Leadership Institute at USC: "Great leaders didn't set out to be leaders. They just did what they loved–and with tremendous drive and enthusiasm–and it led where it led."

The key here is to discover your passion and purpose, clearly articulate it, and develop its strong alignment with the vision of your enterprise. Recall how Herb Kelleher aligned his Passion & Purpose with the Vision of Southwest Airlines:

- Herb's Passion was that he loved people–and his Purpose was to find ways to connect with and serve as many people as he could . It was the thing that gave him joy and fulfillment. *It was his thing!*

- His successor, Bill Kelly, described Herb this way: "Herb wouldn't greet people with the customary handshake. It was typically a bear hug, a boisterous laugh, or even a kiss–men and women and friends and strangers alike."

- Herb's path to alignment with running an airline began when he made the initial connection by articulating that "The business of business is People." He believed that with all his heart–and he extended that to the care and love he manifested to his customers and employees alike. He made his people feel special, and inspired them to make Southwest customers feel special as well.

And that eventually was articulated in the Southwest Purpose:

> *We will become the world's most loved, most flown,*
> *and most profitable airline.*

It may seem paradoxical that something so essential for inspiring others starts out so selfishly... *Isn't it wrong to begin with your*

Personal Passion & Purpose rather than engaging with your key stakeholders in developing the Company Vision?

Indeed, some suggest that the first step in setting an enterprise vision should be to bring together your key stakeholders and develop a "consensus vision." While collaboration is a step along the way to a compelling company vision, it is not the place to start.

Why? Because consensus visions often suck the life out of the leader's passion and purpose. YOU must decide what is most motivating to you, what you are absolutely devoted to, what constitutes *your thing!*

At this point, we often find that our clients catch themselves still questioning if undertaking the task of Visioning is really necessary. Let's consider the common challenges that are often raised:

- If you are a **Start-Up Leader**, you likely have a handful of close associates–and you've already decided that your purpose is to "create the better mousetrap–and make millions of dollars." You might be asking yourself, *what more do we really need?*

- If you are an **Incoming Leader**, you have likely moved into your role from outside your current company, or you have been promoted into your leadership role. The purpose, mission, and values of your enterprise have been set by your predecessors. *It would be imprudent, even impudent, to consider resetting these, right?*

- If you are an **Ongoing Leader**, you may have occupied your position for many years. *Why rock the boat? Aren't we doing fine without readdressing our purpose, mission, and values?*

Let's address each of these challenges:

For the Start-up Leader...

- You have the distinct advantage of laying the foundation for the future of your business *now*–before inevitable day-to-day pressures steer you off course.

- The endless IN The Business activities that will consume most of the early days of your enterprise have yet to fully overtake you. *Now* is the best time to discover and articulate your purpose and passion, thereby aligning the most important stakeholder in your business: YOU!

- The time you invest *now* in self-discovery will pay enormous dividends for you, your team, and those you serve.

For the Incoming Leader...

- While there is great value in making an early assessment of your new assignment, including intensive conversations with each of your key stakeholders, you should strive to observe and discern which policies, practices, and processes are essential, as well as those which are "sacred cows." Recognize that your opportunity is to build on, and improve, what your predecessors have done.

- Ask the following questions as you observe and discern:

  1. Are we experiencing consistent high alignment of all key stakeholders with the strategies and goals of the company?

  2. Are company strategies, systems, and processes delivering the effectiveness and efficiency desired?

  3. Are all key stakeholders "all in;" are they highly engaged in achieving the purpose, mission, and values of the company?

  4. Are the company's purpose, mission, and values clearly articulated, communicated, understood, and acted upon throughout the enterprise?

- If you discover anything less than a strong affirmative answer to each of these questions, you are faced with significant leadership challenges from the get-go. One of your best strategies for asserting your leadership in addressing these issues is to set forth your own passion and purpose as the foundation for re-invigorating your company's vision.

- The solution to company problems and opportunities must begin with YOU, with your Passion and Purpose, *your thing!*

For the Ongoing Leader...

- Ongoing businesses often suffer from what I call "success complacency." We know this all too well at CEObuilder®. We have enjoyed a very successful business model for over three decades. As a result of this, I became blinded to the subtle changes in our business environment. Inadvertently, I adopted a "Why fix it, if it ain't broke" attitude.

  I would never tolerate this attitude from our clients, but unfortunately I didn't recognize it in myself until technology and the recent COVID-19 pandemic forced me to see that changes were needed. As author Marshall Goldsmith has noted, "What got you here, won't get you there."

  As I, myself, am an Ongoing Leader, I have to do what author Guy Kawasaki has advised in his book *Rules for Revolutionaries*, I must "eat my own dog food!" So, as I write this, I am readdressing my own passion and purpose. I don't anticipate changing the core elements of my vision, but I recognize that today's business environment requires innovation and new energy!

- Like the Incoming Leader, you should diligently and objectively observe and discern which policies, practices, and processes are essential, with a critical eye regarding those which may have become "sacred cows." It is often challenging to send these beasts to the slaughterhouse, especially if they seemed to align well in the past. But one of the essential elements of aligning and executing strong effective purpose-driven strategies is to recognize and have the courage to abandon that which is no longer viable.

- Ask yourself these hard questions:

1. Are all of my key stakeholders strongly aligned with the strategies and goals of the company?

2. Are our strategies, systems, and processes delivering the effectiveness, efficiency, value, and profitability desired?

3. Are my key stakeholders "all in;" are they highly engaged in achieving the purpose, mission, and values of the company? Is there any sense of having lost our way?

4. Are the company's purpose, mission, and values clearly articulated, communicated, understood, and acted upon throughout the enterprise? Do we live up to the purpose and mission (our value proposition)? Do we consistently live our values?

- If you discover anything less than a strong affirmative answer to each of these questions, you are faced with significant *ON The Business* challenges. The easy thing to do is put the blinders on, and just pursue business as usual.

  Remember the story I shared in Chapter 2 regarding Intel leaders Andy Grove and Gordon Moore. They asked themselves, "What if we got kicked out and the board brought in a new CEO, what do you think he would do?" That led them to abandon their sacred cow, Intel core memories. This was not the easy thing to do, but it was the right thing–and it saved the company.

- One of your best strategies for asserting your leadership in addressing these issues is to set forth your own passion and purpose as the foundation for re-invigorating your company's vision.

Hopefully, whether you are a Start-Up, Incoming, or Ongoing Leader, you are ready to test the water, to take a stab at setting, or resetting, your Personal Purpose, your WHY...

What is your WHY, your Purpose?

Each leader has the right, even the responsibility to answer this question.

Viktor Frankl, discovered this in the extremity of the Holocaust. He shared his insights in his classic, *Man's Search for Meaning.* He noted that "Man's search for meaning is the primary motivation in life and not a secondary rationalization of instinctual drives. This meaning is unique and specific in that it must and can be fulfilled by him alone; only then does it achieve a significance which will satisfy his own will to meaning."

Rather than ask yourself,

"What do I want out of life?"...

ask,

"What does life want out of me?"

Some have expressed concern that discovery of their WHY, their Purpose, might precipitate a career change... Author Todd Rose, in his book, *Dark Horse,* notes that this has sometimes occurred... if leaders discover that their career aspirations fail to align with their current situation. This, however, is most often the exception rather than the rule. More likely, you will discover that there are deeper answers that will align your WHY with your present work and your enterprise. And these will generally be more compelling than simply making money or achieving advancement.

Typically, these answers are not easily discovered; they will require you to "peel the onion" to find the driving forces that constitute your purpose and passion. You must "mine for them," and then challenge their accuracy before you articulate and act upon them.

Chapter 7 will provide you with a proven process for peeling your onion, discovering your own driving forces, and articulating your own compelling passion, purpose, mission, and values.

Peeling Your Onion-The Model

*He who reveals to me what is in me and helps me to
externalize it in fuller terms of self-trust, is my real helper,
for he assists me in the birth of those things which he knows
are in me and in all men.*

W. John Murray

Most everyone would agree that the ability to persuade others is an essential business skill. Especially in today's knowledge economy, that ability is paramount. Because of technology's acceleration of information through the internet and the ubiquitous use of "smart devices," virtually everyone has access to a plethora of voices. Thus, persuasion today carries the extraordinary challenge of effectively sharing our messages with target markets and stakeholders while they are barraged with many other persuasive messages and distractions. While this is daunting, economically it is imperative that we each step into this arena. According to a recent article by Carmine Gallo in the *Harvard Business Review*, "Some economists believe that persuasion is responsible for generating one-quarter of America's total national income."[69]

---

[69] *Harvard Business Review:The Art of Persuasion Hasn't Changed in 2,000 Years,* Carmine Gallo, July 15, 2019. https://hbr.org/2019/07/the-art-of-persuasion-hasnt-changed-in-2000-years

The ways that persuasion impacts our world are virtually endless. From persuading investors that your entrepreneurial vision has merit, to politicians persuading citizens to vote for them, to salespeople persuading their prospective customers to buy, to leaders striving to motivate their teams...persuasion is a critically important skill. Mr. Gallo notes that "Persuasion is so important to billionaire Warren Buffett that the only diploma he proudly displays in his office is a public-speaking certificate from a Dale Carnegie course. He once told business students that improving their communication skills would boost their professional value by 50% — instantly."[70]

As we have reviewed the purpose, mission, and values of Southwest Airlines, it is clear that Herb Kelleher faced, and company leadership continues to face, the challenge of persuading their stakeholders to buy-in and live their vision. Persuading others is, indeed, an essential part of leadership. However, we have found that an immediate focus on your stakeholders is often premature. **Your initial target for persuasion is yourself.**

Carmine Gallo's HBR article appropriately refers us to the wisdom of ancient Greek philosopher Aristotle for a proven, age-old process of highly effective persuasion. While Mr. Gallo focuses on using that process to persuade others, I will use it here for the most important audience for your purpose and passion: YOU!

Aristotle's Rhetoric has been employed by many of the world's greatest communicators to deliver some of history's most influential speeches. These highly persuasive presentations stressed three fundamental elements that comprise a strong persuasive case for action:

1. **PATHOS:** An appeal to the emotions–or the heart–of the audience to be persuaded.

   Aristotle contended that strong persuasive messages must be steeped in emotion. As Gallo stated in his article, "People are

---

[70] Ibid.

moved to action by how a speaker makes them *feel*."[71] When your audience feels empathy or sympathy (terms derived from the word *pathos*), they are experiencing the deep feelings that stir them emotionally to your message. How is this done? *By story-telling!*

Gallo notes that "Studies have found that (stories) trigger a rush of neurochemicals in the brain, notably oxytocin, the 'moral molecule' that connects people on a deeper, emotional level."[72] The use of stories to set the foundation for persuasion has been proven to engage your stakeholders, but it is important that you recognize that *your* most personal stories have tremendous value in first persuading yourself to engage with energy, enthusiasm, and enduring commitment to your personal passion and purpose. These narratives should not be limited to your successes. Indeed, your tales of failure, embarrassment, awkwardness, and misfortune often provide what author and Harvard Business School professor, Bill George, calls *crucible* events. More discussion of this shortly!

2. **LOGOS:** An appeal to the mind of the audience. Rather than emotional appeal, this is an appeal to reason. It provides the logical facts that provide credibility for the cause being promoted. Why are your purpose, mission, or values important? How will your cause impact your target market, your community, or the world? How will you show that it is economically feasible? What are the logical appeals that cause *you* to wholeheartedly buy into *your own* vision? Here is where business planning and strategy come into play. You will seek the data, evidence, and facts that support your vision and form a rational argument for it. Remember, your first goal here is to convince yourself...before unveiling your vision to others. Does your vision hold up to your own tough, logical scrutiny?

---

[71] Ibid.
[72] Ibid.

3. **ETHOS:** An appeal based on the ethics or underlying values of the cause you are promoting, thereby giving credibility to it. Here you zero in on your core beliefs and values. This is where you introspectively assert what *you will*, and *will not*, do to fulfill your passion and purpose. This assertion sets forth your beliefs and values, as well as your strong commitment to "walk your talk." In his HBR article, Gallo noted that "Aristotle believed that if a speaker's actions didn't back their words, they would lose credibility, and ultimately, weaken their argument."[73]

For you personally, Ethos requires deep consideration of your beliefs and values. It requires that you articulate them. And, it requires you to make a commitment, even a covenant with yourself to live them. Finally, it requires you to recognize that a failure to live them will undercut your leadership effectiveness. Hypocrisy will destroy your ability to ultimately persuade the stakeholders beyond yourself.

Aristotle's Premise...

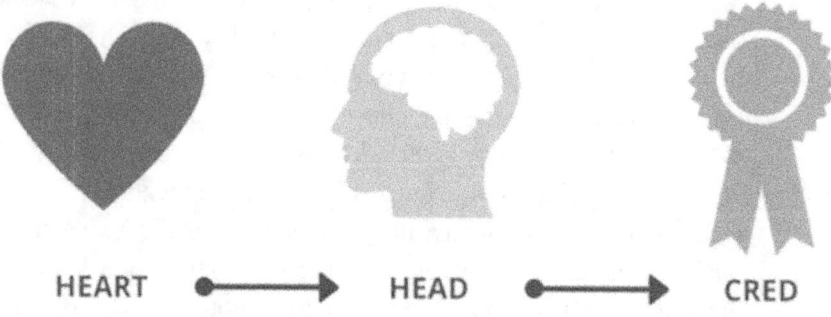

HEART → HEAD → CRED

To Aristotle's model, I add the important elements of Authenticity and Resolve.

---

[73] Ibid.

In each of Aristotle's fundamental elements (Pathos, Logos, and Ethos), you must be totally Authentic, sharing your personal strengths, motivations, and vulnerabilities. And the ultimate measure of your WHY is your Resolve to act on the Purpose and Passion you have articulated.

With these elements in mind, I developed our *PACER Visioning Model:*

- ***P: Pathos***–The emotional stories that have molded your heart, and set your life path

- ***A: Authenticity***–The unique strengths, attributes, and vulnerabilities that define you

- ***C: Your Credible Cause***–The underlying logic (Logos) for your WHY, extending to the personal Value Proposition to which you are dedicated

- ***E: Ethos***–The beliefs and values that set forth how you will behave in pursuit of your WHY; *what you will and will not do*

- ***R: Resolve***–A clear answer to the question: *Therefore, What?*, requiring an assessment of both the benefits and the the costs of moving forward–and a firm commitment to doing so

I recommend that you use the *PACER Visioning Model* twice, first in articulating your personal vision, and then in developing your enterprise vision (addressed in Chapter 8). In your initial efforts, this will be a very intimate process in that it should primarily involve only yourself. Your ultimate articulation of your purpose and passion will provide a strong foundation for the second collaborative use of the model with the key stakeholders in your organization.

Your PATHOS

*The difficulties, hardships, and trials of life, the obstacles
one encounters on the road to fortune, are positive
blessings. They knit the muscles more firmly, and teach self-
reliance. Peril is the element in which power is developed.*

William Matthews

Our objective here is to facilitate the discovery of the pivotal events
of your life, those experiences that have deeply impacted you
physically, mentally, emotionally, and spiritually. As mentioned
earlier in this book, author and Harvard Business School professor,
Bill George suggests that many of these are what he calls *crucibles*.
He defines these as severe trials, traumas, or tragedies that you have
experienced. Additionally, these might include some of the hard
things you have had to deal with in the course of your work life.

The *Handbook of Leadership Theory and Practice*[74] which
explores leadership along many dimensions suggests that in addition
to crucible experiences the following core elements are also powerful
in personal development:

---

[74] *Handbook of Leadership Theory and Practice,* edited by Nitin Nohria and Rakesh
Khurana, page 683.

- **Life and Job Transitions:** Being thrust into unfamiliar responsibilities and having to prove yourself.
- **Task-Related Responsibilities:** Being required to be an agent of change, where:
  - New directions, strategies, or tactics must be developed, or
  - Inherited problems must be solved, or
  - Downsizing is required, or
  - Interpersonal conflicts must be resolved, or
  - High stakes are involved, or
  - External pressures are significant, or
  - The cumulative aspects of your situation are overwhelming.
- **Responsibility without Authority:** The need to influence change without being able to compel it.
- **Other Obstacles:** Adverse life, societal or business conditions, lack of leadership support, an adversarial relationship with your key stakeholders, lack of spousal or family support.[75]

The boy in the boat:

Where these define the circumstances that may have led to your Pathos experiences, the timing and venues for them can vary widely. Regarding timing, your pivotal experiences may have occurred during your early childhood, adolescence, young adulthood, mid-life, or even in your later years.

Consider the story told in the book, *The Boys in the Boat*[76] of a Depression Era boy, Joe Rantz, who at age 15 was abandoned by his father and stepmother. Out of necessity, he learned to fish for chinook salmon and forage for mushrooms, berries, and watercress to feed himself. He occasionally earned a little cash through a variety

---

[75] *Handbook of Leadership Theory and Practice,* edited by Nitin Nohria and Rakesh Khurana, page 683: Source-Adapted from McCauley, Ruderman, Ohiott, and Morrow (1994)

[76] *The Boys in the Boat,* Daniel James Brown

of "entrepreneurial activities" that often required hard manual labor. Somehow, he stayed in school and earned good grades. Living in the house near the Puget Sound where his parents had left him behind, he was stoically alone.

Joe's story follows his path from being a lonely teenager to trying out for the University of Washington freshman rowing team. He saw making that team as his ticket to obtaining a college education and rising out of the poverty of the Great Depression. From the first day of tryouts, it became clear that his goal was anything but easily attainable. He learned, as author Daniel Brown, describes it, that "competitive rowing is an undertaking of extraordinary beauty preceded by brutal punishment. Unlike most sports, which draw primarily on particular muscle groups, rowing makes heavy and repeated use of virtually every muscle in the body…"

Joe made the freshman team in the autumn of 1933 and began his odyssey to Olympic gold in 1936. During that three year period, he faced one challenge after another, some of which boiled down to just staying alive. He worked constantly to provide meager meals and shelter for himself, while expending almost superhuman energy into his sport. He experienced not only the worries of caring for his daily subsistence needs, but also the concern that he might, after all of his work and sacrifice, lose his place on the Washington team.

Joe Rantz's story is one of extraordinary courage and focus, of a young man who somehow overcomes economic, athletic, academic, and relationship strains. He is a worthy example of what psychologist and best-selling author Daniel Goleman calls *emotional intelligence*. Joe was a leader, first of himself, later of his team, and ultimately throughout his life.

For Joe Rantz, the timing of his crucible experiences was both early and often. As for the venues for those experiences, they also are likely to be varied. Some may happen within the context of your family life, others may include situations you faced in elementary school, junior high, high school or college. Other venues might be early work experiences, your first leadership experience, or what you experienced on an athletic team. They may include online interchanges. They may involve your trials and tribulations with bad bosses, mistakes you've made, career setbacks, or the shock of landing in an unfamiliar situation or culture. Or they might spring on you suddenly in the middle of a tea party…like they did for Frances Perkins!

A transformational tea party:

Frances Perkins was 31 years old when her crucible experience descended upon her. She literally went from a tea party to a personal trauma beyond her worst nightmares.

On March 25, 1911, she and a group of friends were gathered for tea at a friend's upscale brownstone in New York City when they were interrupted by frantic screams outside. They rushed out to see the cause of the commotion. Down the street, they could see that one of the tallest buildings was on fire.

Having an instinctive desire to help, Perkins rushed toward the scene. As she came closer, she could see that the eighth, ninth, and tenth floors of the Triangle Shirtwaist Factory were ablaze. As she looked skyward, she was aghast to see dozens of workers crowded against open windows. Surely they weren't going to jump, Frances thought… but suddenly one by one, 46 precious human beings threw themselves into the air, away from the conflagration.

At the top of her lungs, Frances screamed upward, "Don't do it! Help is coming!" But it wasn't. Neither she, nor firefighters, nor thousands of other onlookers could stop the death and destruction. 146 Shirtwaist employees, most of whom were women, tragically died that day. Reflecting on those who had jumped, Perkins later noted, "Every one of them was killed. It was a horrifying spectacle."[77]

The Triangle Shirtwaist Factory fire changed Frances Perkins forever…

Until that day, Frances had been on the path of a good, genteel life. She had possessed a modest interest in the working conditions of factory employees, but Triangle transformed that interest into a passion. Morally indignant over the conditions that led to fiery deaths

---

[77] Frances Perkins, "The Triangle Factory Fire," lecture, Cornell University online archives, http://trianglefire.ilr.cornell.edu/primary/lectures/francesperkinslecture.html.

of so many in that tragic incident, she threw herself into the challenge of preventing such catastrophes. She became politically active–and steeled herself to the cause.

The years ahead became much different than Perkins had expected. She became a fierce advocate who put people before profits, politics, and policy. Ultimately, her advocacy for American workers led her to be appointed Secretary of Labor under President Franklin D. Roosevelt. She contributed in major ways to both the New Deal and Social Security. She was a pivotal figure in all twelve years of the FDR administration.

As author David Brooks noted in his book, *The Road to Character,* Frances Perkins didn't create her life, she was "summoned by life" to a high purpose. She asked herself, "What does life want from me? What are my circumstances calling me to do?"[78]

A third example of a leader's Pathos growing out of crucible experiences:

Daniel Vasella was a chronically ill Swiss farm boy in the 1950's. He struggled with asthma, tuberculosis, and meningitis. During his youth, he spent a whole year in isolation in a sanatorium. He endured continuous fear and pain as his nurses restrained him while administering lumbar punctures. In short, much of his childhood was a living hell.

However, one day a doctor visited him and kindly explained every step of the procedures he was receiving. Through this openness, Daniel was transformed from an object to be poked and prodded to a human being worthy of kindness and compassion. The new physician's combination of respect and tenderness took away his pain and fear.

As he continued through childhood, Vasella's crucible experiences continued. At the age of 10, his older sister succumbed to cancer. The following year, his other sister died in a car accident. And two years later, his father died during a surgical procedure. His widowed mother, left without an income, was forced to take employment in a distant town to support the family. Young Daniel could have become resentful, even angry, at his very personal brushes with the world of medicine. Instead,

---

[78] *The Road to Character,* David Brooks, p.21.

he came to see them as the foundation for who he was, and what he would become.[79]

He says, "I decided to become a physician so I could understand health, and gain some control over my own life after disease had disrupted my family so much. The compassionate physician at the sanatorium became the role model for the kind of doctor I wanted to be."[80]

Vasella entered medical school at the University of Friborg in 1973. During his subsequent years of residency at the Universities of Bern and Zurich, he realized that he wanted to have a greater impact by going beyond lessening patient pain and suffering to restoring people to health. He sought an organization that had that purpose, and was led to the pharmaceutical industry.

In the world of pharmaceuticals, Vasella's path took him to an exciting career in research, global drug development, and product marketing. He emerged as the CEO of Novartis, blossoming as the leader of a global healthcare company that creates life-saving drugs. Drawing on the role model of his childhood, he focused the Novartis culture on compassion, competence, and competition.[81] After his leadership role at Novartis, Vasella joined the board of directors at XBiotech, Inc, a biopharmaceutical company located in Austin, Texas, that focuses on the discovery and commercialization of a next generation of therapeutic antibodies which harness a human's natural immunity to fight disease. He is an honorary member of the American Academy of Arts and Sciences. In 2004, *Time* magazine named him one of the world's 100 most influential people, and he was chosen as the Most Influential European Business Leader of the Last 25 Years by the readers of the *Financial Times*.[82]

Consider the achievements of other notable individuals who were motivated by their personal crucible experiences:

---

[79] *Discover Your True North,* Bill George, p.58
[80] Ibid. p.58
[81] Ibid, p.58-60
[82] https://en.wikipedia.org/wiki/Daniel_Vasella

- **Helen Keller:** Prolific author and social reformer who overcame the loss of her sight and her hearing as an infant.

- **Abraham Lincoln:** President who led America out of the Civil War, who overcame poverty, a lack of formal education, and extraordinary political and interpersonal opposition.

- **Oskar Schindler:** German industrialist and member of the Nazi Party who saved the lives of 1200 Jews during the Holocaust by resisting the inhumanity and anti-Semitic prejudices of Adolf Hitler and the Nazi Party.

- **Mohandas K. Gandhi:** Indian lawyer who became known as the Mahatma; he employed nonviolent resistance to lead India to independence from British rule after facing intense racism and persecution in both South Africa and India.

- **Anjeze (Agnes) Bojaxhiu:** Albanian peasant whom the world came to know as Mother Teresa; she was motivated to serve the "poorest among the poor."

- **Martin Luther King Jr.:** Baptist minister and civil rights leader who led a movement to "overcome" racism and pursue the dream of equal opportunity for all.

And of course, there is **Van Phillips**, mentioned earlier in Chapter 3, who used his water-skiing accident and subsequent amputation of his left leg as the catalyst for developing the Flex-Foot blade prosthetic that allows amputees to pursue high levels of athletic performance.

So, are there Crucible Experiences that have impacted your life? And, while you consider these pivotal stories in your own life, let's also draw your attention to more uplifting life-changing experiences that may have also helped form who you are today.

An example of this was shared by the late basketball player and coach, **Denny Crum**. As a young boy, Denny dreamed of playing basketball for UCLA. His hoops skills eventually drew the attention of coach **John Wooden,** who recruited him. This proved to be the determining factor in Crum's career. After playing at UCLA, Denny became a coach himself at Pierce College, a community college in Los Angeles.

Continuing to provide mentoring for Crum, Coach Wooden eventually offered him the assistant coaching position at UCLA. Denny was at Wooden's side for three NCAA titles. He later moved on to coach at the University of Louisville, leading them to six Final Fours and two NCAA championships.

Denny Crum often expressed deep gratitude for the extraordinary blessing it was for him to know, work with, and coach with John Wooden. Here's the statement UCLA released from former coach Denny Crum on John Wooden:

> "Coach Wooden meant so much to me and to so many others. He was my coach, my mentor, my brother, my father—my comrade in coaching.

> "I was fortunate to play for him and coach with him. I had the best of both worlds.

> "He was a special person. He was a genuine, honest, God-fearing man – that's the way he lived his life. The more you got to know him, the more you respected and loved him.

> "I remember so many occasions, when Coach, Gary Cunningham, and I would walk down to Westwood Village for lunch. We'd go through the backdoor at Hollis Johnson's (drug store/lunch counter). We'd sit on milk carton crates, use another one for a table, and talk about fishing and a lot of different things that were not basketball-related.

> "It was such a pleasure to be around him. Coach was a lot smarter than most coaches; he knew his strengths and weaknesses. He would hire assistant coaches with talents that he felt would make the team stronger.

> "If you asked Coach what he did for a living, he would say he was a teacher, not a basketball coach: a teacher. That's when he was at his best – planning, organizing and teaching.

Every morning we would spend an hour-and-a-half going over the practice from the day before: what to change, what to keep, how to prepare for the next practice. He was such a perfectionist and his attention to detail was genius. He never wanted to overlook anything.

"Coach was so smart. In practice preparation, I would say to him, 'Maybe we should do it this way.' He wouldn't say yes or no, he would look at me and say, 'Please explain your idea to me.' I would then explain and Coach would say, 'OK, we'll try it today and if it works, we'll leave it in and if it does not, we'll take it out.' He never acted like he knew everything; he always relied on his assistant coaches for advice and counsel.

"What I learned the most from Coach was about life and how to properly live it. Coach's teachings and philosophies he got from his Father, and I got those same teachings and philosophies from Coach. Living life the correct way was far more important than basketball.

"Coach is now back with his wife Nellie and with his Lord."[83]

I experienced my own very personal uplifting Pathos experience as an undergraduate student at Weber State University in the late fall of 1971. I was enrolled in an upper division macroeconomics course. On day one of the course, Professor Iwamoto invited any who intended to pursue an advanced degree to stand. Along with several others, I stood up. He then asked if anyone aspired to attend Harvard, Stanford, or MIT. Anyone who did not, he invited to sit down. That left me standing alone.

As I remained standing, the professor made his way to stand directly in front of me. He stared intently into my eyes, making me more than a little uncomfortable. He then asked if I understood the challenge I

---

[83] *Denny Crum on John Wooden*, Orange County Register, Adam Maya and Staff Writers, June 6, 2010, https://www.ocregister.com/2010/06/06/denny-crum-on-john-wooden/

was facing to achieve that goal. I assured him that I did, and after a few more seconds, he invited me to retake my seat.

After class, Iwamoto approached me again, and firmly stated that I would need an A in his class--and that if I earned that grade, he would be honored to write a letter of recommendation to the Harvard Business School on my behalf.

I studied diligently all semester, and kept a solid A in the course through all of the assignments, quizzes, and exams. Finally, just before Christmas break, I took Dr. Iwamoto's final exam. Unfortunately, the complexities of macroeconomics converged on me that day; it seemed that all understanding of economics had left me. I panicked and my answers became rambling and imprecise. When I left the exam room, I knew I had lost my A in the course.

Devastated, I drove home in a dark and dreary snowstorm to my new bride whom I knew would undoubtedly be as sad as I was over my poor performance.

The telephone was ringing...

As I walked into our apartment, my wife was answering the phone. She handed the receiver to me. "It's for you, Rich; it's Professor Iwamoto."

The professor wasted no time in small talk. He said, "Mr. Tyson, you did not do well on your exam. I am quite discouraged for you. Can you return to campus so that we can review your work together?"

I responded that I was sure that Dr. Iwamoto wouldn't want to do that; that it was snowing and that he must need to get home. "No," the professor replied, "if you are willing to return, I will wait for you."

I arrived back at the office half an hour later. Iwamoto had me sit down next to him, and for the next two hours, he patiently walked me through every question and its corresponding answers. It was an extraordinary in-depth conversation on macroeconomics. Professor Iwamoto finally asked if I understood where I had erred on the exam— as well as the answers that I should have given. When I responded affirmatively, he gave me a new copy of the exam and led me to an adjacent office. He smiled and said,"Please retake the exam."

Learning from a kind, dedicated master teacher...

Another hour or so passed before I finished the exam. When I emerged, Dr. Iwamoto asked, "How did you do, Mr. Tyson?" I responded that I thought I had now aced it. The professor took the exam from me, and without reading it, wrote a large A on the top page.

Then he handed me a sealed envelope addressed to the Harvard Graduate School of Business. He said, "Mr. Tyson, here is your letter of recommendation. Please see that it gets in the right hands at Harvard. It's been an honor to be your teacher!"

Right up to that moment, I had no expectation that my grade would change—and certainly no anticipation that Professor Iwamoto would write the desired letter of recommendation. What I knew *before* those outcomes was that this man was an outstanding teacher. *After* this extraordinary experience, I realized that he was a truly great teacher, one who sincerely cared about what his students learned, as well as what we each aspired to accomplish and become.

I will be forever grateful for the sacrifice and friendship of Dr. Iwamoto. His kindness and commitment to my understanding of a complex subject matter gave me a new paradigm regarding what real teaching is all about. In my subsequent work as a coach to leaders, I have often thought of this great teacher–and have strived to emulate him. This snowy evening with a dedicated professor was pivotal for me, as it set a standard for how I would later approach my own teaching, coaching, and mentoring of others.

PATHOS relies heavily on your personal stories...

Whether your pivotal life event was a crucible or positive/uplifting experience, there is always a story that accompanied these events. And, even though, at this stage, you are the sole audience for these stories,

I encourage you to write them down, along with the reasons they were pivotal events in your life.

Search your memory for these pivotal events…what emotions did each event stir within you? How did each event act to forge your personality, your passion, your purpose, your WHY?

Reflect on your life in segments…

- Childhood
- Adolescence
- Young Adulthood
- Mid-Life
- Later-Life

By following this process, you will begin remembering the events that have made you who you are today, why they are important, and what they mean to you regarding your purpose and passion.

I have found that the following PATHOS worksheet is often helpful in considering these time segments as you work through the chronology of your life:

Life Segment	Pivotal Event	Crucible -or- Positive?	Why was this Pivotal?
Childhood			
Adolescence			

Young Adulthood			
Mid-Life			
Later-Life			

In the interest of providing a useful example for you, I've included an example of a few Pivotal Events from my own life. I have purposely not shared examples from clients who have completed this activity because their answers are often very personal, and as such should be kept private.

PATHOS WORKSHEET for Rich Tyson

(a partial list excerpted from my more comprehensive use of the PATHOS Worksheet)

LIFE SEGMENT	PIVOTAL EVENT	CRUCIBLE -or- UPLIFTING	Why was this pivotal?
Childhood	Reading the newspaper to Mother: I have a big "cabulary"	U	Age 4–Love of reading and learning--and love of my mother
	Lost on a Train to Tokyo	C	Age 10–Gratitude for unselfish kindness, important to be a problem-solver and rescuer of others
Adolescence	Marion Storey	U	Age 16–An extraordinary, committed teacher, who balanced kindness with incisive directness and objectivity
	Football Prowess Came at a Cost: Anger	C	Age 16-17–I was only a good player when I was mad, and when I was mad, I never liked myself. I soon recognized how important it was to be authentic with myself.
Young Adulthood	Vietnam & the Crate Manufacturer	C	Age 18–Indignation led me to stand up and be courageous, even in the face of negative consequences
	Professor Iwamoto	U	Age 21–Unselfish service, commitment to learning, teaching, and facilitating the success of others

Mid-Life	Micronesian Seafood Flop--and How I Made an Ash of Myself	C	Age 30-32–Taught me to temper my enthusiasm with deliberation and humility--and to seek coaching and support
	Playing, Coaching, and Loving Baseball	U	Age 33-64–Baseball has many life lessons: including how to deal with imperfection, continuous opportunity to improve, the need for teamwork and coaching. *Everyday is an At Bat...Swing for the Fences!*
Later-Life	The Birth of Briley & Cole	C	Age 62-67–The power of prayer, love, family, and friends during the births of these handicapped children
	Being a Coach & a Mentor	U	Age 40-73–Serving others, growing leaders, helping them do their jobs effectively and efficiently, facilitating their problem-solving, and seeing them grow and succeed are my greatest payoffs

These Pivotal Events provide thematic insights for my life and purpose, my PATHOS. While they represent a variety of both Crucible and Uplifting experiences in my life, at this point they are merely a stroll down memory lane. It is important now to analyze each experience a bit further, to glean the key themes from each event.

My analysis unearthing the themes from the PATHOS Worksheet follows:

LIFE SEGMENT	PIVOTAL EVENT	CRUCIBLE -or- UPLIFTING	THEMES
Childhood	Reading the Newspaper to Mother: I have a big "cabulary"	U	Love of reading and **learning**--and **love** of my mother
	Lost on a Train to Tokyo	C	Gratitude for **unselfish kindness**, important to be a **problem-solver** and **rescuer** of others
Adolescence	Marion Storey	U	An extraordinary, **committed teacher**, who balanced **kindness** with **incisive directness** and **objectivity**
	Football Prowess Came at a Cost: Anger	C	I was only a good player when I was mad, and when I was mad, I never liked myself. I soon recognized how important it was to be **authentic** with myself.
Young Adulthood	Vietnam & the Crate Manufacturer	C	**Indignation** led me to stand up and **be courageous**, even in the face of negative **consequences**
	Professor Iwamoto	U	**Unselfish service**, **commitment** to **learning**, **teaching**, and **facilitating** the **success of others**
Mid-Life	Micronesian Seafood Flop--and How I Made an Ash of Myself	C	Taught me to temper my **enthusiasm** with **deliberation** and **humility**--and to seek **coaching** and **support**

	Playing, Coaching, and Loving Baseball	U	Baseball has many **life lessons**: including how to **deal with imperfection**, continuous daily **opportunity to improve**, the need for **teamwork** and **coaching**
Later-Life	The Birth of Briley & Cole	C	The power of **prayer**, **love**, **family**, and **friends** during **crises**
	Being a Coach & a Mentor	U	**Serving others**, **growing leaders**, **helping** them do their jobs effectively and efficiently, **facilitating** their **problem-solving**, and seeing them grow and **succeed** are my greatest **payoffs**

Extending the analysis of my PATHOS Worksheet beyond the sample I've shared here rendered the following themes or key words which describe my personal *Pathos*. While no theme was repeated more than 2 times, several appeared with that frequency, including Learning, Teaching, Facilitating, Coaching, Growing Leaders, Helping & Supporting Others, Unselfishness, Kindness, Commitment, Service, Problem-Solving, Dealing with Imperfections & Crises, Growth & Improvement, Focus on the Success of Others, Family, and Love.

Other themes that were mentioned once: Rescuer, Incisive, Directness, Objectivity, Authenticity, Indignation, Courage, Consequences, Enthusiasm, Deliberation, Humility, Life Lessons, Opportunity, Teamwork, Prayer, Friends, and Payoffs.

These themes provide important insights into what is important in my life, what I am passionate about. They extend from both my crucible and uplifting experiences and stories.

With these themes in mind, a real sense of my PATHOS emerges.

*At the heart of my motivation, personal drive, and purpose
is my love for others–and my desire to serve them. To do
this, my passion is to pursue a life of continuous learning,
thereby expanding the value I can deliver to my fellowman.
As I continue to learn, I enjoy enthusiastically sharing
what I have learned with others through teaching–and
facilitating their ability to apply true principles effectively
and efficiently in their work and lives. I love to provide
what I call "learning in the moment of need" for those I
serve, as well as helping them unearth long-range strategic
opportunities and challenges. I actively seek the chance to
coach, to grow leaders, and help guide others to growth,
improvement, and fulfillment of their personal purposes.
I do this with all who desire my service, including family,
clients, athletic teams, my community and church.*

At this point, I encourage you to put your reading of this book
on pause, and take a few hours (maybe even a few days) to complete
your own PATHOS worksheet and to reflect on the themes that emerge
for you. As I have done, consider both the Crucible and Positive/
Uplifting events in the various segments of your life. Then discover
your significant themes.

On our website, you may access the PATHOS Worksheet at www.
ceobuilder.com/books.

I wish you well in your discovery process!

An alternative tool for discovering your PATHOS looks forward rather than back...

This tool invites you to your own funeral, to consider the **"eulogy
virtues"** that will be shared on that day.

David Brooks, best-selling author of *The Road to Character*,
provides a definition that is helpful here. He states that there is a
"difference between 'resume virtues' and 'eulogy virtues.'" Resume

virtues are the experiences and education that fill your resume, those skills that contribute to extrinsic success in career pursuits.[84]

Eulogy virtues are intrinsic. They are the deeper virtues that are at the core of your being. ***They are who you really are.*** Most of us would say that eulogy virtues are ultimately much more important than resume virtues.

So...what will they say at your funeral? Consider using the following Eulogy Worksheet to answer these questions:

- My family will say...
- My friends will say...
- My business partners will say...
- My employees will say...
- My customers will say...
- My community will say...

EULOGY VIRTUES WORKSHEET

My family would say:

_____

_____

_____

_____

My friends would say:

_____

_____

_____

_____

---

[84] *The Road to Character,* David Brooks, p.xi.

My business partners would say:

_____

_____

_____

_____

My employees would say:

_____

_____

_____

_____

My customers would say:

_____

_____

_____

_____

My community would say:

_____

_____

_____

_____

From the eulogy insights you've gleaned in this exercise, what are your virtues—or those that you desire to develop? How do these insights help you in discovering your Pathos, your passion, your purpose?

_____

_____

_____

_____

Therefore, what? **What must you do to move in that direction? Are those actions persuasive to your heart? Do they compel you to enthusiastic action?**

_____

_____

_____

_____

Finally, how do you describe your Personal PATHOS? What are the persuasive themes that emerge from the pivotal events of your life, or from what will be said about you in your Eulogy, your *Eulogy Virtues***?**

_____

_____

_____

_____

Completing these exercises and arriving at your articulation of your personal Pathos should not be a process that you rush. To do this right, and arrive at a statement of your personal purpose that reflects the essence of who you are requires much more introspection and soul-searching than just completing the forms suggested here.

You should wrestle with the Pathos process, with an eye to what author Matt Higgins calls "burning your boats." In other words, is your articulation of your personal purpose so inspiring to YOU that you are willing to pursue it with abandon, "all-in", with no contingency plans. Once again, I must clarify that this doesn't necessarily mean that you quit your current job; indeed, I often find that clarity regarding a person's personal purpose focuses and enlivens their behaviors and actions at their current position. But it does mean that you see yourself in the words that describe your purpose—and that you are unwilling to let go of that definition of yourself. And that could mean moving on to other career and life opportunities.

In his bestselling book, *Burn the Boats: Toss Plan B Overboard and Unleash Your Full Potential,* Matt Higgins suggests that we each should ask ourselves the following important questions in arriving at our definition of personal purpose:

- What qualities make me someone I can respect and admire?

- Do I want to spend my days creating from scratch, or executing someone else's vision?

- Can I tolerate the risk of an uncertain future, or do I need predictability to thrive?

- Would I rather be thinking or doing?

- Do I feed off human interaction, or does it drain me?

- When have I been happiest, and what would it take to feel that way again?

- What do I want my epitaph to read?[85]

Your answer to these questions will help you evaluate the veracity of the PATHOS or purpose statement you develop. When your answers bring you to a mindset of both confidence and peace with what you have written, you are ready to move on. The purpose you have articulated will stir your emotions in ways that inspire you to engage in the various dimensions of your life with energy, enthusiasm, and enduring commitment.

Remember that PATHOS is the emotional component that precedes the more cognitive elements of your Purpose. It defines your passion, your drive for fulfillment, and it will provide you with a personal definition of "how you will measure your life," a term coined by author and business guru, Harvard Business School professor Clayton Christensen in his book by the same title.

As we have discussed earlier, sometimes this is as simple as Herb Kelleher's PATHOS, that of "loving people." He made sure that

---

[85] *Burn the Boats: Toss Plan B Overboard,* Matt Higgins, page 13.

everything he did in his life and his career was built on this foundation. It was how he measured his life, and it gave him purpose every day. It has been manifested in one of the most successful airlines in the world.

If, after completing the exercises in this chapter, you still feel that you've not quite zeroed in on your personal PATHOS, I encourage you to take some additional time to repeat each element shared here. Dig a little deeper; we have observed that to reveal what matters most sometimes requires more time, effort, and soul-searching. Remember that persuading your heart must come before you persuade your head, and before you test the credibility of your personal purpose, mission, and values.

When you feel that your heart is persuaded, move on to Chapter 7B, Being Authentic With Yourself.

AUTHENTICITY: A Focus on Yourself

God gave every man individuality of constitution and
a chance for achieving individuality of character. He puts
special instruments into every man's hands by which
to make himself and achieve his mission. (Of course,
this applies to every woman as well.)

Josiah G. Holland

Your true identity is established by <u>becoming</u>
the person you can become....The day will come
when your working days will end. The work that will have
supported you and your family one day will be behind you.
On your final graduation day, when you finally leave this
frail existence, what you will have become will matter much
more than merely your career. From an eternal perspective,
<u>who you really are</u>
is far more important than what you did.

Russell M. Nelson

It is an absolute perfection to know how to get
the very most out of one's individuality.

Michel DeMontaigne

To these quotes, I would add perhaps the most famous words spoken by Polonius in Shakespeare's play, *Hamlet,* in giving his son, Laertes, his blessing and advice:

> "This above all—**to thine own self be true**, And it must follow, as the night the day, Thou canst not then be false to any man."

Thus, Polonius sent his son into the world with the admonition to avoid pleasing other people by changing his sense of who he was or how he would act.

Eloquent words, but very challenging; many of us do not have a clear understanding of who **our own self** is, of clarity regarding the key elements of our individuality. At the most basic level, you recognize the face you see in the mirror. In that regard, you know who you are. However, your development of your personal purpose (as a foundational step toward developing a compelling company purpose) requires that you dig deeper. For most of us, that means relying on others to provide observation and discernment regarding the key characteristics that define our attitudes, behaviors, and choices.

Now, if that sounds like I'm veering off into the world of psychology, let me assure you that this is only a temporary detour in that direction. And, in the context of being certain of your personal purpose, mission, and values, it is critical that you have an authentic understanding of who you really are. This will increase the probability that you possess the attributes that will align with your Pathos, your passion. The process which enables the discovery of your authentic self requires complete honesty and a willingness to feel a bit vulnerable. Even so, it is, for most people, a great illuminating adventure of personal discovery. The key question for you, for each of us, here is: *Who am I...really?* In *A Guide to Finding Yourself*, written by an author using the pseudonym, PsychAlive, he (or she) states:

> "Finding yourself may sound like an inherently self-centered goal, but it is actually an unselfish process that is at the root

of everything we do in life. In order to be the most valuable person to the world around us, the best partner, parent etc, we have to first know who we are, what we value and, in effect, what we have to offer. This personal journey is one every individual will benefit from taking. It is a process that involves breaking down—shedding layers that do not serve us in our lives and don't reflect who we really are. Yet, it also involves a tremendous act of building up – recognizing who we want to be and passionately going about fulfilling our unique destiny – whatever that may be. It's a matter of recognizing our personal power, yet being open and vulnerable to our experiences. It isn't something to fear or avoid, berating ourselves along the way, but rather something to seek out with the curiosity and compassion we would have toward a fascinating new friend."[86]

Finding that new friend in yourself generally takes a lot of insightful questions by trained analysts who have learned to glean insights from your answers to those questions. The field of psychology has led to the development of a huge industry of personality tests to assist us in answering the question, "who am I, really?" Any one of these may provide you with valuable insights. A list of *The 23 Best PersonalityTests in Ranking Order (2023 Update)* is included as Appendix #1 at the end of the book for your consideration.

However, before I send you scurrying to use any (or all) of those tests, I think it is important to understand how they are typically structured, what they typically reveal, and what they don't. Most are personality assessments based on what is known as the Five Factor Model. That model provides insights regarding how an individual rates according to each of the five factors: Openness, Extraversion, Conscientiousness, Agreeableness, and Neuroticism. Those that are most often used extensively by industrial psychologists have eliminated the Neuroticism factor. Among the most popular are Myers-Briggs,

---

[86] *A Guide to Finding Yourself,* PsychAlive, https://www.psychalive.org/finding-yourself/

DiSC, and Enneagram. Each of these are mentioned in the list of the top 23 personality tests shared at the end of this chapter.

I have personally taken, and utilized, each of these three well-known assessments, and can attest to their value. They each provide unique insights into the psychological factors that contribute to an individual's behavior. Myers-Briggs (MBTI), for example, uses noted psychiatrist and psychoanalyst Carl Jung's theory of conscious psychological type. The results of MBTI assessments group individuals into one of 16 personality types based on their answers to a series of questions that measure an individual's "polarities of preference:"

- Extroversion or Introversion (E or I)
- Sensing or Intuition (S or N))
- Feeling or Thinking (F or T)
- Judging or Perceiving (J or P)

The following graphic shows each of the 16 personality types:

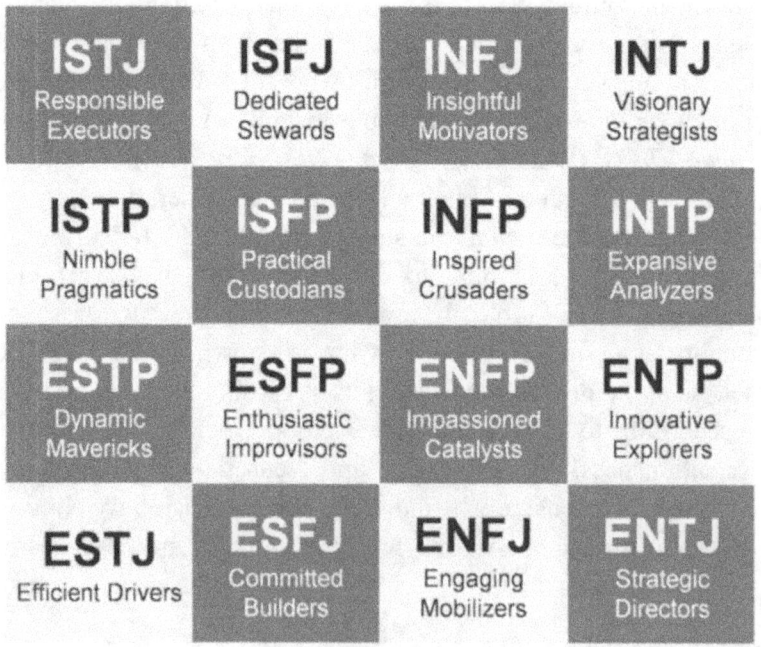

Having participated in the use of this assessment tool, I came away with mixed emotions. On the positive side, I was intrigued by where I landed. I was classified as an ENTJ. That was fine with me… until the company with whom I was working at the time noted that their best executives were almost always ISTPs. I had always been acclaimed as one of the firm's best performers, but now I was worried. I wondered if I had been psychoanalyzed into an uncomplimentary box–and, if so, was the MBTI analysis correct? In chatting with other executives, a similar concern was prevalent.

Might MBTI give you personal insights regarding your unique and authentic individuality? It may, but I found it to be somewhat lacking in providing clear insights regarding my potential and practical ideas as to how to perform in meeting that potential.

My experience with DiSC was similar. The theory on which it was developed was introduced by American psychologist William Moulton Marston in his book, *The Emotions of Normal People*, published in 1928. He set forth the Marston Model of the Four Dimensions of Behavior. Those dimensions were initially Dominance, Inducement, Submission, and Compliance. They were later changed to:

- Dominance
- Influence
- Steadiness
- Conscientiousness

DiSC assessments measure and predict your behavior. They suggest how forceful you are likely to be in expressing your opinion, your tendency to be outgoing or introverted, how patient or impatient you are likely to be with others, and how hard-working and dependable you are. I was categorized as *a Creative*, with high Dominance and Conscientiousness, with somewhat lower scores on Influence and Steadiness. Very interesting insights, to be sure, but the DiSC assessment, while identifying my behavioral tendencies, fell short of providing the useful insights I desired for zeroing in on a clear understanding of my authentic self.

The Enneagram of Personality Theory also fell short of the mark for me. It was created as a key element of Protoanalysis in the 1950s by Oscar Ichazo, a Bolivian teacher. Protoanalysis draws on teachings from Judaism, Christianity, Islam, Buddhism,Taoism, and ancient Greek philosophy, as well as psychology, cosmology, and metaphysics. Ichazo identified Nine Enneagram Types based on the virtues, ego fixations, passions, and holy ideas which he observed in human beings.

These nine personality types are conveyed by an Enneagram, a geometric illustration that shows the intensity of each of the nine personality characteristics of the person taking the assessment. When I took this assessment, my Enneagram defined me as a strong 8, *a Challenger*, one who is self-confident, decisive, willful, and confrontational. Challengers have a strong desire to achieve, a desire for affiliation with others, and a desire to make a positive impact on the world. The Enneagram Report also provided a personality profile that gave insights on what they perceived to be my core emotions, fears, and desires, and how those factors are likely to influence my relationships and my work. As with Myers-Briggs and DiSC, I found this feedback to be interesting, but still not a strong definitive guide to who I am–and what my core purpose should be.

At this point in my search for insights into "who I am, really," I began to wonder….perhaps I'm looking in the wrong place. When I shared the results of these personality assessments with those people who are closest to me, those who have some sense of who I am, their eyes seemed to glaze over. While they corroborated some of what I shared, their common response was that these personality tests seemed to be "a lot of psycho-babble"—and not very useful. I had to agree.

It wasn't long after having spent several hundred dollars test-driving the three assessments mentioned here (as well as several others), that one of my clients asked if I had ever taken the Gallup's StrengthsFinder 2.0 assessment. My first thought was "here we go again." However, this CEO spoke quite highly about the insights he had gleaned from this tool. So…with some reservations, I looked into it.

There were two immediate surprises with StrengthsFinder. The first was how easy it was to take the assessment. I simply had to order the book, *StrengthsFinder 2.0 from Gallup: Discover Your Clifton Strengths.* I jumped onto Amazon and received the book the next day. Each book provides a unique access code for your use only in taking the assessment.

The second surprise was that StrengthsFinder is not a personality test at all. It is a self-discovery process that reveals the strengths that define each individual. It is a performance-based tool that focuses on *how* people are most likely to be at their very best, *what* their inherent strengths are, and *how* to play to those strengths to experience personal fulfillment and success.

Digging in further to learn about StrengthsFinder, I discovered that through many years of research, Gallup has focused on the desirable outcomes of people discovering who they really are, and what gives them joy and fulfillment in their lives and in their work. That research has proven that teams that focus on strengths every day have 12.5% greater productivity than those who don't. It boils down to doing what you love to do...on a consistent and ongoing basis.

Unlike the personality assessments that are typically based on the 5 Factor Model mentioned above, StrengthsFinder makes no claims to be a personality test. Instead, it is based on what Gallup calls *Talent Themes*, the areas in which individuals have the greatest potential for success through their unique strengths. Gallup has discovered that there are 34 of these themes. Each one of them provides insights on how you can use your inherent talents to be productive, fulfilled, and happy. The purpose of StrengthsFinder is to lead you to a clear understanding of who you are–and what brings you personal fulfillment and satisfaction. For my purpose in this book, they are focused on helping you to discover your Authentic Self.

The key premises of StrengthsFinder are:

1. You have inherent gifts, talents, strengths, or attributes that motivate your life.

2. Your greatest potential for growth and fulfillment is in your unique areas of greatest personal strength.

3. You should seek to discover your strengths, and upon discovering them, set high intrinsic goals (and purpose) related to those strengths, and then–*play to your strengths.*

Your unique strengths will fall into any of four major categories, defined as follows:

- **EXECUTING:** People with dominant Executing themes make things happen.

- **INFLUENCING:** People with dominant Influencing themes take charge, speak up, and make sure others are heard.

- **RELATIONSHIP BUILDING:** People with dominant Relationship Building themes build strong relationships that hold a theme together and make it greater than the sum of its parts.

- **STRATEGIC THINKING:** People with dominant Strategic Thinking themes absorb and analyze information that informs better decisions.

Having come to understand these categories and the fundamental premises undergirding this assessment , I was anxious to try StrengthsFinder for myself. **Here are the themes that emerged for me. Details for each of these are shared in Appendix #2 at the end of this book. I encourage you to read through them to understand the valuable feedback you will receive from utilizing StrengthsFinder in zeroing in on your Authentic self.**

MY TOP 10 THEMES:

1. **STRATEGIC THINKING: Learner**–You have a great desire to learn and want to continuously improve. The process of learning, rather than the outcome, excites you.

2. **STRATEGIC THINKING: Context**–You enjoy thinking about the past. You understand the present by researching its history.

3. **STRATEGIC THINKING: Strategic**–You create alternative ways to proceed. Faced with any given scenario, you can quickly spot the relevant patterns and issues.

4. **EXECUTING: Achiever**–You work hard and possess a great deal of stamina. You take immense satisfaction in being busy and productive.

5. **RELATIONSHIP BUILDING: Individualization**–You are intrigued with the unique qualities of each person. You have a gift for figuring out how different people can work together productively.

6. **EXECUTING: Arranger**–You can organize, but you also have the flexibility that complements this ability. You like to determine how all of the pieces and resources can be arranged for maximum productivity.

7. **STRATEGIC THINKING: Analytical**–You search for reasons and causes. You have the ability to think about all of the factors that might affect a situation.

8. **RELATIONSHIP BUILDING: Connectedness**–You have faith in the links among all things. You believe there are few coincidences and that almost every event has meaning. You build bridges between people and groups by helping them find meaning and purpose.

9. **STRATEGIC THINKING: Input**–You have a need to collect and archive. You may accumulate information, ideas, artifacts, or even relationships.

10. **INFLUENCING: Maximizer**–You focus on strengths as a way to stimulate personal and group excellence. You seek to transform something strong into something superb.

Notice that my strengths lean heavily toward Strategic Thinking, with 5 of my Top Ten Themes falling within this category. While not quite as dominant, my strengths also include Executing and Relationship

Building. Influencing is less dominant yet, but is still present in my Maximizer strength.

I have shared the detailed report from the Gallup organization (Appendix #2) with those who are closest to me: my wife, my children, my business partners and coworkers. Without exception, they were stunned at how accurate these descriptors are of how I think, work, and behave. The most common reaction was, "Amazing! StrengthsFinder nailed it!"

I concur with that answer.

These ten themes have articulated who I am, what I enjoy most in my life, and how I prefer to work and interact with others. They have helped me focus on my personal gifts and spend less time on things that don't matter—or things that I am not good at. That is an outcome that the major personality tests haven't delivered for me. For that reason, I unequivocally recommend StrengthsFinder 2.0 for anyone desiring definition of "who they really are," their Authentic self.

Please note that I am not an employee of Gallup or StrengthsFinder. They have not asked me for my endorsement; indeed, until this book is published, they will not know that I have given it. In that regard, I have not–and will not–receive compensation from them.

My preference for StrengthsFinder is pretty simple. By providing insights into my Authentic Self, it allows me to correlate my strengths with my day-to-day activities, thereby increasing my performance and enjoyment in those activities, and helping me to feel confident in moving forward toward fulfilling my personal purpose.

So...in pursuit of articulating YOUR Authentic Self, I suggest that you jump on the internet and go to store.Gallup.com, or use the following link to order a copy of StrengthsFinder 2.0 from Amazon:

https://www.amazon.com/s?k=strengths+finder+2.0+with+access+code&crid=397KIUAZPKDB3&sprefix=strengths%2Caps%2C128&ref=nb_sb_ss_ts-doa-p_1_9

It is generally available for under $20.00.

When you have completed the assessment, you will be ready to move to Chapter 7C, Your Personal CAUSE—And the Logic that Provides Its Credibility.

Your Personal CAUSE–And the Logic That Provides Its Credibility

The measure of a man is not determined by his show of outward strength or the volume of his voice or the thunder of his action. It is to be seen rather in terms of the strength of his inner self in terms of the nature and depth of his commitments, the sincerity of his purpose, and his willingness to continue growing up.

Grade E. Pollard

Who will adhere to him that abandons himself?

Sir Philip Sidney

A man is a lion for his own cause.

Scottish Proverb

Your Cause embodies the underlying logic, or Logos, that makes implementation of that Cause credible in the eyes of key stakeholders—most importantly YOU. It relates directly to how you will create and deliver value–your Personal Value Proposition that aligns with your WHY. To provide the driving force in your life–and for your business, your Personal Value Proposition should clearly relate to and align with the Value Proposition of your enterprise. It should provide an unambiguous answer to the question posed in the title of Clayton M. Christensen 's best-selling book, *How Will You Measure Your Life?*

I have written this book, *Align & Execute*, with a focus on your role in leading your business successfully, whatever that enterprise may be. That being said, however, I have found that the alignment of the key components of business success (as illustrated in the Business Success Pyramid) is always most powerful when it is founded not only on the Logos of the enterprise, but when it is deeply rooted in the underlying logic that drives its leader. And this is, in fact, far more important than providing the foundation for your business success; it does, indeed, define *how you will measure your life!*

It is important to recognize that "how you will measure your life" must be defined in the sequence of two essential areas:

- **First, the value you are creating for yourself**; that is, what gives you a continuous sense of personal fulfillment? What does the definition of that value inspire you to do? What passions motivate you to create that value for yourself? What actions does your pursuit of that value precipitate?

  In his book, Clayton Christensen provided guidance for both of these areas. Regarding the value that you are creating for yourself, he posed three key questions:

  1. How can you be sure that you will find satisfaction in your career?
  2. How can you be sure that your personal relationships will become enduring sources of happiness?
  3. How can you avoid compromising your integrity–and stay out of jail?[87]

- **Second, the value that you create and deliver to others,** those people who are your target market for that value—and what you

---

[87] *How Will You Measure Your Life?* Clayton M. Christensen, page 6.

will do to create and deliver that value for that constituency. With regard to this second area, I have addressed this for your business earlier in this book (Chapter 3: Moving from your WHY to WHAT YOU DO). While there are notable similarities, my intention in this chapter is to put a laser focus on your personal WHY–and moving to WHAT YOU DO (or want to do) as an individual, rather than focus at this juncture on your company. Subsequently, when your personal WHY and WHAT are clearly aligned with the WHY and WHAT of your business, success becomes increasingly inevitable! That alignment almost always proves to be inspiring to both yourself and others.

With regard to the value you will create and deliver to others, a bit more "logos analysis" can be helpful. There are two fundamental starting points for the creation of value for others:

- o **PUSH VALUE, which is the introduction of something new, different, or innovative that the target market has generally not known they needed or wanted.** Often this takes the form of a new technology that heretofore has not existed. This could be like the blade prosthetics introduced by Van Phillips. The Internet or Artificial Intelligence are also examples of Push Value that have brought the world what Clayton Christensen called "disruptive technologies".

- o **PULL VALUE, which identifies and serves a clearly defined market need.** Such products and/or services are often the result of research that ferrets out a problem or "pain" that a given class of customer is dealing with. With that understanding, a value proposition is then developed to eliminate or mitigate the pain. Pull Value might also provide a value proposition that delivers a "gain" desired by a targeted customer group. Or, as Clayton Christensen points out, Pull Value might provide an intense focus on the "job" that the target customer needs your product or service to do for them.

While these value creation insights are most often used in defining enterprise value, you should begin by applying them personally to yourself. What Push Value might you be inclined to deliver to the world? Are there new disruptive technologies that you have thought of or might conceive? What is the fresh idea that you've always wanted to pursue?

What "pain" have you observed that you might address? How might you tackle a long-standing problem that has affected your family, your customers, your community? What "gains" might you deliver to underserved markets? What "jobs" might you fulfill for target customers?

Tim Brown, Co-Chair of IDEO and author of *Change By Design: How Design Thinking Transforms Organizations and Inspires Innovation,* and Warren Berger in his book, *A More Beautiful Question: The Power of Inquiry to Spark Breakthrough Ideas,* provide suggestions that are often very useful in zeroing in on your Cause and the logic required to support it. Brown asserts that there are three essential phases to the design, creation, and delivery of strong value propositions. These are:

- INSPIRATION: Identifying the problem or opportunity that motivates the search for solutions
- IDEATION: The process of generating, developing, and testing ideas
- IMPLEMENTATION: The path that leads...to the market.[88]

Within these phases, Berger suggests key questions when pondering the value you might create for others:

In the INSPIRATION PHASE, ask WHY Questions: *Why* questions challenge the status quo. They demand deep thought that eschews the easy answers. They include:

---

[88] *Change By Design: How Design Thinking Transforms Organizations and Inspires Innovation,* Tim Brown, page 16.

- *Why* does a particular situation exist?
- *Why* does it present a problem or create a need or opportunity, and for whom?
- *Why* has no one addressed this need or solved this problem already?
- *Why* do you personally want to invest more time thinking about, and formulating questions around this problem?[89]

In the IDEATION PHASE, ask WHAT IF Questions: *What if* questions force us to move into creative new ideas. They are often used by facilitators in brainstorming for new ways of thinking and seeing the world.

- *What if* you tried looking at this problem from another perspective? From the perspective of the "other guy?" From the perspective of an outsider? From 30,000 feet? From the atomic level?
- *What if* you worked to discover the key constraint to success and solved it?
- *What if* you were to identify "sacred cows" and traditions that are no longer merited?
- *What if* you eliminated all unnecessary or redundant practices?
- *What if* you looked at the situation as a doctor might, or as a jet pilot, or a biologist, or an anthropologist, or a housewife, or a child?

What if questions should move you from the inspiration of asking *why* to opening your mind to many possible ideas for solving a problem or taking advantage of an opportunity.

---

[89] *A More Beautiful Question: The Power of Inquiry to Spark Breakthrough Ideas,* Warren Berger, page 29.

In the IMPLEMENTATION PHASE, ask HOW Questions: *How* questions transition your thinking into specific strategic options for putting your Cause into action. They provide the operational logic for your personal purpose.

These questions should not be taken lightly, nor should they be answered quickly. Your answers are, in fact, existential–*they often define what you need to be satisfied with how you will spend the years you have ahead of you.* They will not only define how you will measure your life, but also will form the basis for your Personal Value Proposition, your life Mission–and that of your business.

So... what if defining how you will measure your life–and the Cause that extends from those answers is leading you away from your current path?

My objective in this chapter is not to steer anyone away from their current path, at least not immediately. Indeed, I hope your discoveries herein will align well with your current path. However, the essence of Clayton Christensen's counsel–and my own–is that life is too short to be consumed in general unhappiness and dissatisfaction. Personal alignment and execution, if not a source of endless joy, should at least be fulfilling. The late Stephen R. Covey noted, "I have (observed) many climbing up the ladder of success only to find, once they got to the top, that the ladder was leaning against the wrong wall." Conversely, author Todd Rose in his book, *Dark Horse,* put it this way, "Personalized success is living a life of fulfillment and excellence.[90]

The key point is perhaps best summed up by Simon Sinek, in his book *Start With Why: How Great Leaders Inspire Everyone to Take Action:*

"Very few people...can clearly articulate WHY they do WHAT they do. When I say WHY, I don't mean to make money–that's a result. By WHY I mean what is your purpose,

---

[90] *Dark Horse: Achieving Success Through the Pursuit of Fulfillment,* Todd Rose and Ogi Ogas, page 19.

cause or belief? WHY do you get out of bed every morning? And WHY should anyone care?

"When most…people think, act,or communicate they do so from the outside in, from WHAT (they do) to WHY. And for good reason–they go from the clearest thing to the fuzziest thing. We say WHAT we do, we sometimes say HOW we do it, but we rarely say WHY we do WHAT we do.

"But not the inspired leaders. Every single one of them… thinks, acts, and communicates from the inside out."[91]

So the answer you should be seeking first is not WHAT to do with your life, but rather from deep inside you, you should answer *WHY you are here.* What is your cause, your purpose, your mission? With that clearly articulated, you can then proceed to answer the questions regarding WHAT to do–and HOW to do it. Those answers will then constitute the Logos, or logic, for your Cause!

As you articulate your Personal Purpose, I suggest that you endeavor to do so according to the definition of a "just cause" shared by Simon Sinek in another of his books, *The Infinite Game.*

He states that your cause should be:

- **For Something**—Affirmative & Optimistic
- **Inclusive**—Open to all those who would like to contribute
- **Service Oriented**—For the primary benefit of others
- **Resilient**—Able to endure political, technological and cultural change–and–
- **Idealistic**—Big, bold, and ultimately unachievable[92]

The next several vignettes in this chapter will show how several significant leaders have applied these principles. I cannot say that

---

[91] *Start With Why: How Great Leaders Inspire Everyone to Take Action,* Simon Sinek, page 39.
[92] *The Infinite Game,* Simon Sinek, page 37.

they employed the precise terms that I've shared here, but you will see that the processes inherent to their respective successes are very much the same.

The first story is that of one of the most extraordinary, purpose-driven CEOs of the past 200 years. She (yes, this remarkable leader was a woman) is probably not described as a CEO in any of the literature that shares her story, but she deserves to be described as a Chief Executive Officer as much or more than anyone with whom I've worked or studied. Her name? Florence Nightingale.

Florence Nightingale

Florence Nightingale was born in 1820 in Florence, Italy, to a wealthy and well-connected family, part of the "'upper ten thousand,' the social, political, and economic class that ruled England."[93] The family owned two country homes as part of an inheritance handed down over generations.[94] The pattern of the Nightingales' life was well-established along the lines of the rich and powerful; when they weren't traveling on the European mainland, they spent summer and fall at one home, and the rest of the year at the other, enjoying each social season and special events.[95] They regularly associated with elites of London, Paris, and much of Europe, including heads of state and such notables as novelist Victor Hugo, author of "Les Miserables" and "The Hunchback of Notre Dame," and Alexis de Tocqueville, author of "Democracy in America."[96]

Florence was a precocious little girl, learning to read and write almost in her infancy. By age 7, she had become "a serious and prolific letter-writer who showed powers of observation and analysis far beyond her years.[97] Her father recognized her innate appetite for learning and readily invited her into his library by the age of 12. There

---

[93] *Florence Nightingale: Mystic, Visionary, Healer*, Barbara Mongomery Dossey, page 4.
[94] Ibid
[95] Ibid, page 8.
[96] Ibid, page 42.
[97] Ibid, page 8.

her education began. She studied Roman, French, German, Italian, and Turkish history, as well as English political and constitutional history, philosophy, ethics, grammar, composition, mathematics, and the Bible.[98] As she later remembered it, "For 7 years of my life I thought of little else but cultivating my intellect."[99]

Personal Purpose Begins to Emerge: The Value Florence Desires for Herself

Florence was a loving, obedient, and diligent child, but her personal purpose began to diverge from the expectations of her parents and those of the high society to which she was born. Around the age of 15, she often slipped away from home in the evenings to the bedsides of villagers who were sick or injured, saying "she couldn't sit down to a grand 7 o'clock dinner while this was going on...to visit them in a carriage and give them money is so little like following Christ, who made Himself like His Brethren."[100]

The Nightingales were not oblivious to the plight of their less fortunate neighbors; indeed, Florence's mother sometimes "paid visits to villagers, usually to distribute food from the Nightingale's table or to offer practical advice. However, 'poor-peopling' was only a sidelight in her life; she was consumed with ambition for social success–not social service–for herself and her daughters."[101]

Social success, however, was of no interest to Florence. This became clear to her, late in her 16th year, when a great influenza epidemic struck the London area. Seeing the enormity of suffering around her, Florence immersed herself in nursing. Soon, these days of selfless service began to evolve from a job to a calling. She articulated it this way: "That a quest there is, and an end, is the single secret spoken."[102] She had begun to discover her Personal Purpose, her WHY.

---

[98] Ibid, page 18.
[99] Ibid, page 17.
[100] Ibid, page 30.
[101] Ibid, page 31.
[102] Ibid, page 33.

Around the age of 19, Florence wrote in a private note that she must "overcome the desire to shine in society."[103] And although she had suitors who desired her hand in marriage, her heart was elsewhere. She was drawn to nursing. Nursing, however, she observed, was far from a respectable occupation–and no one saw it as a desirable profession. Author Barbara Montgomery Dossey has noted that "At this time, in England, 'nurses' were generally drawn from the ranks of the poor and unskilled, and usually remained in that state…they also had a reputation for drunkenness and immoral conduct. This sad state of affairs had evolved for three centuries as nursing passed into its 'dark ages' in England. Since the Reformation and the suppression of monasteries, the quality of nursing and hospitals had suffered in all the Protestant European countries, but most severely in England."[104]

In spite of this, Florence became increasingly drawn to nursing. She began to see an opportunity in the lamentable state of the field, and a nascent value proposition began to form in her mind.

To go from these ideas to creating value, however, she recognized the need to first learn the rudiments of nursing in its present sorry state. She arranged to work alongside a doctor at a hospital at the age of 25, much to the dismay of her mother, who was horrified. She exclaimed that such a venture was beneath her daughter's class and unequivocally forbade it. She rejected the idea as "unladylike," scorning nurses as "merely women who would be servants if they were not nurses." She disdained Florence's desires saying, "It is as if you want to be a kitchen maid."[105]

Crushed by her mother's condemnation, Florence nevertheless found herself questioning *why* nursing had come to be viewed with such negativity. She observed that the well-heeled of British society were nursed at home, while the poor and destitute found themselves in shabby and often unsanitary hospitals. Even the doctors who served in such hospitals were regarded as little more than tradesmen by the

---

[103] Ibid, page 43.
[104] Ibid, page 53.
[105] Ibid, page 54.

upper class. For the next seven years, she wrestled with her deep desire to change things for the better, while still obeying the admonitions of her parents.

However, at the age of 32, her mother and father finally relented to her ceaseless entreaties, allowing her to spend 3 months at the Institution of Deaconesses at Kaiserswerth in Düsseldorf, Germany. Even so, they instructed her not to tell anyone, lest any family or friends should find out.[106] Clearly they hoped that this experience would dissuade their headstrong daughter. But it did not…

Inspiration Leads to Ideation as Florence's asks *Why* and *What If* Questions

At Kaiserswerth, Florence discovered that nursing could be so much more than it was in England. She wondered *why* this essential service was so backward and poorly regarded in Great Britain. And that led her to *what if* questions: including *what if* the care of the sick could be smoothly managed with goals, rules and an organizational structure?

Kaiserswerth provided a vision of quality care for the sick and the poor–and rehabilitation for orphans, prostitutes, and others who were usually written off by society. During her 3 months at Kaiserswerth, Florence wrote over 100 pages of detailed notes, a record that revealed not only illnesses, surgical procedures, and treatments, but how patients responded emotionally and spiritually. And perhaps most importantly to her sense of personal purpose, she also recorded her own sense of the sacredness of the work.[107]

After Florence returned to England from Kaiserswerth, she began to cut the apron strings with her parents. In a letter to her sister, she stated, "… you don't think that with my talents, I'm going to stay dangling about my mother's drawing room all my life–I shall go and look out for work to be sure."[108]

---

[106] Ibid, pages 74 & 75.
[107] Ibid, pages 75 & 76.
[108] Ibid, page 78.

Ideation Provides the Seeds for Implementation, as Florence Begins to Ask *How* She Can Put Her Personal Purpose into Action

On August 12, 1853, at the age of 33, Florence broke free from the gender, class, and familial shackles that had bound her. On this day, she began her professional career in London as superintendent (what I see as her first CEO position) of the Institution for the Care of Gentlewomen in Distressed Circumstances.[109] This institution served as a sanatorium for sick, unmarried middle-to-lower class women, most of whom served in low-paying governess positions, if they could find work. The 1851 British census noted that there were over 365,000 of them, with only about 25,000 actually working. In other words, there was a huge market for the services of this hospital.[110] The opportunity immediately aligned with Florence's sense of her purpose, her Cause. It did not take long for her Logos, the logic that would define her Cause to emerge.

Florence's genius lay in her ability to create administrative systems whereby her patients (her customers, if you will) would be effectively and efficiently served. Her defining purpose in creating an outstanding organization was to mitigate or eliminate the pain and suffering of her constituents. This included attention not only to their physical health, but their mental, emotional, and spiritual health as well. She dived headlong into the work, filing copious quarterly reports to the governing committee for the hospital. These addressed virtually every imaginable issue including patient care, working conditions, wages, and hours for nurses, training for nurses and other employees, a medication purchasing system, inventory management, nutrition guidelines, and kitchen design and management. She stressed employee competence over connections, setting specific work standards and accountability. She was a patient trainer, willing to work with any nurse or employee who showed a willingness to

---

[109] Ibid, page 88.
[110] Ibid, page 86.

engage and work hard. But she did not tolerate those who failed to meet this standard; she felt no constraint in firing slackers.[111]

Florence Articulates Her *Just Cause*

Florence's only unfulfilled passion at the Institute was her desire to more intensively focus on training nurses to understand and grow into highly competent and respected professional caregivers. Using Simon Sinek's definition of a Just Cause, her purpose was "for something", optimistically focused on the nursing profession which, if transformed, would benefit all of British society. She recognized the incredible challenge of changing minds and attitudes, and engaging others in her cause. She was realistic, but inherently resilient; she did not shrink from the resistance she expected to face from English politicians and society. To most observers, her cause was overly bold–and most likely unachievable. Even so, she had become determined to change nursing and caregiving for the better.

After one full year with the Institution for the Care of Gentlewomen in Distressed Circumstances, she submitted this letter to the governing committee:

> "I have not effected anything toward the object of training nurses–my primary idea in devoting my life to Hospital work... I therefore wish, at the close of the year for which I promised my services...that I may retire (to) meet with a sphere which is more analogous to the formulation of a Nursing School."

Thus she gave notice to her employers. The opportunity at the Institute had provided her with significant growth and development, but after one rigorous year, her Cause had further evolved into what would be the driving force for the rest of her life. However, her next next step toward the creation of a school that would bring nursing

---

[111] Ibid, page 92.

into prominence as a vital and respected profession was not what she anticipated. As so often is the case, world affairs intervened.

Florence Nightingale's Crucible Experience Provides the Logos for Her Personal Purpose

Coincident with her year at the Institute, Czarist Russia began an incursion southward toward the Mediterranean and the Middle East through what is now Ukraine and Romania. Britain and France opposed this action, seeing this as upsetting the balance of power in that region.

Jerusalem notably stood at the center of the ferment between the nations involved. It functioned at that time under the administration of the Turkish government, with influence from England, France, and Russia. For their part, France claimed the right to protect Roman Catholics in Jerusalem, while Russia similarly claimed the right to protect the Greek Orthodox Church, of which Czar Nicholas I was the ex officio head. The relationship between the churches and their respective protectors was contentious at best.

Thus the stage was set for conflict. It erupted in the summer of 1853 when Roman Catholic adherents in Jerusalem attempted to place a star over the manger in the Church of the Nativity. Orthodox monks took offense, and in an attempt to prevent what they saw as sacrilege, a fight broke out. Several Orthodox monks were killed, infuriating the Russians. Accusing the Turkish authorities of failing to keep order, they used the incident as a pretext to mobilize their troops, moving southward into Wallachia (what is now Romania). This led to a declaration of war by the Turks in October of 1853. In response, the Russian fleet in the Black Sea destroyed the Turkish navy, massacring their sailors in the water. This atrocity inflamed public opinion in Europe, leading to a declaration of war against Russia by France and Britain in March of 1854. Thus, as allies of Turkey, England and France entered what became known as the Crimean War.

Recognizing the urgent need to prevent the Russians from gaining control of the Dardanelles and the Bosporus Strait that bisects Turkey and provides access to and from the Black Sea, France and England rushed troops to Turkey. Soon, battles raged, taking a terrible toll on both sides. Disease compounded the casualties. While some hospitals operated in Turkey, they became quickly overwhelmed. The Barrack Hospital in Scutari (modern-day Istanbul), for instance, maintained an average patient load of 2000 in a facility designed for 1200. Individual wards with capacity for 30 routinely had to accommodate over 70.[112]

One notable doctor, a Dr. Hall, sent this plaintive report to London:

> "It is with feelings of surprise and anger that the public will learn that no sufficient preparations have been made for the cure of the wounded. Not only are there not sufficient surgeons…not only are there no dressers and nurses; there is not even linen to make bandages for the wounded…

> "Can it be said that the battles (are events) to take the world by surprise? Has not the expedition to the Crimea been the talk for the last four months? And when the Turks gave up to our use the vast barracks to form a hospital…, was it not on the grounds that the loss of English troops was sure to be considerable when engaged in so dangerous an enterprise?

> "Not only are men kept, in some cases for a week, without the hand of a medical man coming near their wounds, not only are they left to expire in agony, unheeded and shaken off, though catching desperately at the surgeon whenever he makes his rounds through the fetid ship; but now, when they are placed in the spacious building, where we are led to believe that everything was ready which could ease their pain or facilitate their recovery, it is found that the commonest appliances of a workhouse sick-ward are wanting, and that the men must die through the medical staff of the British Army having forgotten that old rags are necessary for the dressing of the wound."[113]

---

[112] Ibid, page 108
[113] Ibid, page 110.

Other reports of the terrible inadequacies of medical care for the wounded began to find their way into the British press, causing an outcry for significant improvements, including in nursing. Reading these, Florence was stirred. She had yearned for a situation that would allow her to bring nursing into prominence within the medical world. The Crimean War seemed to provide that. Amazingly, she was approached to lead a volunteer group of nurses to Turkey.

Florence had earlier given what amounted to six months' notice to the Institute governing committee, which period would not have been fulfilled until February of 1855. But now, on October 14,1854, she petitioned the committee to allow her to leave early. Her request was given additional emphasis when the day after she submitted her petition, she received a letter from Britain's Secretary of War, Sidney Herbert, formally inviting her to go to Turkey and supervise a group of female nurses on behalf of the government. The next few days were a whirlwind of activity, as she recruited a staff of 38 nurses (the inclusiveness of her cause began to grow), with whom Florence crossed the English Channel to France on October 21, 1854.[114] There, she met with merchants in Marseilles, arranging for supplies to be used in their work, and on October 27, she and her team sailed for Turkey.

Florence Nightingale now came face-to-face with her purpose, her Cause. She arrived in Scutari at the Barrack Hospital on November 5. Nothing she found there was even the slightest bit hopeful. The medical officers there disdained the women, especially their leaders. Conditions were filthy, supplies were inadequate, and overcrowding was severe. Five days after they arrived, injured soldiers from two major battles began arriving in the thousands, overwhelming the facility. Florence called it the "Kingdom of Hell."[115]

The demands placed on her and her nurses were relentless. By December, she penned the following words in a letter:

---

[114] Ibid, page 119.
[115] Ibid, page 125.

"I have not a moment. The whole army is coming into the hospitals. The task will be gigantic. Alas, how will it all end? We are in the hands of God. Pray for us. We have at the moment five thousand sick and wounded. My only comfort is, God sees it, God knows it, God loves us."[116]

Florence's Purpose Finds Its Logic, Its Meaning, and How It Fulfills Her

In spite of her misgivings, she didn't shrink from the task before her. It was what she had longed for. She sometimes worked 20 hours a day. She exhibited a commanding authority and a healing empathy that medical officers soon came to appreciate. On one notable occasion, surgeons laid five soldiers aside to die, deeming their conditions hopeless. Florence and a few of her nurses cared for these men through a long night–and by morning they were fit for surgery. When doctors would sometimes say, "we can't," her response was "we must."[117]

Florence Nightingale remained self-assured, working her way through virtually every challenge that the Crimean War could dish out. Finding that the Barrack Hospital's cesspools were blocked, she was greeted with raw sewage overflowing into hospital corridors. Although this naturally repelled her and her nurses, Florence aggressively addressed the problem, not only demanding that the blockages be cleared, but going further to establish standards of sanitation and cleanliness.[118]

Her influence quickly extended beyond the Barrack hospital to multiple hospitals throughout the Crimea, each providing new and different challenges for her leadership. Where supplies were scarce, for instance, she became a master of procurement, acquiring "6000 shirts, 2000 socks, 500 pairs of drawers, nightcaps, slippers, knives, forks, wooden spoons, trays, tables, forms, clocks, operating room tables,

---

[116] Ibid, page 121.
[117] Ibid, page 129.
[118] Ibid, page 126.

scrubbers, towels, soap, screens, spoons, tin baths, combs, precipitate for destroying lice, scissors, bedpans, and stump pillows.[119]

Florence's organization and administrative skills also were evident in how she deployed her nurses. She kept the least disciplined of them under her watchful eye. Three were dismissed for drunkenness in the first few weeks. While she would not tolerate such behavior, she worked with the others to support them in what was a horrid working environment. She established her own performance rating system, whereby she rated "16 very efficient and 5 or 6 excellent." And one notable member of her team, Mrs. Elvira Roberts, became a trusted resource, one to whom she could delegate important tasks.[120]

She gave orders for the regulation of female nurses in the wards. She established administrative order and accountability that extended beyond her nurses to doctors and medical officers. She worked under the scrutiny of politicians, sometimes with very little support. She could be extraordinarily outspoken, even aggressive in pressing for reforms in medical care. And yet, she was most notably known for her compassion and care of the wounded, the sick, and the weary.

The *London Times* famously described her as such:

> "Wherever there is disease in its most dangerous form and the hand of the despoiler distressingly nigh, there is that incomparable woman to be seen. Her benignant presence is an influence for good comfort, even amid the struggles of expiring nature. She is a 'ministering angel' without any exaggeration in these hospitals, and as her slender form glides quietly along each corridor, every poor fellow's face softens with gratitude at the sight of her. When all medical officers have retired for the night and silence and darkness have settled down upon those miles of prostrate sick, she may be observed alone, with a little lamp in her hand, making her solitary rounds."[121]

---

[119] Ibid, page 129-130.
[120] Ibid.
[121] Ibid, page 153.

These words led to the title given her by her patients, her fellow nurses, and the world: *The Lady With The Lamp*. I see her through business and organizational leadership lenses, but her Personal Purpose and Cause is best manifested in that description. Her continuous commitment to being a healing influence illuminated everything she did–from administration to ministering to those for whom she cared. She diligently strived to engage with the soldiers in her care, talking to them and cheering them with her calm voice, warm smile, and gentle touch. She regularly wrote to the mothers or wives of the soldiers who died. Her energetic, loving, and inspiring leadership continued in Scutari until the end of the Crimean War.

When the war ended in 1856, one might have thought that Florence was due for a long rest; that she might even have felt that her Personal Purpose had been fulfilled. She, however, was only just beginning in what became two personal quests: to reform the British Army's Medical Department–and to transform nursing.

Regarding the first, she was haunted by her memories of the thousands of soldiers who had died because of the unpreparedness and deficiencies in battlefield and hospital medical care. Of the nearly 98,000 British soldiers who had fought in the Crimean War, 4,500 had died of wounds on the battlefield, but almost 18,000 had died of exposure and disease.[122] She recognized that horrible sanitation, poor nutrition, and lack of organization were major causes of such high mortality and that, if not addressed, they would be repeated in any subsequent conflict. She began to spearhead efforts to reform the army's Medical Department, using facts and figures that she had diligently compiled at Scutari and in the Crimea. She used these statistics to support her recommendations, establishing what I am referring to as her Logos, or underlying logic for her Cause.

Her task was formidable because the army Medical Department was largely staffed by a long-standing system of aristocratic patronage rather than competent and committed administrators. Nevertheless, the flaws in the department were significant enough for the government to

---

[122] Ibid, page 186.

form a Board of Enquiry to investigate.[123] The investigation did little, in and of itself to inspire reforms, but it did bring substantial attention to the issues involved. These issues caught the interest of Queen Victoria, who invited Florence to meet with her and Prince Albert with the request that she report on her experiences in the Crimean War and share her ideas about reform. The meeting provided Florence with the opportunity she had most wanted. What could have been nothing more than a social encounter with the queen became the catalyst for "5 years of complex, arduous, and continuous work,"[124]

Of the meeting, Prince Albert wrote in his diary, "She put before us all the defects of our present military hospital system and the reforms that are needed. We are much pleased with her; she is extremely modest."[125] Florence had made her case for her Cause; she had successfully presented the Logos that gave that cause credibility. And she had done it with those who could help her!

With the support of the Queen and Prince, Florence once again threw herself headlong into reforming the British Medical Department. She ultimately presented five proposals for army reforms and twelve additional suggestions that were a combination of army and medical reforms. The first five addressed the nutrition, clothing, life support, and housing of soldiers in the field, as well as supply chain issues, and sanitation. The twelve focused on management and administration of hospitals, as well as cleanliness, hygiene, and sanitation. She further addressed the need for clearly defined policies, procedures, and job descriptions, including compensation and promotion standards. And of course, she recommended both administrative and medical staff training, including the training of nurses.[126]

I cannot do justice in describing the exceptional challenges Florence Nightingale faced in pressing for health care reform. While she had strong support from the Royal family, she had to continually

---

[123] Ibid, page 187.
[124] Ibid, page 190.
[125] Ibid, page 193.
[126] Ibid, pages 190-192

evangelize her proposals to both the British government and the army. She masterfully used her experiences in the Crimean War to turn adversaries into fellow advocates, presenting a strong case for the Logos of her recommendations . She summarized those experiences this way:

> "We have much more information on the sanitary history of the Crimean Campaign than we have on any other. It is a complete example–history does not afford its equal—of an army, after a great disaster arising from neglects, having been brought into the highest state of health and efficiency. It is the whole experiment on a colossal scale."[127]

Eventually under her unrelenting leadership, the following reforms were enacted in the British army:

- The army barracks (wherever soldiers were housed) was put into sanitary order
- A statistical department was established for the army (whereby injuries, illnesses, and mortality were tracked–and standards of care were correlated with patient outcomes)
- An army medical school was instituted.
- The army medical department was restructured, revising hospital regulations, and providing merit-based standards for the promotion of medical officers.[128]

The results of these reforms were truly amazing. In the first 3 years, the fatality rate of British soldiers fell to less than one-half the number of earlier years, and the mortality from all diseases dropped to less than the previous mortality from tuberculosis and other respiratory diseases alone.[129]

---

[127] Ibid, page 201
[128] Ibid, page 202.
[129] Ibid, page 218.

One high Parliamentarian, Sir John McNeill, paid her the following high compliment:

> "Be assured that the progress from a worse to a better system in almost every department of human affairs (is) a progress slow and interrupted. You have done more than anyone else ever did or could have done, and the good you have done will live ever after you, growing from generation to generation."[130]

At this point, Florence Nightingale had reached a high level of both private and public esteem. It was not her nature, however, to rest on her laurels. Nor did she feel that she had achieved her Personal Purpose. In 1860, she published her seminal work, *Notes on Nursing*, wherein she outlined her ideas for improving patient care, nursing ethics, sanitation and hygiene. She supported the principles in that work with research and statistics, making strong arguments for advancements in healthcare policy and administration. With the insights she shared in her book, she launched the Nightingale School of Nursing at St. Thomas's Hospital in London in June, 1860.[131]

While Florence began to feel personal fulfillment as she moved forward in the School of Nursing, this new venture carried more than a few challenges that demanded her attention. Not only was she faced with the grind of curriculum creation and implementation; she also had to figure out how to market her school to appropriate nursing candidates. Her marketing challenges were exacerbated by the fact that graduates of her nursing program were not in high demand. Indeed, they were shunned by most English hospitals. Clearly, it wasn't enough to just seek to attract nursing candidates; she had to convince mainstream hospitals that they should hire graduates of the school. Like most CEOs who launch an innovation, she had to convince end-users as to why they should adopt the new thing. It was a classic example of a *Push Value*

---

[130] Ibid.
[131] Ibid, page 221.

(described earlier in this chapter), the introduction of an innovation that the target market generally does not want or know they need.

Nursing, at this point, was still not seen as either a worthwhile pursuit, or as a profession. She saw this, in part, as a failure of society to understand how nursing could ennoble the role of women. As was her practice, she was quite bold in her position:

> "The whole reform in nursing both at home and abroad has consisted in this; to take all power over the nursing out of the hands of men, and put it into the hands of one female trained head and make her responsible for everything (regarding internal management and discipline)."[132]

Initially, Florence was that woman. However, her own health had become quite compromised by this time. Her role was changing from being the driving force to providing the knowledge and spirit that would inspire and drive others. She soldiered on in transformative ways, her challenges compounded by chronic illness.

Her influence had now become international, and once again, world affairs came calling. The American Civil War broke out in April, 1861. President Abraham Lincoln found himself faced with the same battlefield medical chaos that Florence had witnessed and dealt with in the Crimean War. Through publishing contacts, the Americans reached out to Florence for her guidance.[133] As always, she kindly responded, recommending not only her publications, but others that she felt might help.

By the end of 1861, Florence was fighting what at that time appeared to be a losing battle with her health. Her illness markedly slowed her down, but somehow she continued to be a worldwide influence on health care reform, as well as the education and promotion of nursing as an essential profession. This continued from 1862 to 1879, and included counsel to British leaders as they pursued their colonial interests in India and Australia.

---

[132] Ibid, page 292.
[133] Ibid, page 248.

Florence's later years were marked by continuous health concerns, leading her to withdraw from public life. Even so, she continued to pursue her Personal Purpose, focusing on her writing and correspondence. Although largely out of the public eye, her contributions were widely recognized in England and throughout the world. These included revolutionary improvements in health care (both military and domestic), nursing, and the use of statistics and metrics to support medical and administrative outcomes. She received numerous awards and honors, including being the first woman to be awarded the British Order of Merit in 1907. She passed away on August 13, 1910, at the age of 90.

I recognize that Florence Nightingale would probably not be on anyone else's list of extraordinary CEOs. But I feel that her story is a compelling example of a leader who through the crucible experiences of her life journey found her Pathos (or passion), who was Authentic regarding who she really was, had a Cause for which she developed the Logos (or credible path) to its fulfillment, and then proceeded with great resolve to that end.

As we return now to more conventional business leaders, consider how Florence Nightingale's Personal Purpose developed into the value proposition that she delivered to her target market—and how that fulfilled her life. How might you similarly tap into your Personal Purpose? How might you define the strategy and tactics, the Logos, that will move you down the path to fulfilling your purpose?

Thomas D'Eri, co-founder of Rising Tide Car Wash

While you may have heard of Florence Nightingale before reading this book, it's likely that you have not heard of Tom D'Eri. Further, you might be surprised that I would share the story of a car wash as an example of a visionary, purpose-driven business. But that is precisely what Rising Tide Car Wash is!

Personal Purpose Begins to Emerge: The Value that Tom D'Eri Wants for Himself

Let me introduce you to Tom. As of this writing, he is a 29 year old entrepreneur, a son, and a brother.

Each of those descriptors are important, beginning with "brother." Tom's younger brother, Andrew, has autism. Unfortunately, that doesn't tell you much about Andrew. That's because each person on the autism spectrum has their own unique profile of strengths, as well as areas where they struggle and need support. One thing that is quite similar among those with autism, however, is that as adults they are virtually unemployable. According to *Politico*, "Existing data suggests that only about one-third of adults on the autism spectrum work in paid jobs for more than 15 hours a week–and the rate has barely changed since 1991."[134]

Andrew is fortunate to have grown up in a loving home where he was appreciated and accepted for all he was, including the challenges that autism brought. Although he struggled with mainstream school and was subject to tantrums and meltdowns as a child, he graduated from high school to the joy and approval of family and friends. And then…he was faced with the seeming limbo-world of autistic adulthood, where no productive options were available. While his friends left for college and work, he was stuck at home, doing nothing but eating, sleeping, and playing video games. While others, including Tom, moved on with their lives, Andrew appeared to be in a state of "perpetual pause."

Now, we need to see Tom in his role as"son." To do that, you have to know a bit about his father, John D'Eri. Thomas lovingly describes his dad this way: "My father's focus on (Andrew's) future extended to the way he viewed his responsibility as a good father. He spent many sleepless nights worrying over the challenges Andrew would face as an adult. He started to look at Andrew not as a young boy or someone in his early twenties, but as a forty- or fifty-year old man. What would

---

[134] *Americans with Autism Have Never Had More Support–Except When It Comes to Employment,* Michael Bernick, *Politico.com,* October 4, 2021, http://www.politico.com/news/agenda/2021/10/04/americans- autism-employment-support-514667.

Andrew do? How would he support himself? How could my father support him?"[135]

Asking *Why* questions lead to the seeds of Inspiration

These concerns swirled around a more fundamental question: **Why** were there no good employment and life development options for those with autism like Andrew? This societal inadequacy haunted Tom's dad, and it became a central theme in the relationship between John and Tom.

Returning to Tom's roles, we must understand him as an "entrepreneur." His interest in business began during his undergraduate studies, and like so many others, he looked forward to pursuing an MBA after graduation. However, the roles of brother and son kept nagging him. As he put it, "...every time I came home from college, I felt a lump rise in my throat when Andrew and I hugged."[136] Although his mind was firmly focused on pursuing the next phase of his business career, he, like his father, felt a growing obligation to Andrew–and others like him. Thus the stage was set for their Personal Purpose to emerge. It did so at a most unlikely venue!

Inspiration Leads to Ideation as John and Tom ask *What If* Questions

Early in his junior year at college, Tom received a call from his dad, who was at a car wash. John excitedly shared what had come to him as an amazing revelation, "Thomas," he said, "I'm at the car wash, and you know what? I think Andrew could definitely do this!"[137] **What if** they were to start a car wash where people with autism like Andrew would be the primary workforce?

The idea germinated over the next two years before John and Tom decided to put it to the test. John was willing to pony up as much as $1 million to launch a car wash business staffed primarily by people with

---

[135] *The Power of Potential: How a Non-Traditional Workforce Can Lead You to Run Your Business Better,* Thomas D'Eri with Sara Grace, page xiv.
[136] Ibid, page xiii.
[137] Ibid, page xiv.

autism. He invited Tom to join him in the experiment. Tom didn't have to ponder his decision for very long. He recalls, "Watching Andrew retreat into his bedroom every night was all the convincing I needed."[138]

Ideation Provides the Seeds for Implementation, as John and Tom Begin to Ask *How* They Might Put Their Personal Purpose into Action

It is important to understand the process whereby the business was launched. John and Tom didn't immediately acquire a car wash. Instead, they began by being crystal clear regarding their shared personal purpose–that of employing people with autism. With that firmly in mind as their "north star," they then carefully went about developing *how* that purpose was to become a business enterprise. They needed the logic, or *Logos*, that would define the essential strategy and tactics for the business. In broad general terms, they saw their considerable task as "disrupting the status quo in employing people with autism."[139]

They realized that they needed the credibility that would only emerge as they became experts in what would become an innovative, first-of-its-kind business. This realization led them to a two-pronged learning process, the first key element of which was to strengthen their general business and entrepreneurial skills. They dived into a concerted study of forward-thinking management and leadership authors like Michael Gerber (*The E-Myth*), Todd Rose (*The End of Average*), and Laszlo Bock (*Work Rules*).

The second key element was to learn as much as possible about autism. Although they were quite familiar with Andrew and both his strengths and weaknesses, they recognized that people with autism fall within a broad spectrum. They knew that, worldwide, around 75 million people have autism, with as many as 1 in 44 children being diagnosed with autism spectrum disorder. Clearly, there were many like Andrew who needed the opportunities they envisioned creating. However, they needed to gain a broader and deeper understanding of the challenges inherent in

---

[138] Ibid, page xv.
[139] Ibid.

working with people with autism. To bridge this gap, they spent over a year seeking out experts who could give them some assurance that such a business could be successful and create satisfying employment for people on the spectrum. They came to realize that such expertise would also be needed to help them develop the skills they would need to recruit and train a staff of people with autism. They were most often greeted with amazement at their idea, followed then by pessimism that such a business would be sustainable.

In spite of this, John and Tom moved forward. Sometime, well into more than a year of establishing the *logos* for their purpose, they realized that there was one more glaring deficit in their logic and readiness: neither of them knew anything about car washes–or the car wash industry. Once again, research was required. They began a search for industry experts, and after some effort, they discovered Sonny's Enterprises, the largest manufacturer of car wash equipment in the world, which offered a program called CarWash College. They soon arranged a meeting with Sonny's president, Paul Fazio, during which they shared their vision of a car wash staffed with people with autism.

Paul responded by saying that he felt both Tom and John were crazy, but then expressed his desire to help. He offered them the opportunity to attend a two-week crash course at CarWash College. What they learned there convinced them that "the car wash business and autism were a match made in heaven." In his book, *The Power of Potential*, Thomas shared their insights:

> "...professional car washes operate using consistent and detailed processes. The entire first course (at CarWash College) was focused on specific operating processes and training team members to use them. Many people on the (autism) spectrum were extremely well suited for this particular context. While typical workers often chafe against process, many people with autism thrive on it."[140]

---

[140] Ibid, page 7.

The D'Eri's Articulate Their *Just Cause*

After the short, but intense, learning experience at CarWash College, John and Tom began searching for an existing car wash to purchase. They acquired what they described as a "crappy car wash," renamed it Rising Tide, and began the process of transforming it into a profitable, high-performing organization employing primarily people with autism.

As we review the *Just Cause* of Rising Tide against Simon Sinek's definition, their purpose was "for something", focused on "helping our employees reach their full potential, whether they're neurodivergent (his term for people with autism and other handicaps) or neurotypical (those not diagnosed with such challenges)." Tom goes on to say that "targeted hiring is the heart of our mission, but what we've discovered…is that creating more inclusive work spaces benefits everyone."[141] In that regard Rising Tide is extremely inclusive. It is service-oriented, both in providing a quality car wash for their customers, as well as serving their employees. It is necessarily resilient, as it requires continuous responsiveness to the challenges and opportunities inherent in working with both employees and customers. And the whole concept is idealistic; it challenges many of the underlying assumptions regarding the employability of people with disabilities, most notably those with autism.

Rising Tide's Purpose Finds Its Logic and Its Meaning, Fulfilling the Personal Purpose of Tom and John D'Eri

Rising Tide's purpose aligns perfectly with Tom and John's personal purpose. Tom says, "My work is my calling. I'm proud of the contribution Rising Tide Car Wash makes to the community. Young people start their careers here. When you extrapolate the impact of even a single business

---

[141] Ibid, page 176.

acting in this way over twenty or thirty years, the results are dramatic."[142] As for John, he is no longer haunted by his earlier fears regarding Andrew's future.

So…how has this worked out? Here's a summary of Rising Tide's track record as of the publication of *The Power of Potential* in 2023:

> "The struggling business that we bought in 2012 was washing only 35,000 cars per year. Rising Tide's original location is now a thriving operation that washed more than 170,000 cars in 2021. Our second location, built from scratch, achieved operational break-even sales after only two months of opening its doors in 2017, and it's even more successful than our first. We have a third location…(that opened) in 2022. We've been on the cover of *Entrepreneur*, prominently featured in *Inc.*, on the *Today Show*, and *The Nightly News* (twice!). The videos we make about our business go viral on Facebook. People fly in from other states and rent cars when they land, just so they can experience Rising Tide for themselves. (We are) a wildly profitable, high-performing service organization that customers love to support and that employees love to work for. Our (employee) retention rate is five times our competitors'.[143]

And what about Andrew? Tom puts it this way:

> "My dad wanted to give Andrew a future. That included a livelihood, but more importantly, a positive, purposeful community where he belonged. He didn't want his son to spend his entire life as an outsider. A little more than a decade later, we are now living in the future my father envisioned. In fact, I think it might have exceeded his dreams. I'm convinced we overcame the challenges it took to get here–and there

---

[142] Ibid, page 157.
[143] Ibid, pages xvii and xviii.

were many–because the business was born out of love and was lifted up by the strength of our family.

"Andrew is something of a local celebrity–and he knows it and demonstrably enjoys it. Showing warmth and confidence, he has made himself the de facto mayor of Rising Tide. At team events, he actively tries to include people. Whether it's bowling or a pizza party or the video game truck, he sees himself as a host. Andrew and his teammates are no longer onlookers or outcasts in our community. They are participants. Contributors. Producers. They are part of something bigger."

"I can't honestly say that Andrew is ready to live alone, but why should that be the goal? No human is truly independent, not should they be. A few years back, my father made a push to move Andrew into his own apartment but ultimately listened when his son made his own wishes clear; he'd rather live with his parents. Who wouldn't? They live in a beautiful beach condo, and my mom is a great cook. He likes it there. Someday, he may live with me–but if he does, it won't be as my dependent. He's got his own life.

"Andrew–and the dozens of employees who work at our car washes–now have colleagues, caring managers, friends, admirers, and allies. Their achievement of a 'normal' life shouldn't be as rare as it is."[144]

Rising Tide is an exceptional example of a visionary enterprise based on the very personal purpose of its founders. That purpose continues to drive John and Tom D'Eri to expand their influence and impact on people with autism. Don't be surprised if you find a Rising Tide car wash opening in your community!

---

[144] Ibid, pages 197-199.

Yvon Chouinard, founder of Patagonia

Yvon Chouinard began his business career as a most atypical entrepreneur. He was an adventurer–a rock climber and surfer, who first developed steel pitons in the 1950's for rock climbing, not as a business, but for his own use. These were good enough for him and for a few friends...until they weren't. He realized that his pitons were damaging the rock faces that he loved to climb.

Inspiration Leads to Ideation as Yvon asks *Why* and *What If* Questions

He soon faced the question: ***Why*** *can't we climb without pitons?* That was followed by the question: ***What if*** *we create a way to use the natural cracks in rock faces for anchors?* These questions provided the initial *inspiration* to actively seek a solution. *Ideation* grew out of Yvon's in-born curiosity and creativity–and *implementation* took the form of aluminum chocks. He introduced them to his fellow climbers, and soon the word spread. Others were anxious to purchase Chouinard chocks–and the business began to grow. Even so, Yvon displayed no real interest in being a businessman. He saw his enterprise "as just a way to pay the bills so (he) could go off on climbing trips."[145]

Personal Purpose Begins to Emerge: The Value that Yvon Chouinard Wants for Himself

Notwithstanding his lack of deep interest, the climbing gear business continued to grow. Soon it became clear that the company was uniquely positioned as one of the premier gear companies for the sport of climbing. With the feedback of a loyal customer base, Yvon discovered that there was also a substantial demand for clothing designed for the rigors of climbing and other extreme outdoor sports. Indeed, by 1972, revenue from the Patagonia clothing business had outgrown their climbing gear products. By the 1980's, the company had become so successful that Yvon considered retiring. However, it was at this time that his overriding passion began to emerge.

---

[145] *Let My People Go Surfing: The Education of a Reluctant Businessman,* Yvon Chouinard, page 25.

Once again, the all important *Why* questions began to surface. Yvon found himself increasingly concerned about what he saw as the greatest existential threat facing the world, the burgeoning environmental crisis. He asked himself, ***Why are we destroying the planet through climate change, world hunger, and pollution?*** And then the *What if* questions followed: ***What if*** *we used our company, Patagonia, as a catalyst for addressing these issues?*

Yvon's whole life has been characterized by seeking adventures–and then jumping in with both feet. Like climbing El Capitan in Yosemite, he took on the challenge of addressing the earth's environmental crisis. That became his driving personal purpose, his reason for staying at the helm of Patagonia. That purpose led him to the Logos, or undergirding logic for the business.

Ideation Provides the Seeds for Implementation, as Yvon Begins to Ask *How* He Might Fulfill His Personal Purpose through Patagonia

Yvon Chouinard playfully calls attention to what he describes as his "MBA theory of management, *management by absence.*"[146] Having hired competent executives and managers to lead Patagonia on a day-to-day basis, he often took farflung trips to Africa, the Himalayas, Russia, South America, and other places where he could test company manufactured clothing and equipment. These junkets also provided him with a front-row seat to observe the environmental deterioration of the natural world. He saw that forests and grasslands were diminishing, that glaciers were receding, and that disease and famine were prevalent in many areas. He was profoundly impacted by what he witnessed–and he felt compelled to do something about it. The question was ***How?***

Yvon has never been a "lip-service" guy. Where others have expressed similar concerns, he found that they most often dismissed the idea of doing anything because of the enormity of the challenge. But that is not Yvon Chouinard.

---

[146] Ibid, page 53.

This was, to him, a similar challenge to that of eliminating the use of steel pitons. There must be proactive ways to reverse the factors that are destroying the environment. With that in mind, Yvon took a dozen of his top managers to Argentina–to the mountains of the real Patagonia, to walkabout and discuss what he felt were the most pressing issues facing the company. There he posed the following questions:

- Why are we in business?
- What kind of business do we want to be?
- What can we do to stem the environmental challenges faced by the planet?
- What can we do to stem the environmental harm that we, as a company, are causing?

With answers and ideas in hand, they returned to their Ventura, California headquarters. Yvon then called a board of directors meeting where the following commitments were made:

- All decisions of the company are made in the context of the environmental crisis. We must strive to do no harm. Wherever possible, our acts should serve to decrease the problem. Our activities in this area will be under constant evaluation and reassessment as we seek constant improvement.

- Maximum attention is given to product quality, as defined by durability, minimum use of natural resources (including materials, raw energy, and transport), multifunctionalism, non-obsolescence, and the kind of beauty that emerges from absolute suitability to task. Concern over transitory fashion trends is specifically not a corporate value.

- The board and management recognize that successful communities are part of a sustainable environment. We consider ourselves to be an integral part of communities that also include our employees, the communities in which we live, our suppliers, and our customers. We recognize our responsibilities to all these relationships and make our decisions with their general benefit in mind. It is our policy to employ people who share the fundamental values of this corporation, while representing cultural and ethnic diversity.

- Without giving its achievement primacy, we seek to profit on our activities. However, growth and expansion are not basic to this corporation.

- To help mitigate any negative environmental consequences of our business activity, we impose on ourselves an annual tax of 1 percent of our gross sales, or 10 percent of profits, whichever is greater. All of the proceeds of this tax are granted to local community and environmental activism.

- At all levels of operation–board, management, and staff–Patagonia encourages proactive stances that reflect our values. These include activities that influence the larger corporate community to also adjust its values and behavior, and that support, through activism and financially, grassroots and national campaigners who work to solve the current environmental and social crisis. (They have expanded this, creating a program called "One Percent for the Planet," an alliance of businesses that contribute at least one percent to groups that are listed as "approved environmental organizations.")

- In our internal operations, top management will work as a group and with maximum transparency. This includes an "open book" policy that enables employees easy access to decisions, within normal boundaries of personal privacy and "trade secrecy." At all levels of corporate activity, we encourage open communications, a collaborative atmosphere, and maximum simplicity, while we simultaneously seek dynamism and innovation.[147]

---

[147] Ibid, pages 61, 63-64.

Yvon Chouinard went from Inspiration to Ideation–and then to Implementation. He developed the answers for *how* he, and his company, would begin to fulfill his personal purpose, his just cause.

Yvon Chouinard Articulates His *Just Cause*

Yvon simply articulates his purpose this way:

> *Patagonia's stated mission today is "to use business to inspire and implement solutions to the environmental crisis."*

This purpose aligns with, and extends from, Yvon's own deeply felt personal purpose. He states:

> "It saddens me especially to observe the plight of our own species; we appear to be incapable of solving our own problems. Patagonia exists to challenge conventional wisdom and present a new style of responsible business. We believe the accepted model of capitalism that necessitates endless growth and deserves the blame for the destruction of nature must be displaced. Patagonia and its two thousand employees have the means and the will to prove to the rest of the world that doing the right thing makes for a good and profitable business."

While Yvon's purpose draws attention to what he feels is an existential crisis, it is still affirmative and optimistic, fitting Simon Sinek's requirement that a just cause must be *for something*. It also is *inclusive;* indeed, it invites other companies and people to join with Patagonia in their crusade. It is *service-oriented* in that it is focused on benefitting the earth and its inhabitants. And while it undoubtedly faces an upstream battle against political, social, and cultural norms, it increasingly displays its resilience as a just cause. Finally, Yvon's and Patagonia's purpose is clearly big and bold–and perhaps unachievable.

Yvon is committed to share what Patagonia has done in the last decade and what they plan to do in the decades to come in leading out as a problem-solver. He says, "I knew, after thirty-five years, why I was in business…I wanted to create in Patagonia a model other businesses could look to in their own searches for environmental stewardship and sustainability, just as pitons and ice axes were models for other equipment manufacturers."

Patagonia has been regularly noted in the "100 Best Companies to Work For" and the "Top 25 Medium Sized Businesses," as well as receiving numerous awards for their business priorities. Some might disagree with Patagonias's purpose; no doubt Yvon would not be surprised. But there is no question that this business is successfully fulfilling that purpose under the continuing direction and inspiration of its founder, Yvon Chouinard. In 2024, at the time of this writing, he is 85 years old, and has recently been named by *Time* magazine as "One of the 100 Most Influential People in the World."[148]

Tony Hsieh, founding partner of Zappos, the online shoe retailer

Tony Hsieh's quest for personal purpose and fulfillment was a central theme in his life. It began with his childhood dream of making "lots and lots of money by breeding and selling earthworms" at age nine[149]– and progressed through a series of entrepreneurial ventures, including:

- A newspaper route
- His own newsletter, *The Gobbler* (while in middle school)
- Selling Christmas cards, door-to-door
- Making and selling photo-buttons through mail order
- Tour guiding for a Halloween haunted house (while in high school)
- Video game testing for Lucasfilm company (while in high school)

---

[148] https://en.wikipedia.org/wiki/Yvon_Chouinard
[149] *Delivering Happiness: A Path to Profits, Passion, and Purpose*, Tony Hsieh, page 5.

- Computer programming at a company called GDI (while in high school)
- Selling magic tricks through mail order (while in high school)
- Creation of a comprehensive virtual study guide based on crowdsourcing inputs from his fellow students, which he coordinated, compiled and sold (as a freshman at Harvard)
- Catering at weddings (during his undergraduate years at Harvard)
- Bartending (also during his Harvard years)
- Computer programming for Harvard Student Agencies, Spinnaker Software, BBN, and Microsoft (the latter job was a summer internship)
- Running the Quincy House Grille (the dining facility for the Harvard Quincy House dormitory), where he invested in making the grill attractive to students by adding pizza ovens and MTV music videos
- At graduation from Harvard, a first "real" job with Oracle
- Launched a side hustle called Internet Marketing Solutions (IMS) for creating websites for other companies

It was at this point that Tony decided to fully commit himself to running his own company.

The common centerpiece of each of Tony's enterprises was the pursuit of wealth. As Tony put it, "I always fantasized about making money, because to me, money meant that later on in life I would have the freedom to do whatever I wanted."[150] However, his job at Oracle, which paid him very well, was far from fulfilling. He was bored with his job. As he put it, he was "ready for adventure," regardless of the compensation.

It didn't take him long, however, to discover that designing websites at IMS, while not exactly boring, wasn't what he wanted to

---

[150] Ibid, page 10.

do either. One weekend, with his business partner, he decided to do some computer programming that would cause banner ads to pop up on websites. Every time a visitor came to a website that subscribed to the service and saw an ad, that subscriber would get credits for the exposure. Correspondingly, those credits would be used to gain the website additional exposure. They called this experiment LinkExchange and introduced it to about 50 small websites to test the concept.

Amazingly, within a week, it was clear that they had stumbled on a highly appealing service. Over half of the websites they contacted signed on. They quickly pivoted to the development of the LinkExchange network. It grew rapidly, and before long Tony and his partner were literally working around the clock, answering customer questions and doing programming. They soon found that they couldn't keep up with the demand. Hiring began with friends to help field e-mails, and then was extended to computer programmers. It was, in Tony's own words, "an exciting, fun, magical, and surreal time for all of us. We knew we were on to something big, we just had no idea how it would turn out."[151] It wasn't long before they were approached by a suitor who offered to buy them out for one million dollars. They turned down that offer, only to be offered $20 million five months later. This big number required some real soul searching, but ultimately they turned down that offer as well.

So…Tony's purpose, and that of his partner, that had started out being all about the money, had been transformed. In announcing the decision to turn down the offer, Tony said:

> "We are living in a very special time. The Internet industry is exploding. Companies like Netscape, eBay, Amazon, and Yahoo! are changing the course of human history. Never before have so many companies become successes in such a short period of time. We have the opportunity to be one of those companies while having the time of our lives. There will never be another 1997."[152]

---

[151] Ibid, page 39.
[152] Ibid, page 44.

The next seventeen months were a time of self-discovery for Tony Hsieh. What began as a joyful journey with a group of roughly 25 friends grew into a large and somewhat unwieldy business with offices in San Francisco, New York, and Chicago. They had evolved from a small, energetic company of people who wanted to be part of something fun and exciting to a disjointed group of talented people who, for the most part, had their own selfish career and compensation reasons for joining LinkExchange. Tony found himself dreading to show up for work.

Inspiration Leads to Ideation as Tony asks *Why* and *What If* Questions

Although LinkExchange was, by all accounts, a huge success, Tony had once again determined that this business was unfulfilling. He had to ask himself, ***Why?*** And that led him to ask, *What is success? What is happiness? What am I working toward?*

These questions led Tony to make a list of the happiest periods of his life. One thing stood out: none of these times involved money. He realized that "building stuff and being creative and inventive"[153] made him happy. And those days at LinkExchange had passed. Fortunately, the big money offers had not...Microsoft acquired the company in 1998 for a whopping $265 million dollars. Tony walked away with personal wealth beyond his wildest imagination...and *he was not happy.*

He was at a turning point in his life. As he put it, "I had decided to stop chasing the money, and start chasing the passion."[154] The precise definition of his passion, however, did not emerge easily. He invested in various ventures, hoping to find the platform that would provide an environment that would allow him to foster his own growth, happiness, and development, along with those with whom he would work and serve. Nothing seemed quite right until in 1999, Tony received a voicemail from a guy named Nick Swinmurn, who had started a website to sell shoes online. Nick passionately shared his vision which was based on the $40 billion annual U.S. market for shoes, of which catalog sales were about $2 billion.

---

[153] Ibid, page 53.
[154] Ibid, page 54.

Nick shared his own *Why* and *What if* questions:

- *Why* should buying a pair of shoes be so hard?
- *What if* we created a single place online that people could come to find exactly the shoe they want in exactly the right size, and have it show up on their doorstep in a few days?

Nick's questions resonated with Tony. This is something that I could help build, he thought. Working with Nick, he moved from the *Whys* and *What if's* to asking ***How*** this enterprise could be built. They recognized that the shoe industry was extremely fragmented and, to this point, had remained quite hidebound to old school traditions. The key to success would be to create a network among all of the shoe brands in one common internet platform. This idea gave birth to Zappos.

Personal Purpose Begins to Emerge: The Value that Tony Hsieh Wanted for Himself

Tony joined Zappos, first as an investor, and later becoming CEO. Under his leadership, his personal purpose began to become clear: the company focused on delivering exceptional experiences for customers, employees, vendors, and partners. He dedicated himself to creating a culture focused on creating a positive impact, what he called *delivering wow!* This also became known as *Delivering Happiness,* the title of his best-selling book. Financial success was to be a by-product of that culture, not its primary aim. Tony's leadership was pivotal in leading Zappos from a struggling startup into a successful e-commerce giant with an unrivaled customer service culture.

Ideation Provides the Seeds for Implementation, as Tony Begins to Ask *How* He Might Fulfill His Personal Purpose through Zappos

Tony Hsieh worked diligently to establish a unique foundational culture at Zappos based on strong core values. He believed that creating a unified sense of community within the company would lead to increased productivity, greater job satisfaction, and a more fulfilling work environment. Tony's book, *Delivering Happiness* reflects his philosophy of prioritizing happiness and satisfaction, both in business and in life. He stated:

> "I made a note to myself to make sure I never lost sight of the value of a tribe where people truly felt connected and cared about the well-being of one another. To me, connectedness — the number and depth of my relationships—was an important element of my happiness, and I was grateful for our tribe."[155]

He emphasized the importance of providing excellent experiences for customers, employees, vendors, and partners, and he believed that genuine connections and positive interactions were the keys to achieving this. His innovative customer-centric approach included offering free shipping, a 365-day return policy, and a commitment to delivering outstanding customer service. This philosophy became the hallmark of Zappos' success and garnered widespread attention, including from internet giant Amazon. In 2009, Amazon acquired Zappos for around $1.2 billion, allowing the company to maintain its unique culture and brand identity while benefiting from Amazon's resources and infrastructure.

Tony Hsieh's Ephemeral *Just Cause*

Zappos provided Tony with a clear and compelling *Just Cause*. It established a strong sense of affirmative optimism regarding how all stakeholders would be treated. It was open to anyone who could fully buy-in to the company's purpose, mission, and values. Indeed, new employees were given the opportunity to become thoroughly familiar with how the company works, and, if after doing so, they felt that they couldn't fit in or commit, they were given a $2,000 check as an incentive to move on. The service orientation of Zappos was its centerpiece, benefiting customers, employees, vendors, and partners alike. And their *just cause* has proven to be quite resilient.

---

[155] Ibid, page 76.

There was, however, for Tony, a major problem. The company's success led to his exit–and the end of his pursuit of his personal purpose…at the age of 46. Tony Hsieh's quest for personal purpose and fulfillment was a multifaceted journey that extended beyond the typical measures of business success. For him, "delivering happiness" was defined as creating positive change in the world, fostering enjoyment and connection, and building communities that embodied his values. He largely accomplished this during his time at Zappos, but substance addictions and mental illness began to sap his sense of personal fulfillment. In that sense, his Just Cause proved to be fleeting for him, to be quite ephemeral.

There is a sad and cautionary end to the extraordinary purpose-driven life of Tony Hsieh. While his incredible wealth provided him with the means to do so much in pursuit of his purpose, it also provided easy access to addictive substances. Eventually, these challenges began to separate him from the day-to-day energy and engagement that were so much a part of his leadership and success. Worse yet, they removed him from the support and regular interactions with his "tribe."

In November 2020, Tony was trapped in a house fire in Connecticut that resulted in severe injuries. He passed away due to complications from his injuries at the age of 46. Although his death was ruled accidental, it spelled a tragic ending to a remarkable life; Tony Hsieh, once so purpose-driven, somehow ran off the tracks. There are important lessons to be learned from Tony's story. First, it is a tribute to the power of personal purpose in creating a highly successful personal and professional life. Tony's legacy continues to inspire individuals to consider not just financial achievement, but also the broader impact they can have on the lives of others and on their own sense of well-being.

And second, personal purpose must be continuously fed and regenerated. Over my years of coaching CEOs, I have witnessed many "harvest events" where leaders have sold their businesses for mega-bucks. There is no question that when this occurs, it is an occasion for great celebration. But it should also be a time of deep reflection. WhenTony harvested LinkExchange, he realized that his passion and purpose needed to be reset. But somewhere in the course of his extraordinary time at Zappos, his focus slipped off his personal purpose. He allowed other distractions to pull him away. That's not to say that he didn't invest some of his wealth in other worthwhile projects, but his engagement waned—and left the door open for substance abuse and mental health issues. Too often, I have observed that when a leader's personal purpose is *fulfilled* by a "harvest event," the death of that leader is imminent…unless he or she determines what the next chapter in their purpose will be.

Perhaps, if Tony Hsieh had stayed focused on his great personal purpose, he would still be with us. With the stories of the preceding leaders in mind, I now pose a series of important questions for your consideration, as YOU form the Logos that undergirds your Cause. Your answers to these questions provide the logic that gives your purpose, your Why, its credibility—for you and, ultimately, for other key stakeholders. In facilitating this process with my clients, I have asked the questions that I now pose to you. In every case, their answers were very personal, and as such are not appropriate to share here.

However, I have also used this process myself, and I feel that it is important to share my answers to these questions with you in order to provide some modeling for you. That said, my responses will not be yours. After you have read through the questions—and my answers— please give yourself a few introspective hours to develop your own unique answers….and the Logos for your Cause that they represent.

Question #1: What value do you want to create for yourself?

The value I want to create for myself is that I become increasingly serviceable for my fellowman. In order that I might be continuously growing in my abilities to serve others, I must dedicate myself to spiritual, physical, intellectual, emotional, and career development. The true measure of the value I create for myself is manifest in the growth, development, and achievements of those with whom

I interact. As I help them in their growth, development, and success, I will be worthy of their trust, respect, and love. Ultimately, that will be how I measure my life.

Question #2: What aspects of your career choices, to this point in your life, have given you the most satisfaction, happiness, or joy?

What gives me satisfaction is learning and sharing true principles. This is done by moving from ignorance to knowledge, from knowledge to wisdom, and then sharing wisdom with others in a way that facilitates their growth, development, competence, confidence, engagement, and leadership.

What makes me happy is time with family, friends, and conversant people with diverse interests, good senses of humor, and caring and compassion for others. I'm especially happy when I'm with my grandchildren, my wife, my friends, and my neighbors. Vacations, travel, baseball, good food, and good books are also sources of happiness.

What gives me joy is the energy, happiness, and smiling faces of little children—and witnessing the acts of others manifested in selfless service, heroism, patriotism, and sincere love. I also experience joy when I am immersed in nature; I find great joy when I am able to take long hikes in our national parks. And beautiful orchestral music stirs my heart and gives me joy as well.

Question #3: What do others look to you for? How might they describe the way you interact with them, or serve them? What value do they enjoy from you?

Others look to me for guidance, coaching, wisdom, empathy, and support. They would describe the way I interact with them as being "all in"—focused, fully attentive, and listening intently. They would say that there is no doubt that I care. They get all of me.

They would say that I almost always ask a lot of questions. In that regard, they would also say that while I am willing to share knowledge and wisdom, I am not "an answer looking for a question." I ask questions to discern their specific needs, thereby helping them to gain clarity regarding their challenges. With that clarity, my efforts are focused on facilitating their discovery of solutions and action plans. I help them discover their own best answers.

Question #4: With whom are your most important relationships? To what extent are they also part of the target market for the value you bring?

My most important relationships are the following, in this priority order:

1. **My relationship with God.** *As the ultimate source of true principles, I dedicate a portion of every day to learning from Him. I do this during an hour or so at the dawn of each day, wherein I pray and study scriptures. I seek not only to learn true principles, but to learn God's will for me and what I will do each day. This devotional time serves as a foundation and a launching point for everything else I do in my daily life.*

2. **My relationship with myself.** *To fulfill my personal Vision, I must maintain a high level of spiritual, physical, intellectual, emotional, and career fitness. Spiritual fitness grows over time as I remain disciplined in the devotionals described above. Physical fitness requires attention to diet, rest, and exercise. In that regard, I work out vigorously for at least one hour every day except Sundays. While working out, I listen to audiobooks on topics relevant to my Purpose, Mission, and Values. This may include business books, histories, and/or the stories of great leaders in all walks of life. When such audiobooks resonate with me, I purchase the hard copy and review it thoroughly for insights that might add to my*

knowledge and wisdom. I endeavor to read 4-5 books each month, and I write at least one book review monthly. On those occasions when I feel overwhelmed, I take a walk in the hills to recharge my batteries.

3. **My relationship with my wife.** *My wife is my best friend and the most important person in my life. We each have our separate interests and endeavors, and we support one another in those things. We plan together for family, church, work, and recreation together, and we enjoy traveling together, watching movies, playing games, building puzzles, and discussing many diverse topics including religion, politics, and world affairs. I make sure that I allot time for my wife's needs, including lightening her load by helping with household chores and being available to her when she needs me. I love her—and she knows it. And she loves me—and I know it!*

4. **My relationship with my children.** *I have six wonderful adult children with whom I strive to maintain close one-to-one relationships. While I don't see all of them every day or every week—and sometimes not even every month—I reach out to them via texting on a regular basis. They almost always respond, and they do so quickly. They know that I love them and that I'm here for them, almost at any time, day or night.*

5. **My relationship with my grandchildren and great-grandchildren.** *My children maintain a "Grandparents' Calendar" that includes all of the grandchildren's activities, including sports, concerts, science fairs, church activities, etc. My wife and I try to attend as many of these as possible. I also maintain a steady interchange with each grandchild via texting (for those old enough to have a smartphone). Whenever possible, I arrange to take them on Grandpa Dates, doing things they enjoy. I love being a grandpa!*

6. **My relationship with friends and neighbors.** *I strive to be "out in my community" as often as possible in order to stay connected with friends and neighbors. I try to be available to*

help them when needed. I do so with a smile and a sincere desire to serve them.

7. **My relationship with clients.** *When it comes to my clients, I show up! I strive to understand their needs and be timely in responding to them. It may seem strange that I show them as priority #7, and I must admit that there are many times when I must make them priority #1. When situations arise that demand this, I approach each as an opportunity to serve rather than a drudgery or an obligation. I always strive to gain a clear understanding of their needs, to facilitate the discovery of actionable solutions to their problems, and help them grow into being highly successful leaders.*

8. **My relationship with everyone else, to the greatest extent possible.** *With all of this, I still try to interact in positive ways with everyone I meet. With so much darkness in society today, this is sometimes very difficult. Nevertheless, I feel it is absolutely essential that I approach the world with optimism and a smile.*

I feel that, with the exception of my relationship with God, every one of these relationships is a target market for my guidance, coaching, and wisdom. Obviously only #7, my clients, are paying customers for this, but that's more than okay. By extending what I've learned over five decades to my wife, family, friends, neighbors, and others, I not only serve them, but I also hone my skills as I use them.

Question #5: How are you reconciling and aligning your career choices with your personal relationships? If there are tradeoffs to be made, how will you (or are you) managing these so that your relationships not only survive, but become enduring sources of happiness?

This is an ongoing challenge. Every relationship requires time and attentiveness in order to flourish. Within each, urgencies and emergencies can and do occur, forcing time to be allocated to one or more relationships at the expense of the others. When these happen, I strive to be available and responsive, to always see them as opportunities rather than infringements on my planned use of time. Each person inevitably needs a calming voice and demeanor—and I hope to always provide that. When I am successful, these interruptions become sources of blessings to others, and a joy to me.

Question #6: What is the problem or opportunity that is compelling you to discover a solution? Why does it exist?

So much of the unhappiness in the world is a function of a gross misunderstanding of what constitutes outstanding leadership. According to a Gallup report, about 50% of employees have left a job specifically to get away from their manager at some point in their career. Bad bosses/poor leaders are a major factor in employee turnover.

In the best of circumstances, bosses are good, well-intentioned people who simply have never learned the principles of effective leadership. Unfortunately, there are also those who have bought into crippling counterfeits that destroy morale and undermine success. Either way, there is a huge opportunity for growing leaders!

Why does this opportunity exist? Because most of the most important and efficacious principles of leadership are not taught in MBA or undergraduate business programs. And once bosses are on the job, they are too often too busy, too stressed, and too distracted to make the concerted effort necessary to change their attitudes, behaviors, and leadership tactics and strategies. Admittedly, the factors that define this opportunity also make it challenging to gain the attention of the target market. However, with incisive marketing, gaining the attention of even a small fraction of the 32 million small business owners in the United States will set us on the path to interest in and desire for our value proposition.

Question #7: Why are you personally attracted to solving this problem? What if....you did _____?

I am attracted to the opportunity of addressing this problem because I have made the study of true principles of highly effective leadership my focus for over 50 years–and I continue in that endeavor.

The questions, then:

***What if** I wrote a series of books and articles sharing those principles?*

***What if** I developed online training workshops that teach those principles?*

***What if** I reinstituted small group face-to-face forums for intensive discussion of those principles?*

***What if** I continued to coach a limited number of leaders, and while serving their needs, developing a strong influencer role for them in helping CEObuilder® to grow?*

***What if** I created a program of developing coaches who were trained to facilitate the development of leaders who they would guide using the principles that I have learned over the course of my career and life?*

Question #8: How do your answers to Questions #6 and #7 translate into your personal value proposition for others? How does it create value for the target market? What job does your value proposition do, or help do, for your prospective customers? What pain does it eliminate? What gain does it offer to your prospective customers?

***My personal value proposition:** I facilitate the development of highly effective leaders, who in turn, facilitate the* *development of their people into highly effective leaders within their respective areas of authority and influence. As bosses (and others) transform into outstanding leaders, they will apply the principles they are learning in their families, their communities, and their business enterprises. The foundational premise of this value proposition is heliotropic influence through facilitation. Heliotropism, the phenomenon where flowers orient themselves in the direction of the sun, defines for me the appropriate role and behaviors of great leaders wherein they gain appropriate, trusted, and respected influence with their constituents. Facilitation excellence is the key skill whereby I serve as a coach, teacher, and leader. It is the foundational skill on which virtually all other leadership skills are built—and it is the primary skill which I strive to teach other leaders.*

When done well, this value proposition eliminates the pain of anger, depression, and poor engagement in virtually any family or organization. In businesses, it will also reduce (if not eliminate) high employee turnover, litigation, and enterprise failure. The gains enjoyed as a result of this value proposition are readily apparent. Each element of the Business Success Pyramid will improve including, of course, financial outcomes.

Question #9: How will my value proposition change things for the better?

See the answer to the prior question.

Question #10: How large is the market for your value proposition? As specifically as possible, define the target market for your personal value proposition.

The market is huge. Wherever there are bosses, there is a market for improving leadership skills. Entrepreneurial CEOs or startup founders alone represent a group of 5 to 6 million in the United States. The U.S. Small Business

Administration (SBA) notes that there are around 32 million small businesses in the U.S., many of which are led by their founders or entrepreneurial CEOs. Of these, a significant portion are considered startups or newer businesses. Larger companies add significantly to this number.

That said, my value proposition, when extended to virtually anyone within my realm of influence, makes the market even larger for me. A successful marketing campaign to entrepreneurial CEOs, startup founders, and small business executives make this value proposition financially viable for CEObuilder®.

Question #11: What investment of time, effort and resources might you consider seeking from others to align with your Purpose (your Cause) and your Value Proposition?

I'm "all in." It is my career and my life! I seek the support of clients, past and present, in assisting with editing, being a sounding board, providing testimonials, and promoting my books, workshops, forums, and training. I am self-funded in this endeavor.

Question #12: What is the idealistic legacy goal associated with your value proposition that may never be achieved?

My legacy is the leaders that I have helped develop through my facilitation, coaching, and support. I hope that the principles I have shared–and will share–will be similarly facilitated, coached, and supported by each of them as they develop future leaders. In that way, my legacy will continue beyond my life.

Question #13: How persuaded are YOU in the credibility of your Cause?

I feel that my Cause is very credible. I am "all in"— and have been for many years!

Question #14: How will you articulate your Cause in writing in words that convince yourself of its credibility, worth, and value for YOU—and those you serve?

I see the potential in every person to be an outstanding leader. Without being overbearing, I seek to help each individual recognize that potential and grow toward it. In that regard, I will be–and am–a facilitator of the success of others.

My facilitation skills will be primarily focused on myself, my family and friends, and my prospective and current clients. For entrepreneurial CEOs, startup founders, and small business executives, my value proposition is to transform their vision of themselves into becoming outstanding leaders who create outstanding leaders....who create outstanding leaders.

I am not a life coach, although what I do should always improve the lives of others. I am an executive leadership coach. I offer <u>processes</u> that facilitate the discovery of the <u>content</u> that defines each leader's strategies, tactics, and ultimate destination. These processes are built on true, proven principles and models that lead to leadership success.

These are my answers to these important questions. The hours I invested in answering them were what some of my clients have described as a "greasy grind." That said, for me–and for many of them–the grind was worth the investment. I hope you will make that investment in your own Logos. Think deeply and introspectively about your answers. Write them down; wrestle to get the words to a level of credibility that convinces your most important audience: YOU!

You may find it useful to share your answers with one or two people that you trust to give you kind, but straightforward, feedback. Don't be afraid to have them poke holes in your answers. Caring critique will strengthen your Logos. But also don't let them dissuade you from your emerging personal purpose. Florence Nightingale was not about to let her parents turn her into a high society debutante. Nor were Thomas and John D'Eri dissuaded by those who thought they were crazy to focus their purpose on building a business around people with autism. If your purpose is compelling to YOU, that is the key!

Our Visioning process to this point has addressed your compelling purpose (your Pathos), the importance of Authenticity, and should have established the credibility of your purpose and mission (with its accompanying value proposition) through the Logos exercise. It is important now to address the essential Ethos that will define the values that you will live by in pursuit of that purpose and mission.

ETHOS-The Beliefs & Values That Set Forth How You Will Behave in Pursuit of Your Purpose and Mission

*Reputation is built and character is forged as you develop
self-mastery. Courageous accountability for your own
actions becomes a cherished prize.*

Russell M. Nelson

The year was 1831; the place, New Salem, Illinois. A lanky 22 year old young man brought his axe down with incredible force on a log that would become part of the front wall of a rustic, but functional building. It was August, hot and humid, and this fellow was sweating profusely. Even so, he had a hard time not smiling at every stroke of his tool. He was full of positive anticipation, knowing that his boss, Denton Offutt, had picked him to be the clerk of the general store he was building.

Within days of the completion of construction, the next sweaty task was at hand. Dry goods, food items, and other household staples arrived by riverboat–and the young man labored diligently stocking shelves. It wasn't long before he was standing behind the store counter, selling his products and making friends with folks from New Salem and a handful of surrounding towns. He was proud of his opportunity, for which Mr. Offutt paid him the handsome sum of $15 a month.

The young man was meticulous with money; he recognized that the store had to turn a profit for Mr. Offutt. Even so, he was equally committed to assuring that every customer was treated fairly and felt that they were valued. One day, as he was locking up at the end of business, he was stunned to discover that his revenue was slightly more than he had anticipated. He recounted it multiple times, but there was no doubt about it, there was a few cents more in his cash box than there should have been. He worked his way through each of the day's receipts until he determined who had overpaid. When he had identified that customer, he put the change in his pocket, threw on his hat and coat, and headed out the door. Over an hour later, and six miles down a dirt road, he was at the door of a thoroughly surprised woman who accepted the pennies that he returned to her.

Most, including his customer we might surmise, would say that this behavior was unnecessary, and maybe a bit crazy. But for Abraham Lincoln, it identified clearly two values that he personally could not violate. First, he would be governed by complete honesty, and second, he would not allow any mistakes or oversights on his part to harm another person. His values determined both what he would do—and what he would not. And they were fundamental in forging his reputation and character. Ultimately, they contributed to his incredibly important role in leading a nation in crisis.

You may be surprised that I lead off this chapter with a story about "Honest Abe." I do so because his story raises the question regarding how his beliefs and values were formed, and what influenced their development.

It is important to understand that who Abraham Lincoln was to become was forged in the fire of extraordinary personal challenges. He was born in a log cabin in Kentucky into a poor farming family. His parents barely scratched out a subsistence living. As a little boy, Abe learned that being a Lincoln meant that you had to work; almost from the time he could walk, he worked on the family farm. That generally meant little time, and no money, for school. Nevertheless, his accumulation of less than one year of formal education gave him basic reading, 'riting, and 'rithmetic skills. Beyond these, he educated himself through studying books borrowed from neighbors.

As tough as this was, he also faced family tragedies, including the death of his mother, Nancy Hanks Lincoln, when he was only nine years old. He was similarly deeply affected by the deaths of his sister, Sarah, and his first love, Ann Rutledge. How, we might ask, did this boy grow from poverty and peril to become one of the greatest leaders who has ever lived?

There is a clue in his innate drive to learn and develop himself. While his formal education was almost nonexistent, he had an insatiable desire to read everything he could get his hands on. Other than the Bible, there were no books in the Lincoln cabin, but he learned that kind neighbors and friends often had a few books. He borrowed books from anyone who would lend them, and he read every chance that he got, often deep into the night by candle or lantern light.

These books began to stir first, his curiosity, and then his desire to become something more than a poor wilderness farm boy. As a youngster, he penned these words in a notebook:

Abraham Lincoln is my nam (sic)
An (sic) with my pen I wrote the same
I wrote in both hast (sic) and speed
and left it here for fools to read

Abraham Lincoln his hand and pen
he will be good but god knows When[156]

So what did Abe read? In addition to the Bible, he borrowed and read *Aesop's Fables, Pilgrim's Progress, Robinson Crusoe,* Grimshaw's *History of the United States,* Weems' *The Life of George Washington, The Autobiography of Benjamin Franklin,* Blackstone's *Commentaries on the Laws of England,* and the works of William Shakespeare.

It is most notable that Abraham Lincoln studied George Washington and Benjamin Franklin, among others. Their stories began to form Abe's beliefs and values–and clearly contributed to who he became.

---

[156] *Abraham Lincoln: The Prairie Years and the War Years,* Carl Sandburg, page 13.

With that understanding, let's explore how George Washington and Benjamin Franklin formed the beliefs and values that were the basis for their extraordinary lives, and how they ultimately impacted Abraham Lincoln as well.

History tells us that George Washington was influenced heavily by a 16th-century French Jesuit manual that he meticulously copied by hand as a young man. This book, *The Rules of Civility and Decent Behavior in Company and Conversation* was a list of 110 rules that outlined proper manners and behavior for social interaction. These rules were designed to cultivate virtues such as respect, humility, and consideration for others. George Washington ultimately dedicated himself to living by many of these rules, including:

- Respect for your fellowman, regardless of their social status. That respect is manifested in courteous behavior and politeness, with avoidance of any behaviors that might offend or insult others.

- Humility and modesty. Emphasis here is on listening more than you speak, and avoiding boastfulness or drawing excessive attention to oneself.

- Consideration and kindness, including generosity–and living by the Golden Rule.

- Decorum in society. Always exhibiting appropriate posture and demeanor in social situations, both in speech and actions. This also extends to table manners and etiquette.

- Self-control and temperance. Avoid reactiveness, anger, and impatience. Take care in conversation to not interrupt others or speak too loudly or with too much emotion.

- The importance of appearance. Your attire should reflect both who you are and the situation with which you are involved. Cleanliness and personal grooming reflect your values.

Much of what we later see in the character of Abraham Lincoln, he learned from studying George Washington, who developed many of his beliefs and values from his study of such books as *The Rules of Civility and Decent Behavior in Company and Conversation.*

As for Benjamin Franklin, his self-penned book, *The Autobiography of Benjamin Franklin,* which Abraham Lincoln read, shares his personal journey of self-improvement and outlines his 13 virtues, which are:

1. **Temperance:** Eat not to dullness; drink not to elevation.

2. **Silence:** Speak not but what may benefit others or yourself; avoid trifling conversation.

3. **Order:** Let all your things have their places; let each part of your business have its time.

4. **Resolution:** Resolve to perform what you ought; perform without fail what you resolve.

5. **Frugality:** Make no expense but to do good to others or yourself; i.e., waste nothing.

6. **Industry:** Lose no time; be always employed in something useful; cut off all unnecessary actions.

7. **Sincerity:** Use no hurtful deceit; think innocently and justly, and, if you speak, speak accordingly.

8. **Justice:** Wrong none by doing injuries or omitting the benefits that are your duty.

9. **Moderation:** Avoid extremes; forbear resenting injuries so much as you think they deserve.

10. **Cleanliness:** Tolerate no uncleanliness in body, clothes, or habitation.

11. **Tranquility:** Be not disturbed at trifles, or at accidents common or unavoidable.

12. **Chastity:** Rarely use venery but for health or offspring, never to dullness, weakness, or the injury of your own or another's peace or reputation.

13. **Humility:** Imitate Jesus and Socrates.[157]

---

[157] *Benjamin Franklin: His Autobiography, 1706-1757,* pages 79-80.

Franklin devised a method to work on these virtues by focusing on one per week, keeping a journal to track his progress, and aiming to incorporate each virtue into his daily life. He believed that by constantly striving to improve oneself in these virtues, one could achieve personal growth and moral excellence. While we cannot show a direct correlation between Franklin's writing and Lincoln's character, it is clear that study of such notable predecessors had a strong impact on Abe's values—and that those beliefs formed the Ethos that governed his pursuit of his personal purpose and mission.

My assertion here is that as leaders we not only need a sense of our Pathos (our emotional and motivating personal stories), Authenticity (our unique strengths and gifts), and the Cause (the Logos and logic for our Purpose and Mission), we need to be clear on our personal Ethos, our values and beliefs. We each need, as shared earlier in Chapter 4, principles that guide our lives—and provide a Dead Horse Point set of "fence posts" that will provide us with clarity on what we will—and will not—do to achieve our personal goals, purpose, and mission.

While all successful leaders have probably not been as deliberate in the development of their list of inviolable values and the behaviors that extend from them, it is clear that those values and behaviors emerged and set standards for virtually all who achieved greatness. My study of leaders has led me to seek to understand and define their respective core values. The tables in Appendices #3 and #4 share some of the insights I've gleaned from my studies of a sampling of ten notable world leaders, as well as ten notable business leaders. This is admittedly a small sample size in what has become a lifelong study project for me, but it serves to make the point that defining and living by core values is an important component of leadership.

I've taken what I've learned and made a synopsis of the core values that I've discovered for each of these categories:

Common Core Values of World Leaders (Jesus of Nazareth, Mahatma Gandhi, George Washington, Abraham Lincoln, Nelson Mandela, Florence Nightingale, Winston Churchill, Martin Luther King, Benjamin Franklin, Ronald Reagan):

1. Courage
2. Faith & Trust in God
3. Integrity, moral uprightness
4. Justice for all
5. Service, servant leadership
6. Equality; respect, kindness, and courtesy for all
7. Forgiveness, mercy, reconciliation
8. Humility, modesty
9. Perseverance
10. Unity

Common Core Values of Business Leaders (Jeff Bezos/Amazon, Warren Buffett/Berkshire Hathaway, Andrew Carnegie/Carnegie Steel, Yvon Chouinard/Patagonia, Tim Cook/Apple, Henry Ford/Ford Motors, Andy Grove/Intel, Steve Jobs/Apple, Herb Kelleher/Southwest Airlines, Elon Musk/Tesla & SpaceX):

1. Innovation, inventiveness
2. People-centric, development & growth of people (employees/ associates)
3. Quality, product & design excellence
4. Adaptability, flexibility
5. Customer-centric, customer delight
6. Efficiency & productivity
7. Environmental stewardship & social responsibility
8. Integrity & ethics
9. Long-range thinking & investing
10. Simplicity, transparency

It is important to understand that personal values are intertwined with the principles of agency and justice. Key elements of this are:

- **Individual Autonomy.** To be truly powerful in motivating a purposeful life, it is important to understand that "one size does not fit all." Each individual has the right to make choices about their lives, actions, and beliefs without coercion from external forces. This is tricky ground, since as shown in the examples of Abraham Lincoln, George Washington, and Benjamin Franklin, we are influenced by others in the development and articulation of our values. However, as compelling as these examples are, we must take care to respect individual autonomy in the process of values discovery and articulation. Failure to do so disconnects one from who they really are, and what drives them.

- **Responsibility and Accountability.** For any value to be legitimate, it must manifest itself in behavior. That behavior, whatever it is, represents a choice–and every choice has a corresponding consequence. The clear implication here is that each of us is accountable for our actions and their attendant consequences.

  There are times when that accountability carries a heavy burden. Consider, for instance, the men featured in John F. Kennedy's Pulitzer Prize winning book, *Profiles in Courage*. Eight U.S. senators took principled stands on controversial issues at great personal and political risk. Kennedy profiled each statesman as they acted against popular opinion or party lines, making decisions guided by their consciences, convictions, and values rather than political expediency. The book emphasizes the importance of courage and integrity in leadership, celebrating those who stood by their beliefs despite often dire personal consequences.

- **Ethical Decision-Making.** In most cases, strong core values lead to decisions that are ethical; that is, they cause deep reflection on how your actions impact others. While your values are very personal, they do not exist in a vacuum. Because they motivate your actions, they inevitably impact others with whom you interact. Your values should contribute to fair and just relationships. While this necessarily focuses attention on amicable interactions, it also must provide clarity regarding what you will–and will not–do to foster such relationships.

The Process

So, this brings me back to you. What are your core values and beliefs, the principles you live by? You may be able to list them quite easily, or you may want to ponder the question for a while. My objective here is to help you, to facilitate your process of clearly articulating your values, your personal Ethos.

To tackle this, it is important that my process is respectful of your agency, your freedom of choice. While the process I suggest here has proven to be facilitative in helping many leaders articulate their values, it is essential that YOU lead that process, *not* allow it to lead you. As you articulate your values, you must recognize that they are key elements of the foundation for your decision making and behavior. Those decisions and behavior, over time, form your reputation and character. In that regard, as you work through the process I suggest, you should continuously ask yourself:

- Does this value provide a compelling reason for the way I behave on a daily basis?
- Does this value act as a key element in how I make decisions?
- Does this value serve to enhance my relationships and interactions with others?
- Is this value important in how others perceive me; in my reputation with others?
- Is this value clearly a descriptor of the personal character I am striving to develop?

If your answer to these questions is "yes," then you can take comfort in knowing that you have articulated that particular value appropriately. In moving forward, recognize that:

- Your Ethos encompasses the values that set forth how you will behave in pursuit of your Cause
- You must define the core values by which you govern your behaviors and actions on a day-to-day basis.

- You are setting the bedrock for the values which ultimately will govern the behaviors and actions of key stakeholders in your enterprise.

- Although many companies have posted a list of values, it is critical that these be well-defined, clearly articulated, and well-communicated.

- This all starts with YOU, the leader!

To zero in on your values, let's begin by having you consider who has been most influential in your life. To start this process, a little personal brainstorming is generally a good idea. Initially, without any ranking, list as many of the significant influencers (or heroes, if you will) in your life. Influencers may be spouses, parents, teachers, coaches, mentors—or even historical or fictional characters.

The following Influencers/Heroes Mind Map Worksheet may be helpful for this:

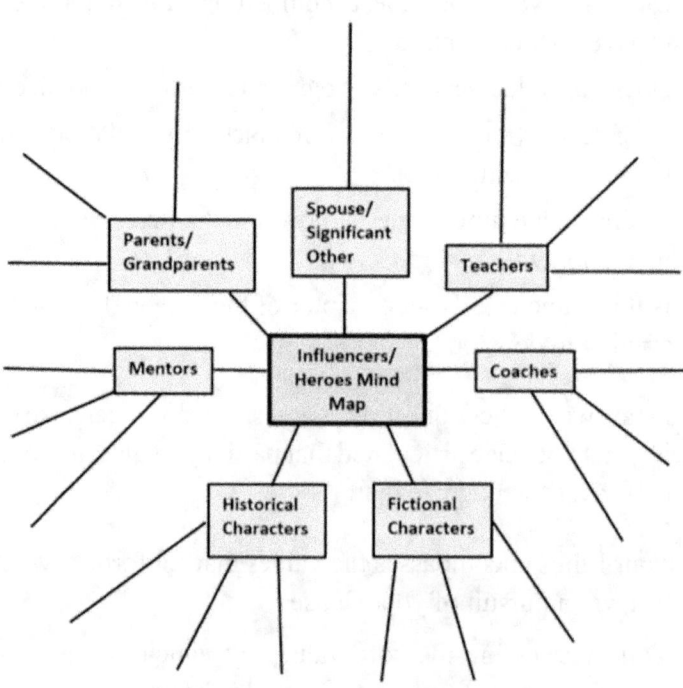

Recognize that while Influencers have often affected you from a positive perspective, a negative influence may have formed one or more of your values. (Example: My father was a 4 pack a day smoker. I witnessed what this addiction did to his health, and as a result, I chose to never smoke. His negative example has had a positive effect on me.)

When you have listed as many influencers as you can, use the worksheet on the following page to:

1. Rank your significant Influencers. The worksheet provides space for 10.

2. Answer the following question for each Influencer: *Why has this person been influential for you?* Space is provided for your answers on your worksheet.

3. Finally, distill your answer into a few words to define the Values, Beliefs, or Principles embodied in the life, behavior, or actions of this person. Your worksheet again provides space for this.

YOUR MOST IMPORTANT INFLUENCERS/HEROES

Rank	Influencer/Hero	Why he/she has been influential	Values they Epitomize
1			
2			
3			
4			
5			
6			

7			
8			
9			
10			

To illustrate the use of this worksheet, I've included an example of five of the most important Influencers in my life.

AN EXAMPLE: A FEW OF RICH TYSON'S MOST IMPORTANT INFLUENCERS/HEROES

Rank	Influencer/ Hero	Why he/she has been influential	Values they Epitomize
1	Jesus of Nazareth	He is the epitome of authenticity; He consistently bore witness of who He was and is, He lived His values, He is the greatest teacher and facilitative leader. His stories (parables) and questions led His followers to discover truth and unfailing values. He was both compassionate and frank.	**Authenticity**, **teacher** of **truth**, **facilitation**, **stories** that **touch hearts**, **questioner/ listener** **Compassion**, **frankness**.

2	Carlos Asay (mentor)	Dear friend and mentor who stood by me in some of my darkest hours.	**Loyalty, kindness, mentor, problem-solver**
3	Tom Peterson (mentor)	Dear friend who saw far more potential in me than I saw in myself—and consistently encouraged me to pursue that potential.	**Recognize** the **potential** in others, **encouragement**
4	Michael Tyson (my brother)	The best brother any man could have. He is kind, open-minded, and generous.	**Kindness, open to the ideas of others, generous**
5	Abraham Lincoln	Masterful leader. Humbly bore rejection and abuse, but led the U.S. out of a seemingly impossible situation. His team was "one of rivals," some who thought him incapable. Even so, through both compassion and tenacity, he led the nation through its most severe trial.	**Humility, courage, facilitative leadership,** a man of **Velvet and Steel**

Now consider the most influential books you have read. Once again, a bit of brainstorming is generally a good place to start. Initially, without any ranking, list the most significant books you have read. The Mind Map Worksheet shown below may help you in this effort. The books that have influenced you may come from a variety of genres including Business, Philosophy, Psychology, Religion, Science, History, or even fiction.

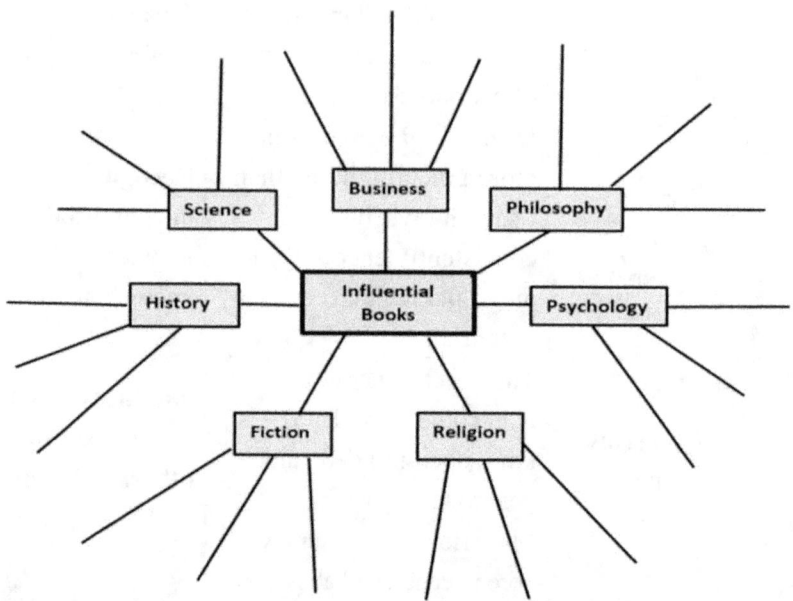

When you have listed as many Influential Books as you can, use the "Most Influential Books Worksheet on the following page to:

1. Rank your Influential Books. This worksheet again provides space for 10.

2. Answer the following question for each Influencer: *Why has this book been influential for you?* Space is provided for your answers on your worksheet.

3. Finally, distill your answer into a few words to define the Values, Beliefs, or Principles embodied in the book. Your worksheet again provides space for this.

YOUR MOST INFLUENTIAL BOOKS

Rank	Genre	Book	Why it has been influential	Values it Epitomizes
1				
2				
3				
4				
5				
6				
7				
8				
9				
10				

Here again, I have provided an example of my personal use of this worksheet.

AN EXAMPLE: A FEW OF RICH TYSON'S MOST INFLUENTIAL BOOKS

Rank	Genre	Book	Why it has been influential	Values it Epitomizes
1	Religion	Scriptures	The Bible was the first book I read with my mother. The stories taught me principles that still govern my life. The stories of Jesus were the centerpiece then and now.	**Obedience**, **honesty**, **kindness**, **humility**, **sacrifice**, **work, service, courage, prayer, repentance, forgiveness**
2	Business	How Will You Measure Your Life?	Clayton Christensen's book asks these important questions: How can I be sure that I'll find satisfaction in my career? How can I be sure that my personal relationships become enduring sources of happiness? How can I avoid compromising my integrity—and stay out of jail?	Above all other business & career outcomes, **personal fulfillment**, **personal relationships**, and **integrity** matter

3	Psychology/ Philosophy	Man's Search for Meaning	Quoting the author, Viktor Frankl: "Man's search for meaning is the primary motivation in his life and not a 'secondary rationalization' of instinctual drives. This meaning is unique and specific; it must and can be fulfilled by him alone; only then does it achieve a significance which will satisfy his own *will* to meaning."	We must **help others discover their own meaning and purpose and help them fulfill it.**
4	Business	Multipliers	The author, Liz Wiseman, compares and contrasts the 5 characteristics of Multipliers (those who grow their people and their companies) and Diminishers (those who subtly destroy their people and companies)	We must **facilitate the development of Multiplier leaders**
5	Business	A More Beautiful Question	Warren Berger's book sets forth the three key innovative questions: Why? What if...? And How?	We must **strive to help leaders solve their own problems** by *questioning their answers, rather than answering their questions*

Now consider the movies that have most influenced you. I have again provided a Mind Map Worksheet for your use. In using it, start without ranking the significant movies you have enjoyed. Recognize that the movies that have influenced you may be from a variety of genres including Drama, Action, Comedy, Religion, Sports, Romance,

History, or Documentaries. They may be fictional or nonfiction. Your worksheet provides space for noting the genre.

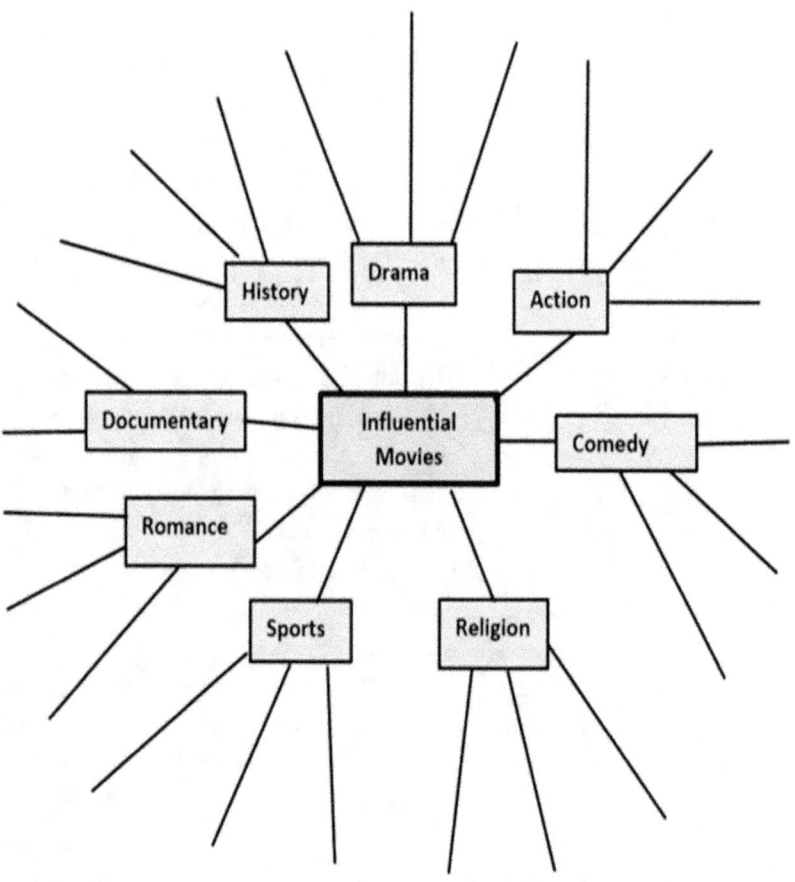

When you have listed as many Influential Movies as you can, use the "Most Influential Movies Worksheet" on the following page.

1. Rank the movies that have been most influential for you. This worksheet also provides space for 10.

2. Answer the following question for each movie: *Why has this film/presentation been influential for you?* Space is provided for your answers on your worksheet.

3. Finally, distill your answer into a few words to define the Values, Beliefs, or Principles embodied in each movie. Your worksheet again provides space for this.

YOUR MOST INFLUENTIAL MOVIES

Rank	Genre	Movie	Why it has been influential	Values it Epitomizes
1				
2				
3				
4				
5				
6				
7				
8				
9				
10				

The following is an example of my personal use of this worksheet.

A FEW OF RICH TYSON'S MOST INFLUENTIAL MOVIES

Rank	Genre	Movie	Why it has been influential	Values it Epitomizes
1	Sports/ Overcoming Over-whelm-ing Odds	Miracle	"Again, again, again!" "The legs feed the wolf, gentlemen." "When you pull on that jersey, the name on the front is a hell of a lot more important than the one on the back." **Coach Herb Brooks**	**Dedica-tion, hard work, selfless sacrifice for a cause beyond oneself**
2	Drama/ Courage	To Kill a Mockingbird	"You never really under-stand a person until you consider things from his point of view … until you climb into his skin and walk around in it." "Simply because we were licked a hundred years before we started is no reason for us not to try to win." "Before I can live with other folks I've got to live with myself." "You just hold your head high and keep those fists down. No matter what anybody says to you, don't you let 'em get your goat. Try fighting with your head for a change." "Best way to clear the air is to have it all out in the open." **Atticus Finch**	**Respect diversity of opin-ions, seek to under-stand before being under-stood, never give up/stay committed to success, fight with your mind, problem-solve, "go to the pain"**

3	War/Courage	Schindler's List	"Whoever saves one life, saves the world entire." **Itzhak Stern** *Itzhak Stern:* There will be generations because of you. *Oskar Schindler:* I didn't do enough. *Itzhak Stern:* You did so much. "…if this factory ever produces a shell that can actually be fired, I'll be very unhappy." **Oskar Schindler**	**Selfless-ness, sacrifice, courage, do no harm**
4	Western/ Overcoming Setbacks	The Man From Snowy River	**Jessica**: *[viewing from horseback, after Jim saves Jessica and they kiss, a change is coming in the Aussie mountain weather]* "It changes so suddenly. One moment it's para-dise, the next it's trying to kill you." **Jim**: "Yep, that's how it can be up here. If it was easy to get to know it, it would not be challeng-ing. You've got to treat the mountains like a high-spirited horse; never take it for granted." **Jessica**: "It's the same with people, too."	**Never take circum-stances— or people for granted** **Recognize change is more likely than stability** **Embrace change and ambiguity**

When you've arrived at this point in the Ethos process, you will have completed three worksheets:

1. Your Most Important Influencers Worksheet
2. Your Most Important Books Worksheet
3. Your Most Important Movies Worksheet

Based on these three worksheets, it is now time to triangulate toward your most prevalent and important values, those that have been revealed on two or more of your worksheets.

Use the Values Distillation Worksheet on the following page to describe and rank each of your values based on the frequency (number of times) each value appears on the three worksheets you have completed.

VALUES DISTILLATION WORKSHEET

#	Rank	Description of Value	Frequency/Number of Responses
1			
2			
3			
4			
5			
6			
7			
8			
9			
10			
11			
12			
13			
14			
15			
16			
17			
18			
19			
20			
21			
22			

#	Rank	Description of Value	Frequency/Number of Responses
23			
24			
25			
26			
27			
28			
29			
30			
31			
32			
33			
34			
35			
36			
37			
38			

Here's how this worksheet distilled out my personal values:

#	Rank	Description of Value	Frequency/Number of Responses
1	1	Courage	….. ….. … (13)
2	1	Kindness	….. ….. … (13)
3	3	Vision/Visionary	….. ….. (10)
4	3	Work	….. ….. (10)
5	5	Relationships	….. …. (9)
6	6	Overcoming Adversity	….. … (8)
7	6	Meeting Challenges	….. … (8)
8	6	Love	….. … (8)
9	6	Loyalty	….. … (8)
10	10	Commitment	….. .. (7)
11	10	Leadership	….. .. (7)
12	10	Opposition in all things	….. .. (7)
13	10	Problem-Solver/Problem-Solving	….. .. (7)
14	14	Focus	….. (6)
15	14	Forgiveness	….. (6)
16	14	Questioner/Questioning	….. (6)

#	Rank	Description of Value	Frequency/Number of Responses
17	14	**Value Creation**	.... (6)
18	18	**Caring/Empathy**	..... (5)
19	18	**Encouragement**	..... (5)
20	18	**Humility**	..... (5)
21	18	**Sacrifice**	..... (5)
22	18	**Service**	..... (5)
23	18	**Succeed, Success**	..... (5)
24	18	**Teacher, teaching**	..... (5)
25	25	**Change**	.... (4)
26	25	**Compassion**	.... (4)
27	25	**Facilitation**	.... (4)
28	25	**Honesty/Integrity**	.... (4)
29	25	**Learning/Learner**	.... (4)
30	25	**Repentance**	.... (4)
31	25	**Selflessness**	.... (4)
32	32	**Ambiguity**	... (3)
33	32	**Diversity**	... (3)
34	32	**Energy/Optimism**	... (3)
35	32	**Engagement**	... (3)
36	32	**Enthusiasm**	... (3)
37	32	**Faith, Faithfulness**	... (3)
38	32	**Family**	... (3)

As the distillation process reveals your values to you, you should be able to articulate those principles and beliefs into an Ethos Statement. Here's what that looks like for me:

THE PERSONAL VALUES OF RICH TYSON

PEOPLE are most important in my life. I **LOVE** my fellow man and seek to **SERVE** him or her wherever possible. This is the **FOCUS** of my personal **VISION** and my **WORK**. This sets the foundation for the other personal values that govern my thoughts and actions.

- I desire to live with **INTEGRITY** characterized by **COURAGE** combined **with KINDNESS**
- I desire to **LEAD** with **CONFIDENCE** combined with **HUMILITY** in **TAKING ON AND MEETING CHALLENGES**
- I am a lifelong **LEARNER, TEACHER,** and **FACILITATOR**
- I seek to be an **ENERGETIC** and **OPTIMISTIC PROBLEM-SOLVER**
- I seek to be a **VALUE-CREATOR**
- I want to be worthy of the **FAITH, TRUST,** and **RESPECT** of my fellow man
- I recognize the extraordinary **POTENTIAL** and inherent **FLAWS** in myself and my fellowman. Because of this, I strive to be a source of continuous **ENCOURAGEMENT** to **IMPROVEMENT** coupled with **UNFEIGNED COMPASSION,** and **FORGIVENESS.** In that regard, I desire to be **HELIOTROPIC, a LEADERSHIP SOURCE OF TRUTH** and **LIGHT.**

These are the Core Values that have emerged from my worksheets, and they are the values that I have committed to live by. They are effectively the Dead Horse Point fence posts that dictate what I will do–and what I won't do–in the pursuit of my personal purpose and mission, with its associated value proposition.

So…what are the Core Values that govern what you will–and will not– do in pursuit of your personal Cause, your Purpose and Mission? How will you articulate them into your personal Ethos Statement? Until you transform the discovery process shared here into a written document that resonates deeply with yourself, you have not completed this essential task.

You should note that your Ethos Statement does not need to be long or wordy. And you should remember that at this point, the audience for this is one person: YOU. It is most important that it stirs your heart and mind! When that occurs, you are ready to move to the last step in the *PACER Visioning Model*: Resolve. I address this in the next chapter.

RESOLVE–With Your Purpose, Mission, and Values Articulated, It is Time to Define & Commit to WHAT YOU WILL DO!

Nothing in this world can take the place of persistence. Talent will not; nothing is more common than unsuccessful men with talent. Genius will not; unrewarded genius is almost a proverb. Education will not; the world is full of educated derelicts. Persistence and determination alone are omnipotent. The slogan "Press On" has solved and always will solve the problems of the human race.

U.S. President Calvin Coolidge

The most difficult thing is the decision to act, the rest is merely tenacity.

Amelia Earhart

Recently, at the end of a long day, I was searching for a movie to unwind to. I came upon a recent release called "A Million Miles Away." I was tired, so I figured that even if this flick proved to be less than entertaining, it would lull me to sleep.

As its story unfolded, it became clear that the main characters were a family of migrant farm workers, Mexican nationals, who each year came north to pick the crops that end up on America's dining room tables. Not more than a few minutes into the film, a young son in the family, Jose Hernandez, tripped and fell face first into a muddy patch in the field where his family was working. Leaping to his feet, he screamed out in anger about being consigned to the life of a picker. He protested that he was sick of it; that he was tired.

His father responded by asking Jose, "Don't you think that your mother and I are tired?"

This brought Jose to ask, "How do you do it? You say you are tired, but I don't see you tired."

To this, his father replied, "It's because I have a recipe, mijo." At this point his dad had Jose's full attention—and mine as well.

Here is the recipe that the senior Hernandez shared:

Ingredient #1: *The first thing is that you have to know what you want. You have to clearly define your goal, your purpose.*

This, of course, is what all five subsets of Chapter 7 of this book have been about. The boy's father was telling his son to make a firm *resolution* to get out of the muddy fields that he hated by finding a goal that would take him where he really wanted to go in his life. No doubt the elder Hernandez was a bit stunned to soon learn that Jose's resolution was to go far above the mud and drudgery of those fields, all the way into outer space! That resolve became everything to Jose.

Ingredient #2: *Look where you are standing right now; recognize how far you are from your goal.* As Jose matured, this ingredient was repeated multiple times. It was daunting to him to recognize how far he needed to come to have any chance of realizing his dream. Even so, his resolve became the driving force that literally carried him over the years.

Ingredient #3: *You have to think how you're going to get from where you are to where you want to be. You have to draw a road map that* *leads to your desired destination.* This is where resolve transforms into an action plan. As he progressed through grade school and junior high, Jose studied everything he could about the NASA astronaut program. He learned that he would need outstanding grades throughout school, and that his education would need to focus on science, technology, engineering, and mathematics. He also discovered that the likelihood of being selected would be enhanced if he achieved academic excellence in an advanced degree program. Clearly, his resolve was to be intensely tested!

Ingredient #4: *If you don't know how to proceed on the path defined in Ingredient #3, you have to dedicate yourself to learning. You can't shortcut this step; it is essential.*

As Jose completed his early school years, he began to work toward achieving the academic elements that would impress NASA. When he felt that he had compiled the right resume, he applied for the astronaut program. Immediately, he was rejected. Although discouraged, he recognized that he could repeat the application process and that he needed to better understand what would change NASA's impression of him.

Over the next three decades, Jose beefed up his resume. He continued to work diligently on his education, ultimately gaining a masters degree in engineering. He landed a job with the prestigious Lawrence Livermore Radiation Labs. He took on additional assignments as they became available, and through one of those opportunities he was able to participate in a government project to curtail nuclear developments in Siberia. He used this experience to become a competent speaker of the Russian language. Knowing NASA looked favorably on aviators, he learned to fly, logging over 800 hours as a pilot. He also learned to scuba dive. And he knew fitness was important as well, so he dedicated himself to become exceptionally fit, ultimately completing 11 marathons. He channeled all of these efforts into a relentless series of applications for the NASA astronaut program over more than a decade. Jose had literally transformed himself both personally and professionally, yet the response from NASA was always the same. He was rejected eleven more times!

Finally, at the age of 36, NASA responded differently; they informed Jose that he was one of 120 finalists from over 2500 applicants. You can probably imagine how thrilled Jose and his family were!

But not so fast....

Ingredient #5: *When you think you've made it, you'll probably have to work even harder to finally reach your goal.* This is where resolve truly gets tested. If you have dedicated yourself to a vision of what you (or your enterprise) is to become, have clearly articulated your mission (what you need to do), and the values that you will live by in pursuit of that vision and mission...you should now expect to be faced with heavy opposition before you actually achieve success. As a finalist, Jose went through physical and psychological testing at the Johnson Space Center. He was grilled by former astronauts on everything from technical engineering and aviation to his interpersonal and teamwork skills. He took tests to identify his problem-solving competence, or lack thereof. By all outward indicators, Jose did well, but in the end he received a phone call from Duane Ross, the director of astronaut selection at NASA. *He had been rejected again...*

However, this time Ross offered Jose a job, not as an astronaut, but as an engineer. Jose's disappointment at being rejected was replaced by a new sense of hope. Perhaps this new job would provide an enhanced opportunity, an inside track. And it did! But it took six years of excellent work as a NASA engineer to render the result that Jose had dedicated his career, even his life, to achieving. Finally, after 15 years of applying, he got the call he had dreamed of; he was invited to join the astronaut program.

Jose, along with his wife, children, and extended family rejoiced. It was a time of great celebration. However, Jose was soon reminded once again of his father's 5th Ingredient. Although he was basking in the glow of having "made it," he still needed to pass muster in the NASA astronaut training program to prove himself capable of actually going into space. Nearly five years of rigorous training were required before the opportunity he had dreamed of was offered. He was asked to serve as Mission Specialist on the Space Shuttle Discovery.

On August 28, 2009, at the age of 47, Jose Hernandez fastened himself in the Space Shuttle, felt the G-forces of a violent launch, and realized the dream of his life. Jose became the first migrant farm worker to go into space. This young man took the wisdom of his father and turned it into reality. He had a little boy dream that many found ludicrous–he wanted to become an astronaut. This purpose became his WHY– and it filled his imagination and provided his life goal, his Ingredient #1. As he grew older, he said, "I think about it every day, every hour. I can't stop thinking about it!"

There is much to be learned from the story of Jose Hernandez. His father's wisdom provides a simple recipe for success. In my career as a business leader and coach, I have developed and used a similar recipe.

I graduated from the Harvard Graduate School of Business with a master's degree in business in the spring of 1977. During the brief period before I started working in my new job at the Avery Label Corporation in Southern California, I took some time to decompress from the intense two-year experience I had just completed at Harvard. Like my fellow classmates, I had been "drinking at the firehose" of what has often been described as the "bootcamp of capitalism." So for a few weeks, I found myself pondering, *what did I learn?*

By this time, I had two full four-drawer file cabinets full of case studies that HBS had required us to read and analyze, every step of the way to the MBA. This material covered everything from finance and accounting, marketing and manufacturing, personnel policy, organizational behavior, global and national economics, entrepreneurship, public policy and taxation, etc., etc., etc.! The challenge that I pondered was to synthesize this overwhelming treasure trove of learning and knowledge into a simple mindset that would provide me with an intellectual foundation on which to build my career. *This was no easy task!*

After several days of jotting down my thoughts, scratching through and deleting most of them, I experienced a revelation. There was a thread of wisdom that was connected to every topic that I had studied. Each subject and its attendant case studies required me to develop a plan of how to attack a problem or opportunity. Those plans would then need to be carried out, to be acted upon. As those actions unfolded, it would become necessary to track them against the plan, and evaluate the results that emerged. And, because those results were hardly ever likely to deliver precisely what was desired, there was almost always the need to revise the initial plans. With that revision, the process would recycle until a greater degree of success was achieved.

With these insights, I developed a management model that I have used ever since that time. It uses the acronym *PACER*. That should sound familiar, as I have used a subsequent and different use of that acronym as a guide for the development of your personal vision, purpose, mission, and values. I have shared it over the past 5 sub-chapters of this book: Pathos, Authenticity, Cause, Ethos, and Resolve.

The management model, or *PACER Action Model,* I developed, however, uses the acronym differently:

P: Plan — To address and resolve any situation, problem, challenge or opportunity, you must have a plan. That plan must answer two fundamental questions:

1. What are the current conditions, the facts that dictate where you are right now? And...

2. What new set of conditions do you desire to achieve? How are these conditions different from where you are today?

Notice the similarity to the first two ingredients in the recipe recommended by Jose Hernandez's father. You have to know what you want to do, or achieve–and you have to acknowledge where you are in relation to that goal or purpose. It's important that you are brutally honest and thorough with yourself in answering these two questions. Too often, many tend to shortchange this process, moving quickly into development of plan details. If, however, you are clear in your understanding of the gap between today and where you want to be tomorrow, you will avoid overlooking essential components in planning your strategies for spanning that gap.

With the gap reasonably well-defined, planning should then answer the following questions:

- WHY do you want to move from today's conditions to a different, new and improved tomorrow? Jose Hernandez clearly wanted to get out of picking the fields, but his greater purpose emerged as he looked into the heavens and learned about astronauts. His WHY became compelling, all-consuming.

- WHAT will need to transpire to make this happen? What are the key milestones, and what are the necessary processes needed in order to achieve them? Early on, Jose realized that he would need to gain an education, starting with simply learning English and getting through elementary and high school. He still had to work as a picker, but he saw himself working his way *out* of the fields, not staying in them. As he met each milestone, he moved to the next. His high school diploma was replaced by both undergraduate and graduate degrees. He became an engineer, and he sought opportunities for growth and development. More milestones were achieved–and year after year he progressed toward his goal. Notice that he became a continuous lifelong learner and planner.

- WHO will you need to engage with to facilitate the desired progress? Jose needed the support of his family. Most importantly, his wife encouraged him when the path seemed especially daunting. He also engaged with mentors along the way, including a former elementary school teacher who described him as "a force of nature." Later mentors included those within the Livermore Labs and NASA who helped him see his "next steps."

- WHAT resources will be required to keep you moving forward? What budget will be needed? Jose's story appropriately highlights his determination and tenacity. But it would be easy to overlook the fact that through all of his adult years, he also had the roles of husband, father, and son. He was the breadwinner for his family, and they counted on him to sustain them as they supported him in pursuit of his incredible goal.

- HOW will that work be accomplished? What are the essential actions that you believe will deliver your desired outcomes? What are your *cause and effect* assumptions? Like Jose, much of this will necessarily unfold as we move forward. Some of the HOWs will be apparent early on, but many will have to be discovered. The Jose Hernandez who gazed at the stars as a little boy could not have imagined the incredible journey his life would take as a prelude to traveling into space.

- HOW long do you project it will take to accomplish the work required? Time frames are important, but they must be broken down into the time likely to be necessary for each milestone. There must be a sense that they will lead to an ultimate triumph, but care must be taken to not be either overly optimistic or pessimistic. While Jose's story spanned over four decades, he couldn't have known that as a child– and it's certainly good that he did not. Great achievement is often killed by a too distant destination. It is also killed at times when time frames are vastly underestimated.

- WHERE will the work be done? In order to move from planning to execution, you need to define where you will work. If you require a college degree, you had better see yourself in a class, doing the requisite work. If you need to generate income to fuel your venture, you must see yourself at a job that will provide you with that income. Jose had to see himself in a variety of important places beyond the farm fields!

A good plan will pass muster with the SMART goal-setting model:

- It is SPECIFIC.
- It has MEASURABLE cause and effect actions and outcomes.

- It is ACHIEVABLE. It is important here to recognize that overarching goals and visionary purposes (gap-bridgers that will close the gap between today and tomorrow) will not likely be achieved overnight. However, appropriately chosen mid-journey milestones can be accomplished more easily; they should be achievable.

- It is RELEVANT. The plan clearly relates to the WHY, to your visionary overarching purpose.

- It is TIME-BOUND. The plan should have an initiation date (when you will start) and a projected completion date (when you will end), as well as periodic review dates within the overall time frame.

A: Action — With your plan in hand, it's time to get busy!

Your plan should provide a map of what you will do every day, each week, each month, and throughout the year. It should help you avoid distractions, as well as help you make firm decisions on what you will–and will not do.

For most people, initially, it will be a challenge to discipline yourself to strictly adhere to your plan. This is where *resolve* gets its first test. To achieve your purpose, this must not be like most New Year's resolutions. While it is rarely possible to meet every demand set in your plan, you must commit to being dedicated. That means when something disrupts your intended actions, you strive as quickly as possible to "get back on the horse."

I have found that with a growing family, there is an endless list of "to dos" that I haven't factored into my business vision or into my personal goals. Over the years, this has occasionally been distressing to me. However, I have found that as I have increasingly made the relationships in my life a priority on par with my business, such interruptions have transformed into opportunities to be a better husband, father, and grandfather. They may slow down my time frame for achieving my business vision, but they enhance my vision of the most important relationships in my life. And, in addition to this, I have worked harder to find ways to be more efficient in pursuit of all my important goals. For me that means I rarely have a boring day. I am too busy ACTING to get bored!

C: Control — Noted leadership trainer and former judge, John E. Jones famously observed "that which gets measured gets done." This was an elaboration on what management guru, Peter Drucker said, "That which gets measured gets managed." The point here is that to *control* your progress toward the accomplishment of your vision, you must measure your progress. However, simply measuring progress is insufficient to move you forward. To control your progress, you must compare your plans to your actions.

Early in my business career, I served as the financial controller for a university. Coming into that position, I understood my job was to oversee the accounting functions of the institution. While that made sense, I was unclear as to why my title was Controller. I didn't feel that I was controlling anything. I oversaw the university's annual budgeting process as well as the day-to-day financial transactions of our business office, and I facilitated the timely production of monthly financial reports. But I didn't have the sense that I really had the authority to control anything.

It wasn't until my first year at the Harvard Business School that I began to understand the term *control.* When I commenced my studies there, one of my courses was entitled "Control," which was clearly an accounting course. I approached the professor, questioning the name they had chosen. Somewhat surprised, he challenged me: "Mr. Tyson, surely you understand the true role of accounting. It is to measure company financial performance against budgets and forecasts so that management can understand what is working and what is not. That is the essence of control. Without accounting, there would be no control."

The lights came on for me. Control is measuring what is done against what has been planned so that you can understand cause and effect, as well as effectiveness and efficiency. Throughout every other course at the Harvard Business School, *control* emerged as a central principle. Whatever you plan, you must measure your actions and their attendant outcomes against those plans. It applies to finance, customer interactions including marketing and sales, operations including manufacturing, distribution, and support functions, competency training and employee engagement, recruitment and achievement of purpose, mission and values.

John E. Jones later expanded his views on *control.* He said, "What gets measured gets done. What gets measured and fed back gets done well. What gets rewarded gets repeated." I'll address feedback and rewards shortly. For now, recognize that quantifying and measuring various aspects of your performance against your plan is essential for progress and ultimate achievement.

E: Evaluate — Having set key metrics in place that compare your actions and outcomes to your plans, you will gain several essential insights:

- First, you will be able to assess your commitment, as well as your ability to carry out your plan.

- You will then be able to evaluate *cause and effect.* Plans are based on assumptions regarding how actions will drive results, and a good *control* system will corroborate or invalidate those assumptions.

- Where actions are measured against your plan, you will see *variances.* These emerge as shortfalls from expectations, as well as those areas where your performance exceeds expectations. Shortfalls will lead you to ask *why?* — and your answers should lead you to consider changes to your plan or your actions, or both. Where you have exceeded expectations, you should also ask *why?* Was this an aberration or random occurrence, or is this level of performance sustainable? Should the plan be revised?

- As you continue to control, on a periodic basis, you will gain an increasingly clear picture of your strengths, weaknesses, and areas for improvement. This will focus your attention on areas for plan revision.

Evaluation is an important learning exercise. It is akin to the elder Hernandez's fourth ingredient. To stay on the path to your destination, you must be a dedicated learner. And your first and foremost source of learning is the illumination you will get from an effective control system that measures your actions against your plans.

To enjoy maximum value from Evaluation, your insights must be shared with others. Selected stakeholders should be invited to review your metrics, and to help in the evaluation process.

R: Revise — In his excellent book, *The Lean Startup,* Eric Ries introduces the concept of *validated learning*, emphasizing the importance of quickly testing assumptions and iterating. One of the book's key principles is the build-measure-learn feedback loop. Revision of plans and actions are key elements of this loop. It allows innovators to test hypotheses and gather data before investing significant time and resources in rolling out a full offering. This minimizes waste and allows for adaptation based on what is observed and discerned from the insights gleaned from the control system. Ries stresses the significance of *the pivot*, a change in strategy without changing the vision, when faced with evidence that the current approach isn't working. This concept empowers innovators to embrace change and evolve their business models based on feedback from their key metrics.

It should be noted that the need to revise plans, or pivot, is the norm, not the exception. You should not be discouraged or disappointed when you find it necessary to pivot. It is, in reality, a key step in reaching your goal. Consider again Jose Hernandez. His pivots were countless, but they ultimately led him to his desired outcome: his **Reward.** That is the final use of the letter R in the *PACER Action Model,* but it comes only after many necessary revisions, and only after Ingredient #5: *working even harder after you feel you have arrived.* In that regard, Ries stresses the importance of *persistence.* Persistence, of course, means that you aggressively stick to what you've decided to do.

This, however, is not to imply that persisting in your resolve will be easy. In fact, it is almost assuredly the opposite. Often, the fulfillment of purpose, mission, and values takes years, decades, or even a lifetime. But such commitment inevitably bears fruit.

I take comfort in the words of 19th-century American philosopher, essayist, and poet, Ralph Waldo Emerson

"That which we persist in doing becomes easier for us to do; not that the nature of the thing itself is changed, but that our power to do is increased."

Herein, Emerson emphasized the concept that persistence and consistent effort lead to an increase in one's ability to accomplish tasks, even if the nature of the task itself remains unchanged. Over time, continued dedication and practice will enhance one's skills and capabilities–and ultimately lead to the fulfillment of personal purpose, mission, and values.

At this point, it is important that we return to the insights you should have gained by using the *PACER Visioning Model & Process*, described in the past 5 sub-chapters of this book: Pathos, Authenticity, Cause, Ethos, and Resolve. Those insights should have rendered for you the key elements of your Personal Vision, including your Purpose (your WHY), your Mission (your Value Proposition), and the Core Values that describe the principles you live by.

Here's how those elements have unfolded for me, as I have utilized my own process, a synthesis of that process:

My PATHOS, my passion, my WHY (from Chapter 7A):

At the heart of my motivation, personal drive, and purpose is my love for others–and my desire to serve them. To do this, my passion is to pursue a life of continuous learning, thereby expanding the value I can deliver to my fellowman. As I continue to learn, I enjoy enthusiastically sharing what I have learned with others through teaching–and facilitating their ability to apply true principles effectively and efficiently in their work and lives. I love to provide what I call "learning in the moment of need" for those I serve, as well as helping them unearth long-range strategic opportunities and challenges. I actively seek the

*chance to coach, to grow leaders, and help guide others
to growth, improvement, and fulfillment of their personal
purposes. I do this with all who desire my service,
including family, clients, athletic teams, my community and
church.*

My AUTHENTIC STRENGTHS (from Chapter 7B):

My greatest personal strengths are:

- **Learner:** I have an insatiable desire to learn and improve my understanding and application of true principles which may be shared with others in pursuit of their own learning, improvement, and success.

- **Contextualist:** As I pursue learning, I seek to understand the context of the principles I discover. Often this goes deep into historical context, allowing me to gain insights about current challenges and opportunities from the lessons of the past.

- **Strategist:** Faced with the various scenarios of life and business, I am generally able to discover relevant patterns to which I can apply the principles I have learned, and develop strategies for moving forward effectively.

- **Achiever:** I have the ability to focus and work hard on various aspects of business and life. I am highly motivated to accomplish a great deal everyday, and I am dissatisfied when I am not busy and productive.

- **People-Focused:** I am intrigued with the unique qualities and potential of each person with whom I interact. I am generally able to ascertain how to organize people into roles wherein they will experience success.

- **Facilitator:** I am a natural questioner, and I utilize that strength to facilitate collaboration which leads to strategies, tactics, and actions. With the strengths of others, I facilitate the development of highly effective project plans and implementation.

- **Analyst:** My questioning approach often unearths root causes for problems and key contributing factors for opportunities. I seek to understand "cause and effect" relationships in applying true principles that will render desired results.

- **Connector:** I have an innate ability to see the relationship between people, stories, and events. I believe that virtually every event and story has meaning, and that there is always "cause and effect." In that regard, I rarely buy into the idea of coincidences.

- **Bridge-builder:** I build bridges between people and groups by helping them find meaning and purpose in their lives and their work.

- **Archivist:** I have a strong need to collect and archive information, ideas, artifacts—and especially books.

- **Maximizer:** I continuously focus on the development of my personal strengths in order to provide service, support, and facilitation to others. My greatest measure of success is witnessing the growth and development of others wherein I have had the opportunity to participate in facilitating that growth and development.

My Personal CAUSE and the factors that establish its CREDIBILITY (from Chapter 7C):

I see the potential in every person to be an outstanding leader. Without being overbearing, I seek to help each individual recognize that potential and grow toward it. In that regard, I will be–and am–a facilitator of the success of others.

My facilitation skills are primarily focused on myself, my family and friends, and my prospective and current clients. For entrepreneurial CEOs, startup founders, and small business executives, my value proposition is to transform their vision of themselves into becoming outstanding leaders who create outstanding leaders.... who create outstanding leaders.

I am not a life coach, although what I do should always improve the lives of others. I am an executive leadership coach. I offer <u>processes</u> that facilitate the discovery of the <u>content</u> that defines each leader's strategies, tactics, and ultimate destination. These processes are built on true, proven principles and models that lead to leadership success.

In pursuit of this cause, I am committed to becoming increasingly serviceable for my fellowman. In order to continuously grow in my abilities to serve others, I am dedicated to spiritual, physical, intellectual, emotional, and career development.

As a foundational principle, I am committed to learning and sharing true principles. I seek to move from ignorance to knowledge, from knowledge to wisdom, and then sharing wisdom with others in a way that facilitates their growth, development, competence, confidence, engagement, and leadership. I am regularly sought to provide guidance, coaching, wisdom, empathy, and support. I strive to be "all in"—focused, fully attentive, and listening intently. I truly care. People get all of me.

I ask a lot of questions. While I am willing to share knowledge and wisdom, I am not "an answer looking for a question." I ask questions to discern specific needs, thereby helping others gain clarity regarding their challenges. With that clarity, my efforts are focused on facilitating their discovery of solutions and action plans. I help them discover their own best answers.

My most important relationships are the following, in this priority order:

1. **My relationship with God.** As the ultimate source of true principles, I dedicate a portion of every day to learning from Him. I do this during an hour or so at the dawn of each day, wherein I pray and study scriptures. I seek not only to learn true principles, but to learn God's will for me and what I will do on that day. This devotional time serves as a foundation and a launching point for everything else I do in my daily life.

2. **My relationship with myself.** To fulfill my personal Vision, I must maintain a high level of spiritual, physical, intellectual, emotional, and career fitness. Spiritual fitness grows over time as I remain disciplined in the devotionals described above. Physical fitness requires attention to diet, rest, and exercise. In that regard, I work out vigorously for at least one hour every day except Sundays. While working out, I listen to audiobooks on topics relevant to my Purpose, Mission, and Values. This may include business books, histories, and/or the stories of great leaders in all walks of life. When such audiobooks resonate with me, I purchase the hard copy and review it thoroughly for insights that might add to my knowledge and wisdom—and my ability to serve others. I endeavor to read 4-5 books each month, and I write at least one book review monthly. On those occasions when I feel overwhelmed or need to reset my emotions, I take a walk in the hills to recharge my batteries.

3. **My relationship with my wife, children, and extended family—within which I include my co-workers and clients.**

   My wife is my best friend and the most important person in my life. We each have our separate interests and endeavors, and we support one another in those things. We plan together for family, church, work, and recreation, and we enjoy traveling together, watching movies, playing games, building puzzles, and discussing many diverse topics including religion, politics, and world affairs. I make sure that I allot time for my wife's needs, including lightening her load by helping with household chores and being available to her when she needs me. I love her—and she knows it. And she loves me—and I know it!

   I have six incredibly bright and accomplished adult children, a description that also applies to their spouses. I strive to maintain close one-to-one relationships with each of them. While I don't see all of them every day or every week—and sometimes not even every month—I reach out to them via texting on a regular basis. They almost always respond, and they do so quickly. They know that I love them and that I'm here for them, almost at any time, day or night.

My children maintain a "Grandparents' Calendar" that includes all of my grandchildren's activities, including sports, concerts, science fairs, church activities, etc. My wife and I try to attend as many of these as possible. I also maintain a steady interchange with each grandchild via texting (for those old enough to have a smartphone). Whenever possible, I arrange to take them on Grandpa Dates, doing things they enjoy. I love being a grandpa!

When it comes to my co-workers and clients, I show up! I strive to understand their needs and be timely in responding to them. I include them as "part of my family," thereby extending to them the right to call on me not only when it is convenient or scheduled, but whenever the need arises. In that regard, it may seem strange that I show them as a subset of priority #3, and I must admit that there are many times when their needs dictate that they be priority #1. When such situations arise, I approach each as an opportunity to serve, rather than a drudgery or an obligation. I focus on facilitating discovery of actionable solutions to their problems and helping them become highly successful leaders.

4. **My relationship with friends and neighbors.** I strive to be "out in my community" as often as possible in order to stay connected with friends and neighbors. I try to be available to help them when needed. I have a sincere desire to serve them, and I see such occasions as important opportunities to show that I care.

5. **My relationship with everyone else, to the greatest extent possible.** With all of this, I still try to interact in positive ways with everyone I meet. With so much darkness in society today, this is sometimes very difficult. Nevertheless, I feel it is absolutely essential that I approach the world with optimism and a smile.

I feel that, with the exception of my relationship with God, every one of these relationships is a target market for my guidance, coaching, and wisdom. Obviously, only my clients are paying customers for this, but that's more than okay. By extending what I've learned over five decades to my wife, family, friends, neighbors, and others, I not only serve them, but I also hone my skills as I use them.

Every one of these relationships requires time and attentiveness in order to flourish. Within each, urgencies and emergencies can and do occur, forcing time to be allocated to one or more relationships at the expense of the others. When these happen, I strive to be available and responsive, to always see them as opportunities rather than infringements on my planned use of time. Each person inevitably needs a calming voice and demeanor—and I hope to always provide that. When I am successful, these interruptions become sources of blessings to others, and a joy to me.

The true measure of the value I create for myself is manifest in the growth, development, and achievements of those with whom I interact. As I help them in their growth, development, and success, I will be worthy of their trust, respect, and love. Ultimately, that will be how I measure my life.

The problem or opportunity that compels me to discover a solution follows:

So much of the unhappiness in the world is a function of a gross misunderstanding of what constitutes outstanding leadership. While this applies quite broadly to all human endeavors, most of my target market is leaders of business enterprises. According to a Gallup report, about 50% of employees have left a job specifically to get away from their manager at some point in their career. Bad bosses/poor leaders are a major factor in employee turnover.

In the best of circumstances, bosses are good, well-intentioned people who simply have never learned the principles of effective leadership. Unfortunately, there are also those who have bought into crippling counterfeits that destroy morale and undermine success. Either way, there is a huge opportunity for growing leaders!

Why does this opportunity exist? Because most of the important and efficacious principles of leadership are not taught in MBA or undergraduate business programs. And once bosses are on the job, they are too often too busy, too stressed, and too distracted to make the concerted effort necessary to change their attitudes, behaviors, and leadership tactics and strategies. Admittedly, the factors that define this opportunity also make it challenging to gain the attention of the target market. However, with incisive marketing, gaining the attention of even a small fraction of the 32 million small business owners in the United States will set us on the path to expanding interest in and desire for our value proposition.

I am attracted to the opportunity of addressing this problem because I have made the study of true principles of highly effective leadership my focus for over 50 years–and I continue in that endeavor. The questions I ask myself include:

What if I wrote a series of books and articles sharing true and efficacious leadership principles?

What if I, with my team, develop online training workshops that teach those principles?

What if we develop artificial intelligence applications to help scale our ability to share those principles and insights?

What if we utilize small group face-to-face forums for intensive discussion of those principles?

What if I coach a limited number of leaders, and while serving their needs, develop a strong influencer role for them in helping CEObuilder® to grow?

What if I created a program of developing coaches who were trained to facilitate the development of leaders who they would guide using the principles that I have learned over the course of my career and life?

I will pose these questions for deeper discussion with the key stakeholders in my life, including my wife, family, and the key executives within my organization, CEObuilder®.

My personal value proposition:

I facilitate the development of highly effective leaders, who in turn, facilitate the development of their people into highly effective leaders within their respective areas of authority and influence. As bosses (and others) transform into outstanding leaders, they will apply the principles they are learning in their families, their communities, and their business enterprises.

The foundational premise of this value proposition is heliotropic influence through facilitation. Heliotropism, the phenomenon where flowers orient themselves in the direction of the sun, defines for me the appropriate role and behaviors of great leaders wherein they gain appropriate, trusted, and respected influence with their constituents.

Facilitation excellence is the key skill whereby I serve as a coach, teacher, and leader. It is the foundational skill on which I believe virtually all other leadership skills are built—and it is the primary skill which I strive to teach other leaders.

When done well, this value proposition eliminates the pain of anger, depression, and poor engagement in virtually any family or organization. In businesses, it will also reduce (if not eliminate) high employee turnover, litigation, and enterprise failure. The gains enjoyed as a result of this value proposition are readily apparent. Each element of the Business Success Pyramid will improve including, of course, financial outcomes.

The market for my value proposition is huge

Wherever there are bosses, there is a market for improving leadership skills. Entrepreneurial CEOs or startup founders alone represent a group of 5 to 6 million in the United States. The U.S. Small Business Administration (SBA) notes that there are around 32 million small businesses in the U.S., many of which are led by their founders or entrepreneurial CEOs. Of these, a significant portion are considered startups or newer businesses. Larger companies add significantly to this number.

That said, my value proposition, when extended to virtually anyone within my realm of influence, makes the market even larger for me. A successful marketing campaign to entrepreneurial CEOs, startup founders, and small business executives make this value proposition financially viable for CEObuilder®.

My personal commitment to this value proposition is 100%. It is my career and my life! I seek the support of clients—past, present and future—in assisting with manuscript and article editing, being a sounding board for my ideas, providing testimonials, and promoting my books, workshops, forums, coaching, and training. That said, I do not seek outside investment. I am self-funded in this endeavor.

My Legacy is—and will be—the leaders that I have helped develop through my facilitation, coaching, and support. I hope that the principles I have shared—and will continue to share—will be similarly facilitated, coached, and supported by each of them as they develop future leaders. In that way, my legacy will continue beyond my life.

My Personal ETHOS, Beliefs & Values (from Chapter 7D)

People are most important in my life. I love my fellow man and seek to serve him or her wherever possible. This is the focus of my personal vision and my work. This sets the foundation for the other personal values that govern my thoughts and actions, which include:

- I desire to live with integrity characterized by courage combined with kindness

- I desire to lead with confidence combined with humility in taking on and meeting challenges
- I am a lifelong learner, teacher, and facilitator
- I seek to be an energetic and optimistic problem-solver
- I seek to be a value-creator
- I want to be worthy of the faith, trust, and respect of my fellow man
- I recognize the extraordinary potential and inherent flaws in myself and my fellowman. Because of this, I strive to be a source of continuous encouragement to improvement coupled with unfeigned compassion, and forgiveness. In that regard, I desire to be heliotropic, a source of leadership truth and light.

My Personal RESOLVE, What I am Committed to Do (from this Chapter, 7E)

I began this book with a question in the title to Chapter 1, *Therefore, What?* That question is especially applicable here. It boils down to going from a vision to an action plan. That takes me back to my *PACER Action Model.* Using this model takes wishes and begins to transform them into reality. Here's the transformational plan for me. Remember, this is the plan for me personally–and not yet for my business.

P: Plan — My plan for actualizing my personal vision includes:

- **Learning Daily**
  - Spiritually, through prayer and scripture study.
  - Physically by maintaining my weight, blood glucose level, and blood pressure through diet, proper nutrition, exercise, rest, and medications.
  - Intellectually through consistent and continual study and mindful engagement with smart and challenging people.
  - Emotionally through taking time for introspection, meditation, recreation, and time with others.

- ○ Career Growth and Development through study and interaction with business partners, co-workers, clients, and other stakeholders, as well as regular writing to express my thoughts and understandings of true leadership and business principles.

- **Serve Daily:** As a former leader in the Boy Scouts of America, I am reminded of their slogan: *Do A Good Turn Daily.* My goal is to render valuable service to at least one person everyday. That may be as simple as a smile, a word of encouragement, or an expression of gratitude in word, text or email. Or it could be as heroic as helping someone in dire straits–or even saving a life. The objective is to be truly heliotropic, sharing light that lifts and supports others.

- **Facilitate Daily:** Through questioning, listening, and occasionally expounding, help others to discover true principles whereby they are able to grow, develop, and succeed. I strive to do this daily, but want to be sure that I do it at least weekly.

This plan consists of SMART goals. They are specific, measurable (see Control below), achievable, relevant to my Vision (purpose, mission, and values), and time-bound (each are daily or weekly),

A: Act — This is where the rubber meets the road. I will execute the Plan. It is achievable as I resolve firmly to enact it!

C: Control — For Control to be effective, I must have metrics against which I will track my progress. These are the metrics I track and measure myself against:

- **Learning Daily:**

  - ○ <u>Spiritually</u>: Track my consistency of prayer and scripture study by daily journaling and notations in my scriptures.

  - ○ <u>Physically</u>: Track my weight and blood pressure daily, and my blood glucose level periodically through the course of each day (using a Continuous Glucose Monitor), track my intake of carbs and sugars (limit them) and track my intake of protein (maintain high levels). Track my exercise to be sure that each day includes both cardio (steps/mileage) and resistance/weight training. Track hours of sleep and log medications taken each day.

o   Intellectually: Track books being listened to and read each day, week and month. Read at least four books each month, as well as a minimum of 4 *Harvard Business Review* and *Economist* articles each month. Write at least one business article and one book review each month.

o   Emotionally: Review affirmation board and vision board regularly, texting to loved ones every week, journaling/ photographs to keep joyful times readily available to me as personal inspiration and rejuvenation, scheduling and carrying out recreational activities at least four times each year.

o   Career Growth and Development: Copious client note-taking, journaling and writing articles, book reviews, and authorship of my own books. Sharing articles and insights via email with clients as inspiration occurs to do so.

- **Serve Daily:** Hold myself accountable for serving at least one person every day. Don't let any day end without this completed.

- **Facilitate Daily:** Assess each week, *have I facilitated the growth and development of anyone this week?*

E: Evaluate — With the preceding key metrics in place, I am able to compare my actions and outcomes to my plans. This will allow me to:

- Assess my commitment, as well as my ability to carry out my plan.

- I will be able to evaluate *cause and effect* regarding the relationship between my actions and the outcomes I desire.

- I will notice any *variances* between what I planned to do–and what I actually did, shortfalls as well as those areas where my performance exceeds expectations. Shortfalls lead me to ask *why?* — and my answers will help me consider changes to my plan or my actions, or both. When I exceed expectations, I will also ask *why?* Was this an aberration or random occurrence, or is this level of performance sustainable? Should the plan be revised?

- As I continue to control, on a periodic basis, I will gain an increasingly clear picture of my strengths, weaknesses, and areas for improvement, focusing my attention on areas for plan revision.

- I will share my evaluative insights with my wife, family, and business associates—-and regularly seek their inputs.

R: Revise — I will readily revise my plans and/or actions as needed in order to achieve the goals that will lead to fulfilling my Vision. I will not be frustrated by the need to pivot, but will see such revisions as opportunities to improve.

R: Reward — I will enjoy the fruits of this process. While that may occasionally involve celebration, the greatest rewards will be the positive impact that my plan has on others.

So there you have it, the personal Vision of Richard "Rich" Tyson, including my Personal Purpose, Mission and its associated Value Proposition, my core Values–and my Action Plan.

As I have alluded earlier, I have shared my own use of the *PACER Visioning Process & Model* rather than sharing its use by any of my clients because of the intensely personal feedback it tends to reveal. Sharing such deep feelings from clients, while inappropriate here, is exactly what I would hope that you have done for yourself.

In this book, I have shared many benefits of developing an articulate and compelling personal purpose. As you now take your personal vision and develop it into a plan that will engage your business, it's important to reiterate those benefits:

- **Motivation and Drive:** A compelling vision serves as a powerful motivator for both yourself and others. When you have a clear sense of purpose, it provides direction, focus, and a reason to push through challenges. It fuels determination and helps you stay committed to your goals.

- **Resilience in Challenges:** Having a compelling vision strengthens your resilience. When faced with obstacles or setbacks, individuals who are connected to a meaningful purpose are more likely to bounce back, learn from failures, and keep moving forward.

- **Alignment of Actions**: A clear vision guides decision-making and aligns your actions with your values and long-term goals. It helps you prioritize tasks and make choices that are in line with your overarching objectives.

- **Fosters Innovation and Creativity:** A strong vision inspires creativity and innovation. When individuals are deeply invested in a cause or goal, they tend to think outside the box, seek novel solutions, and explore new possibilities to achieve their objectives.

- **Enhanced Focus and Productivity:** Clarity of purpose eliminates distractions and enables better focus. When you know what you're working toward, it becomes easier to concentrate on tasks, resulting in increased productivity and efficiency.

- **Personal Fulfillment and Satisfaction:** Living a purpose-driven life leads to a sense of fulfillment and satisfaction. It provides a sense of accomplishment, contributing positively to mental and emotional well-being.

- **Inspires Others:** A compelling vision has the potential to inspire others. When you are passionate about your purpose, it can influence and motivate those around you, creating a ripple effect and possibly inspiring a collective effort toward a common goal.

- **Long-term Vision and Legacy:** Committing to a compelling purpose allows individuals to envision a long-term impact. It can contribute to creating a legacy, leaving a positive mark on the world or within a specific community or industry.

- **Adaptability and Growth:** A vision-driven mindset encourages continual growth and learning. It fosters adaptability by encouraging individuals to evolve their strategies and approaches in pursuit of their purpose.

- **Sense of Meaning and Belonging:** Connecting with a compelling vision gives a sense of meaning and belonging. It provides a sense of being part of something greater than oneself, fostering a deeper connection with others who share similar values and goals.

Recognizing these benefits, and with your Personal Vision well-articulated, you are ready to use that Vision as the foundation for moving your business forward with super-charged enthusiasm and focus!

CHAPTER 8

Transforming Your Personal Vision into A Vision for Your Enterprise

He who wishes to fulfill his mission in the world must be a man (or woman) of one idea, that is, of one great overmastering purpose, overshadowing all his aims, and guiding and controlling his entire life.

Julius Bate

What our deepest self craves is not mere enjoyment, but some supreme purpose that will enlist all our powers and give unity and direction to our life. We can never know the profoundest joy without a conviction that our life is significant–not a meaningless episode. The loftiest aim of human life is the ethical perfecting of mankind–the transfiguration of humanity.

Henry J. Golding

Earlier, I quoted Henry David Thoreau, where he said, "If you have built castles in the air, your work need not be lost; there is where they should be. *Now put foundations under them.*" The transformation of your personal vision into a compelling vision for your enterprise is where your "castles in the air" receive the foundation on which you build your highly successful business–and life. Having articulated your personal vision, it is important to translate that vision into the vehicle for its fulfillment. In order for your efforts in developing that vision to bear fruit, I return to the word *ALIGN*. Success in your enterprise (business or otherwise), and indeed, even in your life requires a very strong alignment between your personal purpose, mission, and values– and those of your enterprise. Your enterprise is, in fact, the vehicle for much of how you will ultimately "measure your life."

This chapter, then, is about the transformation from your personal vision and its key components, your purpose, mission, and values into the corporate version that will bring that vision into reality–and magnify it to serve others. Consider the stories I've shared in this book:

- Herb Kelleher, whose personal vision and purpose in life was to love people," which transformed into the purpose for Southwest Airlines "to become the world's most loved, most flown, and most profitable airline." That vision of SWA has continued beyond Herb's career, and even beyond his life, by his successors who have led the airline.

- Van Phillips, whose personal vision was to bring his amputated leg to a level of usability that would allow him to return to athleticism, which transformed into creating mobility solutions for all leg and foot amputees.

- Frances Perkins, whose personal vision of putting people before profits, politics, and policy, transformed into the New Deal and Social Security under her leadership as U.S. Secretary of Labor under President Franklin D. Roosevelt.

- Daniel Vasella, whose personal vision of compassionate medical care transformed into the production of life-saving pharmaceuticals at Novartis and XBiotech, Inc.

- Florence Nightingale, whose compassion for others led her to the personal purpose of becoming a nurse, which ultimately transformed the entire profession of nursing forever.

- Thomas D'Eri, who along with his father, had the personal vision to find gainful employment for his autistic brother that was transformed into creating jobs and career opportunities for many autistic and handicapped people.

- Yvon Chouinard, whose personal vision to reverse the destruction of planet earth caused by climate change, world hunger, and pollution was transformed into the Patagonia Corporation's commitment "to use business to inspire and implement solutions to the environmental crisis."

- Tony Hsieh, whose lifelong pursuit was to "build stuff, be creative, and inventive," which transformed into a new disruptive innovation in the world of online commerce, using the internet to sell shoes through his company, Zappos.

- And even Abraham Lincoln, whose early vision was to be an honest, hard-working, and successful store clerk, which transformed into becoming the honest, hard-working President of the United States who saved a nation torn by slavery and disunity.

In each case, personal vision with its inherent purpose, mission, and core values had to evolve into a higher enterprise purpose, mission, and values. It had to be rearticulated for the enterprise in a way to attract supporters–and also exclude those who fundamentally disagreed with it.

Please note that these visionaries represent a mix of entrepreneurial startup leaders, incoming leaders to existing organizations, as well as ongoing leaders who used their personal visions to reenergize their enterprises. It is, of course, easy to recognize the importance of this transformation with entrepreneurs who desire a highly energetic and enthusiastic beginning for their businesses. Herb Kelleher, Van Phillips, and Thomas D'Eri are great examples of such leaders.

It is equally important for the incoming leader who may well be greeted with a measure of cynicism about his or her ability to lead the enterprise they have joined. Such newcomers need to balance an inquiring mindset about the company, its culture, and key functions with their vision for the corporation's future. While this is hardly ever an easy task, incoming leaders must arrive with a personal vision that can, and will be, transformed into a viable, high-energy purpose, mission, and values for the enterprise. Florence Nightingale and Abraham Lincoln are outstanding examples of successful incoming leaders.

Ongoing leaders should also take advantage of the opportunity to reenergize and refocus their organizations with an infusion of their personal visions. This may take the form of significant or subtle changes in the company's purpose, mission, or values. Such changes should include discussions, debate, and decisions among key executives regarding attitudes, behaviors, skills, and key operating principles. For instance, Yvon Chouinard was functioning as an ongoing leader of Patagonia when he took a dozen of his top managers to Argentina to discuss the company's vision. He asked critical questions that stemmed directly from his personal vision of addressing the critical environmental challenges faced by the planet. From those questions, and the answers given, a new recharged vision for the company was created. Please note in the personal example I share below regarding my company, CEObuilder®, that I too, am an ongoing leader.

The following graphic illustrates the process of transforming your personal vision and its key components, your purpose, mission, and values into the corporate version that will bring that vision into corporate reality.

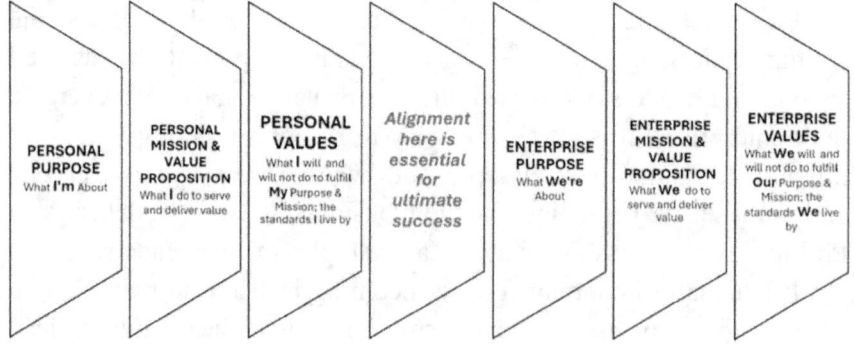

Here's how that process has unfolded for me, and my company, CEObuilder®. Once again, I have used the *PACER Visioning Model* here, focusing it now on how my personal vision transforms into my ideas for the company:

P–PATHOS: *In the prior chapter (See Chapter 7E, page 275), I shared the following:* **At the heart of my motivation, drive, and purpose is my love for others–and my desire to serve them. I do this through continuous learning, thereby expanding the value I can deliver to my fellowman through teaching and facilitating others to apply true principles effectively and efficiently in their work and lives.**

I have transformed my personal PATHOS
to the following PATHOS for my company, CEObuilder®:

CEObuilder®'s purpose is to develop leaders; to serve their inherent need to become highly effective in leading people and enterprises to superior levels of competency, engagement, and success. This caring is displayed in the CEObuilder® commitment to continuously learn true principles of effective leadership–and to deliver those principles to our clients through outstanding teaching, coaching, and facilitation. The fulfillment of this purpose will be manifested as our clients not only become great leaders, but as they, in turn, facilitate the development of other outstanding leaders.

A–AUTHENTIC STRENGTHS: *My personal strengths are* **Learner, Contectualist, Strategist, Achiever, People-Focused, Facilitator, Analyst, Connector, Bridge-Builder, Archivist,** *and* **Maximizer.** *(see Chapter 7E, pages 276-277.)*

A review of these strengths by artificial intelligence site, ChatGPT, rendered the following review of my strengths:

Given these strengths, this leader's likelihood of developing the competency, engagement, and success of other leaders is very high. Here's why:

1. ***Learner & Maximizer:*** *The insatiable desire to learn and continually improve is essential for a leader who seeks to grow others. The ability to learn and maximize personal strengths ensures that this leader stays ahead of trends, constantly seeks new tools, and can share insights, creating a culture of continuous development.*

2. ***Contextualist & Archivist:*** *Understanding historical context and archiving knowledge provides depth and insight. This allows the leader to teach from a rich repository of lessons, examples, and best practices, helping other leaders navigate complexity and avoid repeating past mistakes.*

3. ***Strategist & Analyst:*** *The ability to recognize patterns and analyze cause-and-effect relationships equips this leader with the skill to coach others in developing strategic thinking. This will help emerging leaders anticipate challenges and make informed decisions.*

4. ***Achiever:*** *High personal productivity ensures that goals and tasks are met, providing a strong example for other leaders. This relentless drive for achievement can be infectious, motivating others to work hard toward their own success.*

5. ***People-Focused & Bridge-builder:*** *A keen interest in understanding people's unique qualities fosters empathy and connection. This leader will excel at identifying other leaders' strengths, placing them in roles where they can thrive, and building collaborative environments.*

6. ***Facilitator & Connector:*** *The strength in questioning and facilitating collaboration means this leader is naturally inclined to involve others in the problem-solving process, ensuring buy-in and collective ownership. Their ability to connect ideas, people, and stories can inspire other leaders to think holistically and cultivate stronger teams.*

With such a balanced set of strengths, this leader is well-positioned to not only excel in their own role but also to

effectively nurture, engage, and ensure the success of other leaders. They are likely to be seen as a mentor, a resource, and a strong role model for leadership development.

I have transformed my personal AUTHENTIC STRENGTHS to the following AUTHENTIC STRENGTHS for my company, CEObuilder®:

Our team at CEObuilder® is characterized by the following strengths, which we use consistently and continuously as key elements in serving our clients in becoming highly effective, competent, engaged, and successful leaders. We are:

1. ***Learners & Maximizers:*** *We share an insatiable desire to learn and continually improve ourselves. We strive to stay ahead of trends, constantly seek new tools, and share insights, creating the CEObuilder® culture of continuous development. In this regard, we seek to grow each other, as we grow our clients.*

2. ***Contextualists & Archivists:*** *We recognize the great value of learning from the past. In that regard, we seek to understand historical context and we archive the knowledge that extends from the insights we gain. We utilize what we have learned to teach from a rich repository of lessons, examples, and best practices, helping other leaders navigate complexity and avoid repeating past mistakes.*

3. ***Strategists & Analysts:*** *We are inherently detectives; we seek to identify patterns and analyze cause-and-effect relationships, and we coach others in developing this type of strategic and analytical thinking, helping them to anticipate challenges and make informed decisions.*

4. ***Achievers:*** *We seek high personal productivity whereby goals and tasks are met, and provide a strong example for others within our company, and for our clients. This relentless drive for achievement is infectious, motivating others to work diligently toward their own success.*

5. *People-Focused & Bridge-builders:* We have a keen interest in understanding the unique qualities of each individual, thereby fostering empathy and connection. In this regard, we excel at identifying the inherent strengths of others, helping them to pursue roles where they can thrive.We help build collaboration at CEObuilder®, and within the companies of our clients.

6. *Facilitators:* We recognize that asking insightful questions is an invaluable facilitative skill. Our strength in questioning, listening, and facilitating involves key stakeholders in problem-solving processes, ensuring buy-in and collective ownership–both within CEObuilder® and in our client companies.

7. *Connectors:* Because of our intense focus on others and their needs and desires, we enjoy the ability to connect ideas, people, and stories that can inspire other leaders to think holistically and cultivate stronger teams.

C–MY PERSONAL CAUSE: *I see the potential in every person to be outstanding. Without being overbearing, I seek to help each individual recognize that potential and grow toward it. In that regard, I will be–and am–a facilitator of the success of others. My facilitation skills are primarily focused on myself, my family and friends, and my prospective and current clients. I offer* processes *that facilitate the discovery of the* content *that will define each individual's strategies, tactics, and ultimate destination. These processes are built on true, proven principles and models that lead to leadership success. (See Chapter 7E, pages 277-284)*

I have transformed my personal CAUSE to the following CAUSE for my company, CEObuilder®:

We recognize the potential in every business executive–whether an entrepreneurial startup pioneer, an incoming appointee or new owner of an existing company, an ongoing CEO, or a division or functional executive–to become an outstanding leader. For such business leaders, the CEObuilder® cause is to transform their vision of themselves from being caretaker managers to becoming exemplary visionary leaders who create other exemplary leaders ... .who then create a legacy of exemplary leaders!

THE PROBLEM/OPPORTUNITY THAT COMPELS ME TO DISCOVER A SOLUTION:

So much of the unhappiness in the world is a function of a gross misunderstanding of what constitutes outstanding leadership.

I have transformed that PROBLEM/OPPORTUNITY to the following PROBLEM/OPPORTUNITY for my company, CEObuilder®, to address:

The CEObuilder® target market is leaders of business enterprises. According to a Gallup report, about 50% of employees have left a job specifically to get away from their manager at some point in their career. Bad bosses/poor leaders are a major factor in employee turnover. In the best of circumstances, bosses are good, well-intentioned people who simply have never learned the principles of effective leadership. Unfortunately, there are also those who have bought into crippling counterfeits that destroy morale and undermine success. Either way, there is a huge opportunity for CEObuilder® to take a key role in growing and developing highly effective leaders!

Why does this opportunity exist? Because the most important and efficacious principles of leadership are simply not taught in our colleges and universities–and that includes MBA and undergraduate business programs. And once bosses are on the job, they are often too busy, too stressed, and too distracted to make the concerted effort necessary to change their attitudes, behaviors, and leadership tactics and strategies. Admittedly, the factors that define this opportunity also make it challenging to gain the attention of the target market. However, with incisive marketing, gaining the attention of even a small fraction of the 32 million small business owners in the United States will set us on the path to expanding interest in and desire for our value proposition.

We are attracted to the opportunity of addressing this problem because we have made the study of true principles of highly effective leadership a focus for over 35 years–and we continue in that endeavor. At its most basic level, this opportunity demands an understanding of the problem: *what is the impact of bad bosses on individuals, businesses, and the world economy?*

According to the artificial intelligence site, ChatGPT, "bad bosses" have a significant negative impact on productivity, morale, and the economic success of businesses in the United States. Their influence can create ripple effects throughout an organization, undermining performance and employee satisfaction. ***Some of the key ways in which bad bosses affect businesses include:***

1. Decreased Productivity

- Micromanagement or poor leadership stifles innovation and motivation, causing employees to feel demotivated or disempowered.

- Employees working under bad bosses are more likely to spend time managing interpersonal conflict or simply disengaging from tasks, leading to lower overall output.

- According to studies, bad leadership can reduce team productivity by up to 50%.

2. Low Morale and Engagement

- Poor leadership contributes to high stress, burnout, and decreased engagement. Employees who feel undervalued or mistreated are less likely to go above and beyond, leading to a culture of disengagement.

- A Gallup report found that 70% of employee engagement variance is directly tied to managers. Bad bosses, therefore, are a leading cause of disengagement.

3. High Employee Turnover

- Bad bosses are a leading cause of employee turnover. One survey showed that 50% of employees left a job because of a bad boss.

- Replacing employees is costly: recruitment, onboarding, and lost productivity during the transition can cost businesses 6 to 9 months of an employee's salary per replacement.

4. Direct Economic Costs

- In terms of direct financial impact, it's estimated that $360 billion in lost productivity is attributed to toxic or ineffective managers annually in the U.S.
- Organizations with poor leadership are less likely to meet their business goals, leading to reduced profitability over time.

5. Brand and Reputation Damage

- Bad bosses can damage a company's brand, leading to negative reviews on platforms like Glassdoor or social media. This can make it harder to attract top talent, impacting long-term success.

In summary, the prevalence of "bad bosses" has far-reaching impacts on employee well-being, productivity, and the economic performance of businesses, with costs that extend beyond the immediate workplace to the broader economy. Effective leadership development and coaching are critical in mitigating these effects.[158]

Contrast this with the positive impact of "good bosses":

"Good bosses" are strongly correlated with increased productivity, higher morale, lower employee turnover, and greater corporate profitability. Effective leadership has a transformative impact on both individual and organizational success, as demonstrated by numerous studies and business outcomes. *Here's a breakdown of how good bosses positively influence these key areas:*

1. Increased Productivity

- Empowerment and autonomy: Good bosses create an environment where employees feel trusted to make decisions, encouraging innovation and a proactive attitude toward work.

---

[158] ChatGPT

- Employees led by strong leaders are often 17% more productive than their peers under poor management, as they receive clear direction, support, and feedback.
- Efficient problem-solving: Good leaders facilitate collaboration, effectively removing roadblocks and ensuring that teams work together smoothly.

2. Higher Morale and Engagement

- Good bosses foster a positive work environment by showing empathy, transparency, and support, leading to higher job satisfaction.
- High morale is often the result of recognition and appreciation, with employees more engaged and committed to their roles.
- A Gallup study revealed that highly engaged teams achieve 21% higher profitability and show a 41% reduction in absenteeism compared to teams with lower engagement.

3. Reduced Employee Turnover

- One of the most critical impacts of good bosses is lower employee turnover. Workers are more likely to stay at a job where they feel respected, supported, and valued.
- A LinkedIn survey showed that employees are 60% more likely to stay with their company if they believe their boss genuinely cares about their development.
- Reducing turnover saves organizations significant costs associated with recruiting, training, and lost productivity. By retaining employees, companies reduce replacement costs that can amount to 150% of an employee's annual salary.

4. Corporate Profitability

- Good leadership directly impacts profitability by aligning team efforts with company goals, ensuring high levels of productivity, and fostering innovation.

- Employee engagement has a strong impact on business outcomes, with companies with high engagement scores having 23% higher profitability than those with low engagement.

- Good bosses also help organizations maintain a positive reputation, making it easier to attract top talent and loyal customers, which in turn contributes to long-term profitability.

5. Enhanced Innovation and Agility

- Good bosses encourage open communication and a culture of experimentation, which fosters innovation. This allows businesses to adapt quickly to market changes and stay competitive.

In conclusion, the presence of good bosses is crucial for driving business success. They create environments where employees thrive, and as a result, their leadership is directly tied to key metrics like productivity, engagement, retention, and profitability. Businesses that invest in developing and retaining strong leaders reap the benefits in both their bottom line and overall organizational health.[159]

Clearly there is a strong market for facilitating the development of highly effective, competent, engaged, and successful leaders, namely "good bosses!"

In addressing ways to serve this market, I pose the following questions to my team at CEObuilder®:

> **What if** we were to publish a series of books and articles sharing true and efficacious leadership principles that produce "good bosses" and visionary leaders, building on the work I have done over the past five decades?

---

[159] ChatGPT

What if we were to develop online training workshops that teach those principles?

What if we were to develop artificial intelligence applications to help scale our ability to share those principles and insights?

What if we were to utilize small group face-to-face forums for intensive discussion of those principles?

What if we were to limit the number of leaders I directly coach, but at the same time adding a broadened value proposition for this small focused group of clients that would engage them as partners in not only applying the principles we teach, but also influencing other leaders to engage in utilizing our leadership products and services?

What if we were to create a program of developing highly competent coaches who are trained to facilitate the development of leaders who they would guide using the principles that CEObuilder® has learned, and continues to learn?

MY PERSONAL VALUE PROPOSITION: *I facilitate the development of highly effective leaders, who in turn, facilitate the development of others. As they transform into outstanding leaders, they will apply the principles they are learning in their families, their communities, and their business enterprises.*

The foundational premise of this value proposition is heliotropic influence through facilitation. Heliotropism, the phenomenon where flowers orient themselves in the direction of the sun, defines for me the appropriate role and behaviors of great leaders wherein they gain appropriate, trusted, and respected influence with their constituents.

Facilitation excellence is the key skill whereby I serve as a coach, teacher, and leader in sharing the heliotropic leadership style with others. Facilitation is the foundational skill on which I believe virtually all other leadership skills are built—and it is the primary skill which I strive to teach other leaders.

When done well, this value proposition eliminates the pain of anger, depression, and poor engagement in virtually any family or organization. (See Chapter 7E, page 283)

I have transformed that MY PERSONAL VALUE PROPOSITION into the following VALUE PROPOSITION for my company, CEObuilder®:

We at CEObuilder® facilitate the development of highly effective leaders, who in turn, facilitate the development of their people into highly effective leaders within their respective areas of authority and influence. As these bosses transform into outstanding leaders, they will apply the principles they are learning in their business enterprises.

The foundational premise of this value proposition is <u>heliotropic leadership, primarily manifested through facilitative skills</u>. Heliotropic leadership is a leadership philosophy based on the concept that individuals, like plants, are naturally drawn toward positive energy, growth, and life-affirming experiences, much as plants grow toward sunlight (a process known as heliotropism). In this leadership model, leaders focus on creating environments and relationships that foster positive emotions, personal development, and thriving performance.

Heliotropic leaders, and we who coach them, emphasize strengths-based approaches, inspire through optimism and positive vision, and cultivate psychological safety and trust in their teams. They seek to energize and uplift others by providing support, candid and timely feedback, encouragement, and opportunities for growth, recognizing that people tend to perform better when they are in an environment filled with positive reinforcement, trust, and mutual respect.

This approach, often associated with positive organizational psychology, asserts that focusing on well-being, candor, and positive behaviors in the workplace leads to greater engagement, creativity, and productivity. We at CEObuilder® strive to consistently and continuously provide this value to our clients—and to one another.

Facilitation excellence is the key skill underlying our value proposition whereby we at CEObuilder® serve as coaches, teachers, and leaders in sharing the heliotropic leadership style overlaid on successful alignment and execution of the key strategic components of the Business Success Pyramid. Facilitation is the foundational skill on which we believe virtually all other leadership skills are built—and it is the primary skill which we strive to teach other leaders.

When done well, this value proposition eliminates the pain of anger, depression, and poor engagement in virtually any organization. It builds trust in leaders and reduces (if not eliminates) high employee turnover, litigation, and enterprise failure. The gains enjoyed as a result of this value proposition are readily apparent. Each element of the Business Success Pyramid will improve including, of course, financial outcomes.

THE MARKET FOR MY PERSONAL VALUE PROPOSITION: *Wherever there are bosses– including parents, teachers, athletic coaches, church leaders, administrators, and business executives– there is a market for improving leadership skills. This means that for me, personally, there is a limitless target market. (See Chapter 7E, page 284)*

I have transformed that PERSONAL TARGET MARKET into the following TARGET MARKET for my company, CEObuilder®:

Our target market at CEObuilder®, broadly stated, is business executives, including entrepreneurial startup pioneers, incoming appointees or new owners of existing companies, ongoing CEOs, and division or functional executives. These people typically have 1-20 direct reports for whom they have responsibility for assuring that each report is competent, engaged, and productive as individual contributors to the vision (purpose, mission, and values) of the enterprise for which they work.

Globally, there are millions of business executives who fit this definition, considering the leadership teams of both large corporations and small to medium-sized enterprises. As of recent estimates, there are roughly 50-60 million business executives across all sectors worldwide, but this number can fluctuate depending on how the term "executive" is defined (e.g., C-suite, vice-presidents, general managers, etc.).

Based on the current number of businesses and leadership roles, the number of business executives in the U.S. is estimated to be between 5-7 million, not including small business and entrepreneurial startups. It does include top executives in large corporations and mid-sized businesses.

Fortune 500 companies typically have large executive teams, but the number of executives can vary per company. On average, each Fortune 500 company might have 20-50 executives including C-suite, senior leadership, and board members. This results in an estimated 10,000-25,000 executives across the Fortune 500.

While the global market is huge, as is the U.S. and Fortune 500, these are not the primary focus of CEObuilder®. The companies that populate that market generally have significant barriers that will prevent our entry, including internal HR functions and board oversight that purposely limits their exposure to companies like CEObuilder®.

Small businesses (defined by the U.S. Small Business Administration as companies with fewer than 500 employees), on the other hand, generally have fewer and less zealous barriers—and they are a huge part of the U.S. economy. There are approximately 32 million small businesses in the U.S., nearly all having one to five executives. A conservative estimate of executives in small businesses would be somewhere between 35 and 50 million. Added to this is about 500,000 to 700,000 new businesses started annually. Startups typically have smaller leadership teams, so the estimated number of executives each year in entrepreneurial startups is around 1-2 million.

In summary, the size of the target market for CEObuilder®'s value proposition when focused on small businesses and entrepreneurs alone is at least 50 million—and continues to grow each year by at least 1 million new executives. One-tenth of 1% of this market would be a market of 5,000 executives, which at a conservative estimate of $10,000 per client per year would create a top-line revenue of $50 million annually. Of course, this represents a long-term view of what the CEObuilder® economic engine might generate. More

contemporary revenue estimates will be factored into CEObuilder®
plans and forecasts.

MY PERSONAL LEGACY: *My legacy is–and will be–the leaders
that I have helped develop through my facilitation, coaching, and
support. I hope that the principles I have shared–and will continue
to share–will be similarly facilitated, coached, and supported by each
of them as they develop future leaders. In that way, my legacy will
continue beyond my life. (See Chapter 7E, page 284)*

I have transformed my PERSONAL LEGACY into
the following LEGACY for my company, CEObuilder®:

*The legacy of CEObuilder® is–and will be–the exemplary leaders
that we have helped develop through our facilitation, coaching,
and support. The principles we have shared through our coaching,
forums, education programs, publications, and delivery systems
will have empowered them to become heliotropic "process" leaders
who deliver outstanding "content" (strategies and tactics that fulfill
each element of the Business Success Pyramid) through exceptional
alignment and execution. These leaders employ those principles
in developing future leaders within their enterprises, who in turn,
develop others.*

E–MY PERSONAL ETHOS, BELIEFS & VALUES: *People are
most important in my life. I love my fellow man and seek to serve him
or her wherever possible. This is the focus of my personal vision and
my work. This sets the foundation for the other personal values that
govern my thoughts and actions, which include:*

- I desire to live with integrity characterized by courage combined
  with kindness
- I desire to lead with confidence combined with humility in
  taking on and meeting challenges
- I am a lifelong learner, teacher, and facilitator

- I seek to be an energetic and optimistic problem-solver

- I seek to be a value-creator

- I want to be worthy of the faith, trust, and respect of my fellow man

- I recognize the extraordinary potential and inherent flaws in myself and my fellowman. Because of this, I strive to be a source of continuous encouragement to improvement coupled with unfeigned compassion, and forgiveness. In that regard, I desire to be heliotropic, a source of leadership truth and light. (See Chapter 7E, pages 284-285)

I have transformed my PERSONAL ETHOS, BELIEFS & VALUES into the following ETHOS, BELIEFS & VALUES for my company, CEObuilder®:

People, including our co-workers, associates, clients, vendors, and owners are the most important part of the CEObuilder® business. We strive to treat each and every one with the same love and respect that we hope to receive ourselves. We seek to truly serve him or her whenever and wherever possible. This attitude, and its attendant behaviors, sets the foundation for the other personal values that govern our thoughts and actions, which include:

- We will live with integrity characterized by courage combined with kindness

- We will lead with confidence combined with humility in taking on and meeting challenges

- We are lifelong learners, teachers, and facilitators

- We are energetic and optimistic problem-solvers

- We are value-creators

- We are worthy of the faith, trust, and respect of our fellow man

- We recognize both the extraordinary potential and inherent flaws in ourselves and our fellowman. Because of this, we strive to be a source of continuous encouragement to improvement coupled with unfeigned compassion, and forgiveness. In that regard, we strive to be heliotropic, a source of leadership truth and light.

R–MY PERSONAL RESOLVE as stated in the *PACER Action Model:*
P: Plan — My plan for actualizing my personal vision includes:

- Learning Daily
- Serving Daily
- Facilitating Daily

A: Act — This is where the rubber meets the road. I will execute the Plan. It is achievable as I resolve firmly to enact it!

C: Control — **For Control to be effective, I must have metrics against which I will track my progress. I will apply the metrics shared in Chapter 7E, page 286-287.**

- **Learning Daily:**
  - Spiritually
  - Physically
  - Intellectually
  - Emotionally
  - Career Growth and Development
- **Serving Daily**
- **Facilitating Daily**

E: Evaluate — Using those key metrics, I am able to compare my actions and outcomes to my plans. This allows me to assess my commitment, and my ability to carry out my plans.

R: Revise — I will readily revise my plans and/or actions as needed in order to achieve the goals that will lead to fulfilling my Vision. I will not be frustrated by the need to pivot, but will see such revisions as opportunities to improve.

R: Reward — I will enjoy the fruits of this process.

I have transformed my PERSONAL RESOLVE into the following RESOLVE for my company, CEObuilder®:

P: Plan — The CEObuilder® strategic plan for actualizing our company vision includes:

- **Learning Daily; we are essentially an education company, and as such, we must stay on the "bleeding edge" of knowledge and wisdom that facilitates exemplary leadership. This requires:**
  - o Consistent and continual study of current and historic written, audio, and video material, as well as mindful engagement with smart and challenging people within the disciplines of commerce, behavioral science, problem-solving, and creative/design thinking. While this is especially important at the executive level of our company, we encourage this manifestation of our corporate value of "learning" to be extended to every member of our team. We regularly discuss ways to incorporate new learning into the models and processes that we employ in facilitating the exemplary leadership of our clients. We share what we are learning liberally in our coaching, forums, workshops, and publications. We package our intellectual property in unique and attractive ways whereby it can be marketed and sold effectively.
  - o In order to be continuously engaged intellectually at a high level, we must be physically healthy. To assure that, as an organization, we maintain a level of physical fitness that matches our intellectual demands, we work to sustain the wellness of each member of our team by providing

opportunities for exercise, diet, appropriate professional advice, and recreation.

○ As an organization of intense, focused mental engagement with one another and our clients, we must also maintain a high level of both organizational and individual "emotional intelligence." In support of this necessity, we encourage team members to engage openly (without fear of retribution) in discussion and debate regarding problems and opportunities. We stress the importance of interacting in a heliotropic and empathetic manner with each other, while still candidly addressing challenges. We also encourage team members to regularly carve out time for introspection, meditation, recreation, and social interaction.

○ CEObuilder® is committed to the career growth and development of each team member as is manifested through interaction with business partners, co-workers, clients, and other stakeholders. We encourage each team member to think creatively, and share their thoughts and understandings of true leadership and business principles, both in oral and written form.

- **Serve Daily:** As in most companies, each team member at CEObuilder® has a specific job to perform which represents their primary responsibility. This may be largely focused on the internal functions of our business, or it may be mostly aimed at our clients. While this focus is essential, we encourage each of our team members to broaden their vision to include everyone with whom they come into contact over the course of their working day–and seek opportunities to render valuable service to one or more individuals outside the purview of their job description. This may be as simple as a smile, a word of encouragement, or an expression of empathy or gratitude in word, text or email. Or it could be as heroic as helping someone in dire straits–or even saving a life. The objective is to be truly heliotropic, sharing light that lifts and supports others.

- **Facilitate Daily:** Through questioning, listening, and occasionally expounding, CEObuilder® team members help their co-workers, clients, and others to discover true principles whereby they are able to grow, develop, and succeed. We seek opportunities in this regard as often as possible, both in our work and in our personal lives. And we liberally share the stories of doing so with one another. In this way, we maintain and grow our facilitative culture.

A: Act — We, the team members at CEObuilder®, are responsible to execute the Plan–to live it!

C: Control — For Control to be effective, CEObuilder® must have metrics against which we will track our progress as a business. These metrics include:

- **Learning Daily:**
  - Intellectual Metrics: Each team member will select at least one book and one periodical article to read (or listen to) per month. These may be selected by the individual, or may be assigned to address specific areas for knowledge acquisition. The team member will write a book review and a "key points" summary which he or she may present at an "all-hands knowledge sharing" meeting during the month following their reading. Artificial intelligence or online book reviews may be used in preparing the written review, but the team member must make sure that they address the following key questions in the review:

    1. For what purpose did the author write this book?
    2. What are the most important and compelling insights you gained from reading the book?
    3. What are the weaknesses in the book?
    4. How might this book be valuable to our clients, specifically the leaders in client companies?

5. Therefore, what? How will you use what you've learned? How might CEObuilder® use these insights?

6. Do you recommend that others read this book? Who, specifically, should read it?

The CEObuilder® executive team will assess if–and how–the knowledge gained in this process might enhance our models and processes. Where it is deemed valuable, it will be used in the ongoing development and refinement of those models and processes.

○   Health & Wellness Metrics: At CEObuilder®, we recognize the very personal (and often private) nature of each person's health and fitness. However, we encourage each team member to track their own unique metrics. These might include weight, blood pressure, blood glucose levels, nutrition, exercise, sleep, and any medications for which they have been prescribed. We encourage each team member to be sensitive to wellness concerns they may observe in others–and to be encouraging and supportive. Where possible, the company will invest in wellness programs to help our team members stay healthy.

○   Emotional Metrics: Here again, personal and private concerns make corporate metrics difficult, if not impossible. However, at the ownership and executive levels, we strive to observe and discern the emotional needs of individuals and the engagement level of the team as a whole. We regularly review together the "emotional state" of the company to identify areas for concern and intervention. In this regard, we believe in identifying and responding to such issues early, with both courage and compassion. In the realm of prevention rather than intervention, we are committed to creating and maintaining an empathetic and heliotropic work environment and scheduling and carrying out company recreational activities at least four times each year.

○ Career Growth & Development Metrics: We will track the career progress of each team member in terms of their competence and engagement in their current job assignment, as well as their potential for growing into more significant roles in the future. We will candidly review and assess their performance in job specifics including both actual work and results compared to planned actions and desired outcomes. Each reviewee will also evaluate the leader to whom they report to give a frank assessment of how well they have been sustained and supported in their job performance and their career growth and development. While periodic formal reviews will be conducted, informal day-to-day interactions between reviewers and reviewees are encouraged; a tight feedback loop facilitates effective communication, agility, empathy, mutual respect, and trust.

- **Serving Daily:** As owners and executives we will model heliotropic leadership, and will recognize it and draw attention to it as we observe it in our team members, clients, vendors, and others. Periodically, as the CEObuilder® top leadership group, we will assess our trajectory in being truly heliotropic–and how those behaviors are impacting our business, and the operations of our client companies.

- **Facilitating Daily:** We will consciously use our facilitation skills and will train our team members, coaches, and clients to use those essential skills as leaders in their own areas of responsibility. Each coaching and training situation will provide an opportunity to assess the frequency with which we employ our facilitative models and processes, as well as the effectiveness we are experiencing as we do so. We will assign those at the executive level to share, through oral and written accounts, the growth and development of the CEObuilder® culture. Over the course of each year, these stories will help us track the use and expertise of our company in facilitating exemplary leadership.

E: Evaluate — With the preceding key metrics in place, the ownership and executive team at CEObuilder® will be able to compare actions and outcomes to our plans. This will allow us to:

- Assess our ongoing commitment, as well as our abilities, to carry out our plans.

- We will be able to evaluate *cause and effect* regarding the relationship between our actions and the outcomes we desire.

- We will be acutely aware of any *variances* between what we planned to do–and what we actually did, shortfalls as well as those areas where our performance exceeds expectations. Shortfalls will lead us to ask *why?* — and our answers will help us consider changes to our plan or our actions, or both. When we exceed expectations, we will also ask *why?* Was this an aberration or random occurrence, or is this level of performance sustainable? Should the plan be revised?

- As we continue to control, on a periodic basis, we will gain an increasingly clear picture of our strengths, weaknesses, and areas for improvement, focusing our attention on areas for plan revision.

- We will share our evaluative insights with trusted advisors and mentors--and regularly seek their inputs.

R: Revise — We will readily revise our plans and/or actions as needed in order to achieve the goals that will lead to fulfilling our Vision. We will not be frustrated by the need to pivot, but will see such revisions as opportunities to improve.

R: Reward — We will enjoy the fruits of this process.

Having completed the process of using the *PACER Visioning Model* for both my personal and company vision, I arrived at an important destination. Assuming you are still reading and following that model, I hope you, too, have reached that milestone. If so, you may well relate to the description coined by several of my clients that I have alluded to earlier; they've called it a "greasy grind!."

While I would prefer a more attractive label, I have to admit that, when done right–and thoroughly–the process is intensely introspective, time-consuming, and often even quite emotional. I don't apologize for this; that is how it should be. At this point, you should have arrived at an articulate definition of your personal purpose, and how that purpose is the heart and soul of your career–and your business.

And now with that articulation in hand, you are ready to share your vision with your team!

CHAPTER 9

It's Time to Open Your Kimono-Sharing Your Vision and Your Emerging Strategies with Your Advocates— and Your Adversaries

In every man there is something wherein I may learn of him, and in that I am his pupil.

Ralph Waldo Emerson

A wise man will hear, and will increase learning; and a man of understanding shall attain unto wise counsels.

Proverbs 1:5

Have you learned lessons only of those who admired you, and were tender with you, and stood aside you? Have you not learned great lessons from those who rejected you, and braced themselves against you, or disputed the passage with you?

Walt Whitman

A leader has two important characteristics; first, he is going somewhere, second, he is able to persuade other people to go with him.

Maximilien François Robespierre

You are now at the point in which your vision has been well articulated in terms of your Personal Purpose, Mission, and Values. You have resolved to align your life and your business pursuits with that vision. Although this is unique to you, and very personal, you will not move forward without the enthusiastic engagement of others. If you are launching a new venture, these may be friends and associates whom you will, or have, invited to join you. If you are the leader of an existing enterprise, they will likely be those of your existing executive team. And, if you have been appointed to a new leadership position within an existing business, you may have a combination of those individuals you have inherited and those whom you will select.

In any case, you have the opportunity and challenge of sharing your vision–and requesting honest, unvarnished, and objective feedback on your vision from this constituency. You must grant, even expect, each team member to act in the role of both *advocate* and *adversary* for your vision.

This will be challenging for them, and for you. If and when your team too readily agrees with your vision, you will need to press them to challenge each key element, including the strategies that must grow out of it. And when they present such challenges, you must steel yourself to avoid being offended. Instead, you must field their concerns and ask for their ideas on how to strengthen your vision, making it a source of energy and organizational passion. The goal is not a "rubber-stamped" agreement, but rather a strong sense of shared purpose, mission, and values that each team member will evangelize within the enterprise, as well as with customers, vendors, and other stakeholders.

This necessarily means that revealing your vision and discussing it will not be one brief meeting. Indeed, in all likelihood, it will require a number of long group discussions, and maybe many one-on-one conferences. Plan on your interactions with these stakeholders to be several meetings of what author, Kim Scott, calls "radical candor;" in other words, no holds barred.

It will be essential that both you, and each member of your team, take notes. White board brainstorming and other visuals should be photographed and distributed. If emails or texts are utilized to convey concerns or ideas among the team, you should make sure that they are fully distributed to each team member. In the case of an existing enterprise, care should be taken to keep discussions and documentation confidential until you–and your team–are fully committed to introducing the finalized vision to your entire company.

There is an explicit process goal at this stage: to go from the words of your vision to the strategies, actions, and behaviors that will define not only what you do, but also the culture you desire. To that end, I recommend you consider working with your team using the following 12 Step Process:

1. Share your company Vision with key stakeholders. For me, that is my executive team at CEObuilder®. You will see that I have taken the insights from chapters 7a to 7e, and Chapter 8, and have packaged them in a document for my executive team to read (see PROPOSED REVISED CEObuilder® VISION, pages 323 to 341 at the end of this chapter).

2. Each essential element of vision (purpose, mission, and values) is questioned and debated. Adversarial posturing is not discouraged; indeed, it is expected as much as advocacy for the vision.

3. Major areas of concern are addressed—and if necessary, the vision will be rearticulated to reflect the best inputs of key stakeholders. Any revision, however, must resonate completely with you, the leader.

4. Consensus of key stakeholders is important, if not essential. Anyone unable to support the final articulation of the vision should reconsider playing a key role in moving forward.

5. Collaboratively develop goals and strategies which extend from, and align with, your vision.

6. Define expected costs and benefits of goals and strategies. Assure that benefits have a significant probability of exceeding costs. When this is apparent, commit to move forward.

7. Define the competencies that are required to achieve goals and strategies, including definition of key leadership and operating positions, desired outcomes for those roles, and how leadership will sustain the people who occupy those positions.

8. Share Vision, Goals, Strategies, and Key Roles with the broader team—with all employees. A period of Q&A will be essential to develop early buy-in. Do not discourage questions or challenges. Address everything that your people raise as concerns, options, or opportunities.

9. Pledge allegiance to the Plan. This means that with the exception of unanticipated concerns, compliance by all executives, employees, and other stakeholders is expected in order to "align" the organization and "execute" strategies and key roles.

10. Continuous Feedback & Improvement. Execution will be measured against its Alignment with Plans (vision, goals, strategies, and key roles). Variances from Plans as well as variances in Desired Outcomes will be evaluated regularly for periodic revision and improvement. (Recall the *PACER* Action Model).

11. Metrics will be developed to track the competency and engagement of all key stakeholders, the operational effectiveness and efficiency of enterprise operations, customer satisfaction and resonance with the value proposition, and financial outcomes.

12. Rewards will accrue to all key stakeholders as we Align & Execute!

The emphasis in this chapter, of course, is on step 1. You will proceed with your executive team from sharing your Vision through steps 2 through 7. Resist the temptation to rush that process. My experience has shown that a deliberate process of addressing each step renders better results than a full-court-press to get done quickly.

An early symptom of rushing is if your team readily agrees with everything you have presented to them. If that happens, challenge them to find weaknesses in your thinking. And don't let them off the hook! If they don't identify any soft spots, wait them out; tolerate silence, don't view the lack of response as acceptance.

When you follow the 12 Step Process with open discussion and a willingness to address concerns and differing opinions, the process inevitably delivers the essential foundation for operationalizing your company vision, your enterprise WHY.

The Proposed Revised CEObuilder® Vision that I shared with my team follows, beginning on this page. It shares as much information as I can comfortably give you without getting deeper into our final document and the strategies and tactics that emerged from the process.

As the founder and chief executive of CEObuilder® which is now a 35 year-old company, I am definitely an Ongoing Leader. While the revised vision does not depart significantly from earlier versions, it does serve to reorient and refocus our purpose, mission and value proposition, and also provides new alignment and execution for the company. My team offered several significant ideas to strengthen the language regarding its various components, but there were ultimately few substantive changes.

After several readings and revisions over a period of two and a half weeks, we had navigated our way through the first four steps in the 12 Step Process. Steps 5, 6, and 7 took a bit longer, but rendered an answer to the overarching question: *Based on this CEObuilder® Vision...THEREFORE, WHAT?*

Goals, desired key results, strategies, tactics, roles and competencies emerged and were reviewed against each element of the Business Success Pyramid. From these discussions, we were able to make a full commitment to the plan, and share it beyond the executive team.

PROPOSED REVISED CEObuilder® VISION

PURPOSE

CEObuilder®'s purpose is to develop leaders; to serve their inherent need to become highly effective in leading people and enterprises to superior levels of competency, engagement, and success.

We recognize the potential in every business executive to become an outstanding leader–whether they are an entrepreneurial startup pioneer, an incoming appointee or new owner of an existing company, an ongoing CEO, or a division or functional executive. For such business leaders, the CEObuilder® cause is to transform the typical lesser vision of themselves from being commonplace bosses to becoming exemplary visionary leaders who, in turn, facilitate the development of other outstanding leaders.

The legacy of CEObuilder® is–and will be–the exemplary leaders that we have helped develop through our facilitation, coaching, and support. The principles we have shared through our coaching, forums, education programs, publications, and delivery systems will have empowered them to be heliotropic "process" leaders who deliver outstanding "content" (strategies and tactics that fulfill each element of our Business Success Pyramid) through exceptional alignment and execution. These leaders employ the principles they have learned to develop future leaders, who in turn, develop others.

MISSION

Our mission at CEObuilder® is to care deeply about the leaders with whom we interact. This caring is displayed in the CEObuilder® commitment to continuously learn true principles of effective leadership–and to deliver those principles to our clients through outstanding teaching, coaching, and facilitation.

The Value Proposition that extends from this mission:

We at CEObuilder® facilitate the development of highly effective leaders, who in turn, facilitate the development of their people into highly effective leaders within their respective areas of authority and influence. As these bosses transform into outstanding leaders, they apply the principles they are learning in their business enterprises.

The foundational premise of this value proposition is *heliotropic leadership, primarily manifested through facilitative skills.* Heliotropic leadership is a leadership philosophy based on the concept that individuals, like plants, are naturally drawn toward positive energy, growth, and life-affirming experiences, much as plants grow toward sunlight (a process known as heliotropism). In this leadership model, leaders focus on creating environments and relationships that foster positive emotions, personal development, and thriving performance.

Heliotropic leaders, and we who coach them, emphasize strengths-based approaches, inspire through optimism and positive vision, and cultivate psychological safety and trust in their teams. They seek to energize and uplift others by providing support, candid and timely feedback, encouragement, and opportunities for growth, recognizing that people tend to perform better when they are in an environment filled with positive reinforcement, trust, and mutual respect.

This approach, often associated with positive organizational psychology, asserts that focusing on well-being, candor, and positive behaviors in the workplace leads to greater engagement, creativity, and productivity. We at CEObuilder® strive to consistently and continuously provide the value of adopting this approach within our client companies–and within CEObuilder® itself.

Facilitation excellence is the key skill underlying our value proposition whereby we at CEObuilder® serve as coaches, teachers, and leaders in sharing the heliotropic leadership style overlaid on successful alignment and execution of the key strategic components of the Business Success Pyramid (illustration shown on page 341). Facilitation is the foundational skill on which we believe virtually all other leadership skills are built—and it is the primary skill which we strive to teach other leaders.

When done well, our value proposition will eliminate the pain of anger, depression, and poor engagement in virtually any organization. It builds trust in leaders and reduces (if not eliminates) high employee turnover, litigation, and enterprise failure. The gains enjoyed as a result of this value proposition are readily apparent. Each element of the Business Success Pyramid will improve including, of course, financial outcomes.

We deliver this value proposition through the competency and engagement of the CEObuilder® team, who possess the following strengths which they bring to their jobs everyday.

We are:

1. ***Learners & Maximizers:*** *We share an insatiable desire to learn and continually improve ourselves. We strive to stay ahead of trends, constantly seek new tools, and share insights, creating the CEObuilder® culture of continuous development. In this regard, we seek to grow each other, as we grow our clients.*

2. ***Contextualists & Archivists:*** *We recognize the great value of learning from the past. In that regard, we seek to understand historical context and we archive the knowledge that extends from the insights we gain. We utilize what we have learned to teach from a rich repository of lessons, examples, and best practices, helping other leaders navigate complexity and avoid repeating past mistakes.*

3. ***Strategists & Analysts:*** *We are inherently detectives; we seek to identify patterns and analyze cause-and-effect relationships, and we coach others to develop this type of strategic and analytical thinking, helping them to anticipate challenges and make informed decisions.*

4. ***Achievers:*** *We seek high personal productivity whereby goals and tasks are met, and provide a strong example for others within our company–and for our clients. This relentless drive for achievement is infectious, motivating others to also work diligently toward their own success.*

5. ***People-Focused & Bridge-builders:*** *We have a keen interest in understanding the unique qualities of each individual, thereby fostering empathy and connection. In this regard, we excel at identifying the inherent strengths of others, helping them to pursue roles where they can thrive. We help build collaboration at CEObuilder®, and within the companies of our clients.*

6. *Facilitators: We recognize that asking insightful questions is an invaluable facilitative skill. Our strength in questioning, listening, and facilitating involves key stakeholders in problem-solving processes, ensuring buy-in and collective ownership–both within CEObuilder® and in our client companies.*

7. *Connectors: Because of our intense focus on others and their needs and desires, we enjoy the ability to connect ideas, people, and stories that can inspire other leaders to think holistically and cultivate stronger teams.*

THE TARGET MARKET

The CEObuilder® target market for our value proposition is bad bosses and poor leaders who come to recognize their existential need to change, and good bosses and passable leaders who want to grow to their full potential.

According to a Gallup report, about 50% of employees have left a job specifically to get away from their manager at some point in their career. Bad bosses/poor leaders are a major factor in employee turnover.

In the best of circumstances, bosses are good, well-intentioned people who simply have never learned the principles of effective leadership. Unfortunately, there are also those who have bought into crippling counterfeits that destroy morale and undermine success. Either way, there is a huge opportunity for CEObuilder® to take a key role in growing and developing highly effective leaders!

Why does this opportunity exist? Because the most important and efficacious principles of leadership are simply not taught in our colleges and universities–and that includes MBA and undergraduate business programs. And once bosses are on the job, they are often too busy, too stressed, and too distracted to make the concerted effort necessary to change their attitudes, behaviors, and leadership tactics and strategies. Admittedly, the factors that define this opportunity also make it challenging to gain the attention of the target market. However, with incisive marketing, gaining the attention of even a small fraction of the 32 million small business owners in the United States will set us on the path to expanding interest in and desire for our value proposition.

We are attracted to the opportunity of addressing this problem because the principals of CEObuilder® have made the study of true principles of highly effective leadership our focus for over 50 years–and we continue in that endeavor. At its most basic level, this opportunity demands an understanding of the problem: *what is the impact of bad bosses on individuals, businesses, and the world economy?*

According to the artificial intelligence site, ChatGPT, "bad bosses" have a significant negative impact on productivity, morale, and the economic success of businesses in the United States. Their influence can create ripple effects throughout an organization, undermining performance and employee satisfaction. *Some of the key ways in which bad bosses affect businesses include:*

1. Decreased Productivity

  ○ Micromanagement or poor leadership stifles innovation and motivation, causing employees to feel demotivated or disempowered.

  ○ Employees working under bad bosses are more likely to spend time managing interpersonal conflict or simply disengaging from tasks, leading to lower overall output.

  ○ According to studies, bad leadership can reduce team productivity by up to 50%.

2. Low Morale and Engagement

  ○ Poor leadership contributes to high stress, burnout, and decreased engagement. Employees who feel undervalued or mistreated are less likely to go above and beyond, leading to a culture of disengagement.

  ○ A Gallup report found that 70% of employee engagement variance is directly tied to managers. Bad bosses, therefore, are a leading cause of disengagement.

3. High Employee Turnover

- ○ Bad bosses are a leading cause of employee turnover. One survey showed that 50% of employees left a job because of a bad boss also.

- ○ Replacing employees is costly: recruitment, onboarding, and lost productivity during the transition can cost businesses 6 to 9 months of an employee's salary per replacement.

4. Direct Economic Costs

- ○ In terms of direct financial impact, it's estimated that $360 billion in lost productivity is attributed to toxic or ineffective managers annually in the U.S.

- ○ Organizations with poor leadership are less likely to meet their business goals, leading to reduced profitability over time.

5. Brand and Reputation Damage

- ○ Bad bosses can damage a company's brand, leading to negative reviews on platforms like Glassdoor or social media. This can make it harder to attract top talent, impacting long-term success.

In summary, the prevalence of "bad bosses" has far-reaching impacts on employee well-being, productivity, and the economic performance of businesses, with costs that extend beyond the immediate workplace to the broader economy. Effective leadership development and coaching are critical in mitigating these effects.[160] Contrast this with the positive impact of "good bosses": "Good bosses" are strongly correlated with increased productivity, higher morale, lower employee turnover, and greater corporate profitability. Effective leadership has a transformative impact on both individual and organizational success, as demonstrated by numerous studies and business outcomes. ***Here's a breakdown of how good bosses positively influence these key areas:***

---

[160] ChatGPT

1. **Increased Productivity**
   - Empowerment and autonomy: Good bosses create an environment where employees feel trusted to make decisions, encouraging innovation and a proactive attitude toward work.
   - Employees led by strong leaders are often 17% more productive than their peers under poor management, as they receive clear direction, support, and feedback.
   - Efficient problem-solving: Good leaders facilitate collaboration, effectively removing roadblocks and ensuring that teams work together smoothly.

2. **Higher Morale and Engagement**
   - Good bosses foster a positive work environment by showing empathy, transparency, and support, leading to higher job satisfaction.
   - High morale is often the result of recognition and appreciation, with employees more engaged and committed to their roles.
   - A Gallup study revealed that highly engaged teams achieve 21% greater profitability and show a 41% reduction in absenteeism compared to teams with lower engagement.

3. **Reduced Employee Turnover**
   - One of the most critical impacts of good bosses is lower employee turnover. Workers are more likely to stay at a job where they feel respected, supported, and valued.
   - A LinkedIn survey showed that employees are 60% more likely to stay with their company if they believe their boss genuinely cares about their development.
   - Reducing turnover saves organizations significant costs associated with recruiting, training, and lost productivity. By retaining employees, companies reduce replacement costs that can amount to 150% of an employee's annual salary.

4. Corporate Profitability

- ○ Good leadership directly impacts profitability by aligning team efforts with company goals, ensuring high levels of productivity, and fostering innovation.

- ○ Employee engagement has a strong impact on business outcomes, with companies with high engagement scores having 23% higher profitability than those with low engagement.

- ○ Good bosses also help organizations maintain a positive reputation, making it easier to attract top talent and loyal customers, which in turn contributes to long-term profitability.

5. Enhanced Innovation and Agility

- ○ Good bosses encourage open communication and a culture of experimentation, which fosters innovation. This allows businesses to adapt quickly to market changes and stay competitive.

In conclusion, the presence of good bosses is crucial for driving business success. They create environments where employees thrive, and as a result, their leadership is directly tied to key metrics like productivity, engagement, retention, and profitability. Businesses that invest in developing and retaining strong leaders reap the benefits in both their bottom line and overall organizational health.[161]

Clearly there is a strong market for facilitating the development of highly effective, competent, engaged, and successful leaders, namely "good bosses!"

---

[161] ChatGPT

The size and economic potential of this market:

Broadly stated, the market includes business executives, including entrepreneurial startup pioneers, incoming appointees or new owners of existing companies, ongoing CEOs, and division or functional executives.

These people typically have 1-20 direct reports for whom they have responsibility to assure that each report is competent, engaged, and productive as individual contributors to achievement of the vision (purpose, mission, and values) of the enterprise for which they work.

Globally, there are millions of business executives who fit this definition, considering the leadership teams of both large corporations and small-to-medium-sized enterprises. As of recent estimates, there are roughly 50-60 million business executives across all sectors worldwide, but this number can fluctuate depending on how the term "executive" is defined (e.g., C-suite, vice-presidents, general managers, etc.).

Based on the current number of businesses and leadership roles, the number of executives in large and mid-sized companies in the U.S. is estimated to be between 5-7 million. This excludes executives in small business and entrepreneurial startups.

Fortune 500 companies typically have large executive teams, but the number of executives can vary per company. On average, each Fortune 500 company might have 20-50 executives including C-suite, senior leadership, and board members. This results in an estimated 10,000-25,000 executives across the Fortune 500.

While the global market is huge, as is the U.S. and Fortune 500, these are not the primary focus of CEObuilder®. The companies that populate that market generally have significant barriers that will prevent our entry, including internal HR functions and board oversight that purposely limits their exposure to companies like CEObuilder®.

Small businesses (defined by the U.S. Small Business Administration as companies with fewer than 500 employees), on the other hand, generally have fewer and less zealous barriers–and they are a huge part of the U.S. economy. There are approximately 32 million small businesses in the U.S., nearly all having one to five executives.

A conservative estimate of executives in small businesses would be somewhere between 35 and 50 million. Added to this is about 500,000 to 700,000 new businesses started annually. Startups typically have smaller leadership teams, so the estimated number of executives each year in entrepreneurial startups is around 1-2 million.

In summary, the size of the target market for CEObuilder®'s value proposition when focused on small businesses and entrepreneurs alone is at least 50 million–and continues to grow each year by about 1 million new executives. One-tenth of 1% of this market would be a market of 5,000 executives, which at a conservative estimate of $10,000 per client per year would create a top-line revenue of $50 million annually. Of course, this represents a long-term view of what the CEObuilder® economic engine might generate. More contemporary revenue estimates will be factored into CEObuilder® plans and forecasts.

In addressing ways to serve this market, the following questions are posed to the team at CEObuilder®:

What if we were to publish a series of books and articles sharing true and efficacious leadership principles that produce "good bosses" and visionary leaders, building on the work we have done over the past five decades?

What if we were to develop online training workshops that teach those principles?

What if we were to develop artificial intelligence applications to help scale our ability to share those principles and insights?

What if we were to utilize small group face-to-face forums for intensive discussion of those principles?

What if we were to limit the number of leaders coached by Rich Tyson to those with whom we might partner in emphasizing, highlighting, and marketing our key processes, content, and models, thereby adding a broadened value proposition for this small focused group of clients while also influencing a broader market for CEObuilder® services and products?

What if we were to create a program of developing highly competent coaches who are trained to facilitate the development of leaders who they would guide using the principles that CEObuilder® has learned, and continues to learn?

From the answers that emerge from addressing these questions (and others that may arise), CEObuilder® will begin to zero in on specific strategies and tactics whereby we can intensify serving our target market.

CEObuilder® CORE VALUES

People, including our co-workers, associates, clients, vendors, and owners are the prime focus of CEObuilder® as a business. We strive to treat each and every one with the same love and respect that we hope to receive ourselves. We seek to truly serve him or her whenever and wherever possible. This attitude, and its attendant behaviors, sets the foundation for the other personal values that govern our thoughts and actions, which include:

- We live with integrity characterized by courageous candor combined with kindness and empathy as we interact together
- We lead in our respective roles with confidence harmonized with humility in taking on and meeting challenges
- We are lifelong learners, teachers, and facilitators
- We are energetic and optimistic problem-solvers
- We are value-creators
- We are worthy of the faith, trust, and respect of our fellow man

- We recognize both the extraordinary potential and inherent flaws in ourselves and our fellowman. Because of this, we strive to be a source of continuous encouragement toward improvement coupled with unfeigned compassion, and forgiveness. In that regard, we strive to be heliotropic, a source of leadership truth and light.

OUR RESOLVE

P: Plan — The CEObuilder® strategic plan for actualizing our company vision includes:

- <u>Learning Daily</u>; we are essentially an education company, and as such, we must stay on the "bleeding edge" of knowledge and wisdom that facilitates exemplary leadership. This requires:

  ○ Consistent and continual study of current and historic written, audio, and video material, as well as mindful engagement with smart and challenging people within the disciplines of commerce, behavioral science, problem-solving, and creative/design thinking. While this is especially important at the executive level of our company, we encourage this manifestation of our corporate value of "learning" to be extended to every member of our team. We regularly discuss ways to incorporate new learning into the models and processes that we employ in facilitating the exemplary leadership of our clients. We share what we are learning liberally in our coaching, forums, workshops, and publications. We package our intellectual property in unique and attractive ways whereby it can be marketed and sold effectively.

  ○ In order to be continuously engaged intellectually at a high level, we must be physically healthy. To assure that, as an organization, we maintain a level of physical fitness that matches our intellectual demands, we work to sustain the wellness of each member of our team by providing opportunities for exercise, diet, appropriate professional advice, and recreation.

○ As an organization of intense, focused mental engagement with one another and our clients, we must also maintain a high level of both organizational and individual "emotional intelligence." In support of this necessity, we encourage team members to engage openly (without fear of retribution) in discussion and debate regarding problems and opportunities. We stress the importance of interacting in a heliotropic and empathetic manner with each other, while still candidly addressing issues and challenges. We also encourage team members to regularly carve out time for introspection, meditation, recreation, and social interaction.

○ CEObuilder® is committed to the career growth and development of each team member as is manifested through interaction with business partners, co-workers, clients, and other stakeholders. We encourage each team member to think creatively, and share their thoughts and understandings of true leadership and business principles, both in oral and written form.

• **<u>Serving Daily</u>:** As in most companies, each team member at CEObuilder® has a specific job to perform that represents their primary responsibility. This may be largely focused on the internal functions of our business, or it may be mostly aimed at our clients. While this focus is essential, we encourage each of our team members to broaden their vision to include everyone with whom they come into contact over the course of their working day–and seek opportunities to render valuable service to one or more individuals outside the purview of their job description. This may be as simple as a smile, a word of encouragement, or an expression of empathy or gratitude in word, text or email. Or it could be as heroic as helping someone in dire straits–or even saving a life. The objective is to be truly heliotropic, sharing light that lifts and supports others.

- **Facilitating Daily:** Through questioning, listening, and occasionally expounding, CEObuilder® team members help their co-workers, clients, and others to discover true principles whereby they are able to grow, develop, and succeed. We seek opportunities in this regard as often as possible, both in our work and in our personal lives. And we liberally share the stories of doing so with one another. In this way, we maintain and grow our facilitative culture.

A: Act — We, the team members at CEObuilder®, are responsible to execute the Plan–to live it!

C: Control — For Control to be effective, CEObuilder® must have metrics against which we will track our progress as a business. These metrics include:

- **Learning Daily:**
  - Intellectual Metrics: Each team member will select at least one book and one periodical article to read (or listen to) per month. These may be selected by the individual, or may be assigned to address specific areas for knowledge acquisition. The team member will write a book review on the book and a "key points" summary of the article which he or she will present at an "all-hands knowledge sharing" meeting during the month following their reading. Artificial intelligence or online book reviews may be used in preparing the written review, but the team member must make sure that they address the following key questions in the review:

    1. For what purpose did the author write this book?

2. What are the most important and compelling insights you gained from reading the book?

3. What are the weaknesses in the book?

4. How might this book be valuable to our clients, specifically the leaders in client companies?

5. Therefore, what? How will you use what you've learned? How might CEObuilder® use these insights?

6. Do you recommend that others read this book? Who, specifically, should read it?

The CEObuilder® executive team will assess if–and how–the knowledge gained in this process might enhance our models and processes. Where it is deemed valuable, it will be used in the ongoing development and refinement of those models and processes.

o   Health & Wellness Metrics: At CEObuilder®, we recognize the very personal (and often private) nature of each person's health and fitness. However, we encourage each team member to track their own unique metrics. These might include weight, blood pressure, blood glucose levels, nutrition, exercise, sleep, and any medications for which they have been prescribed. We encourage each team member to be sensitive to wellness concerns they may observe in others–and to be encouraging and supportive. Where possible, the company will invest in wellness programs to help our team members stay healthy.

o   Emotional Metrics: Here again, personal and private concerns make corporate metrics difficult, if not impossible. However, as CEObuilder® owners and executives, we strive to observe and discern the emotional needs of individuals and the engagement level of the team as a whole. We regularly review together the "emotional state" of the company to identify areas for concern and intervention.

In this regard, we believe in identifying and responding to such issues early, with both courage and compassion. In the realm of prevention rather than intervention, we are committed to creating and maintaining an empathetic and heliotropic work environment and scheduling and carrying out company recreational and social activities at least four times each year.

○ <u>Career Growth & Development Metrics</u>: We will track the career progress of each team member in terms of their competence and engagement in their current job assignment, as well as their potential for growing into more significant roles in the future. We will candidly review and assess their performance in job specifics including both actual work and results compared to planned actions and desired outcomes. Each reviewee will also evaluate the leader to whom they report to give a frank assessment of how well they have been sustained and supported in their job performance and their career growth and development. While periodic formal reviews will be conducted, informal day-to-day interactions between reviewers and reviewees are encouraged; a tight feedback loop facilitates effective communication, agility, empathy, mutual respect, and trust.

- **Serving Daily:** As owners and executives we will model heliotropic leadership, and will recognize it and draw attention to it as we observe it in our team members, clients, vendors, and others. Periodically, as the CEObuilder® top leadership group, we will assess our trajectory in being truly heliotropic–and how those behaviors are impacting our business, and the operations of our client companies.

- **Facilitating Daily:** We will consciously use our facilitation skills and will train our team members, coaches, and clients to use those essential skills as leaders in their own areas of responsibility. Each coaching and training situation will provide an opportunity to assess the frequency with which we employ our facilitative models and processes, as well as the effectiveness we are experiencing as we do so. We will assign those at the executive level to share, through oral and written accounts, the growth and development of the CEObuilder® culture. Over the course of each year, these stories will help us track the use and expertise of our company in facilitating exemplary leadership.

E: Evaluate — With the preceding key metrics in place, the ownership and executive team at CEObuilder® will be able to compare actions and outcomes to our plans. This will allow us to:

- Assess our ongoing commitment, as well as our abilities, to carry out our plans.

- We will be able to evaluate *cause and effect* regarding the relationship between our actions and the outcomes we desire.

- We will be acutely aware of any *variances* between what we planned to do–and what we actually did, shortfalls as well as those areas where our performance exceeds expectations. Shortfalls will lead us to ask *why?* — and our answers will help us consider changes to our plan or our actions, or both. When we exceed expectations, we will also ask *why?* Was this an aberration or random occurrence, or is this level of performance sustainable? Should the plan be revised?

- As we continue to control, on a periodic basis, we will gain an increasingly clear picture of our strengths, weaknesses, and areas for improvement, focusing our attention on areas for plan revision.

- We will share our evaluative insights with trusted advisors and mentors--and regularly seek their inputs.

R: Revise — We will readily revise our plans and/or actions as needed in order to achieve the goals that will lead to fulfilling our Vision. We will not be frustrated by the need to pivot, but will see such revisions as opportunities to improve.

R: Reward — We will enjoy the fruits of this process–and we will enjoy celebrating our successes.

Our Business Success Pyramid follows on the next page.

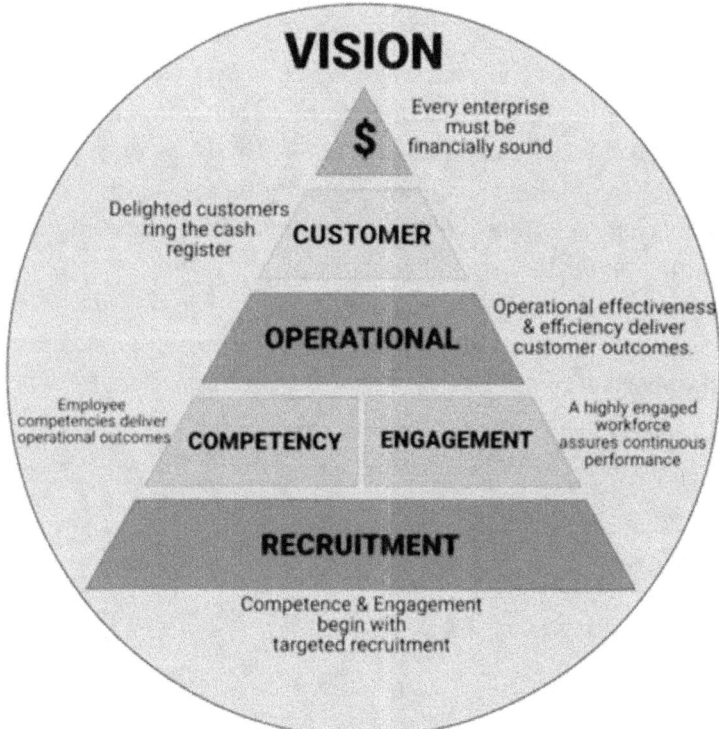

The preceding document shown from page 323 to 341, is the PROPOSED REVISED CEObuilder® VISION which I shared with my ownership and executive team. In discussing and operationalizing it, we followed the first nine steps of our 12 Step Process, and continue to work steps 10, 11, and 12.

As shown in the Business Success Pyramid, this *new* CEObuilder® Vision encompasses all of the key elements of my job description as CEO of the company. That vision also is the mortar between each of those elements, providing the essential cause that holds everything together. It is the foundation from which the business aligns–and it gives meaning to all of the goals, strategies, and tactics that we will execute in the coming day-to-day operations of our company.

For you, the reader, your Vision should similarly accomplish these things as well. Your efforts in diligently applying the 12 Step Process shared in this chapter will provide you with the vision-based alignment and execution that will assure your success.

Thank you for reading–and thanks for accompanying me on this journey. I wish you extraordinary business and personal success in your most important role, that of leader!

AFTERWORD

You will recall that early on in this book, I shared the concept of leading and lagging indicators in the context of my Business Success Pyramid. At that time, I methodically built the case for financial success being the ultimate lagging indicator–and I have clearly reinforced that idea by placing it at the top of the pyramid.

As I discussed the pyramid further, I shared how each strata or layer beneath the pinnacle was, in fact, both a leading and lagging indicator. I worked my way down through the pyramid to what might be considered the ultimate leading indicator: your Enterprise Vision, including your company purpose, mission, and values.

I then took the leading indicator concept even deeper–to your personal purpose, mission, and values. Now, as I conclude my book, I want to "peel the onion" one more time. You see, the actual ultimate "leading" indicator is YOU, the leader–of your enterprise, your team and associates, certainly–but more importantly of yourself.

"To thine own self be true" is much more than great prose. It is the basis for success–in business and in life. You must be true to your purpose, mission, and your values. If you are consistent in doing this, you will grow into the leader you are destined to become, you will be that *ultimate leading indicator!*

And, what is the ultimate lagging indicator? It is, in fact, not the financial pinnacle shown on the Business Success Pyramid. Well beyond financial success is how you have impacted the careers and lives of those with whom you have been privileged to work, teach, facilitate, and lead. As author Simon Sinek said in his best-selling book, *Leaders Eat Last,* "What if we judge a leader not on what they do when holding the torch but on what happens after they pass it on? A leader's legacy is only as strong as the foundation they leave behind that allows others to continue to advance the organization in their name."[162]

The ultimate lagging indicator, then, is the legacy you leave behind, the people you have grown and developed.

You see…It's all about the money, BUT IT'S NOT!

---

[162] *Leaders Eat Last: Why Some Teams Pull Together and Others Don't,* Simon Sinek, page 211

ACKNOWLEDGMENTS

I have been writing articles for business publications for years, and that process has become fairly comfortable for me. Because of that, and the fact that I am a voracious reader, I was foolish enough to assume that I could write a book quickly and easily. That notion, which described my mindset about writing this book, was how I felt...*five years ago*, when I started writing *Align & Execute*.

I have long since abandoned the idea of "quick and easy," as have my family, friends, and associates who may have, in an effort to be supportive, bought into my overconfidence. I am most fortunate that these same folks have not abandoned me. They have consistently and continuously been encouraging, assuring me that I could see this project through to completion.

At the top of this list is my business partner, Kevin Denning. Kevin has had the vantage point of sitting across the desk as one of my CEO clients for years, experiencing the principles I have shared in *Align & Execute*. He, therefore, has applied much of what you have read here, and now as my partner in CEObuilder®, he has provided vital feedback on the content of the book. He is also the point-man for all technology issues and opportunities in our company, including an online workshop that will soon be introduced to teach the principles in this book. I am grateful beyond words for Kevin.

I am also deeply grateful for our CEObuilder® executive team, including Kevin, Christian Tyson (my son), Emily Beattie (my daughter), and Tim Stroshine (who is as close to being my son as anyone who isn't could be). As a team, and on countless one-on-one occasions, we have spent many hours discussing the principles I have

345

written about. They have been my readers, my critics, and my best supporters.

I must also acknowledge my former business partner, Steve Dunaway. Steve is now retired, but his influence has been important throughout our years working together in CEObuilder®. His ideas and support have been invaluable to me.

I also would be remiss to not express my gratitude to all of the clients with whom I've worked over the years. Having worked with leaders from over 60 different industries, they have both broadened and deepened my understanding and perspective. I wish I could list them all here, but I'm afraid that attempt would leave someone out. So, suffice it to say that both individually and collectively, they have blessed me with valuable insights and working examples of leadership challenges, opportunities, and excellence.

I have also been blessed to have a few extraordinary mentors in my life and career. Some have been notably mentioned in this book, like Dr. Iwamoto, my professor of economics at Weber State University many years ago. I didn't share as much about several others, but they have also had a profound impact on how I see the world of business and leadership. They include Tom Peterson, Carlos Asay, Dan Judd, Wick Skinner, and Bob Vanourek. I am very grateful for each of these great men.

I also want to thank my family and friends who have patiently stood by me through the "long march" it has been to complete *Align & Execute*. Foremost is my wife, Janell. I know she has, at times, wondered if this book was to be an interminable project, but she has continued to stay supportive. Beyond her are my children and grandchildren who have recognized my need to "keep grinding" on this project. I also want to thank my brother, Mike Tyson, for his unwavering support of virtually everything I have undertaken throughout my life.

Finally, I must give thanks to God. I feel His influence every day– and I acknowledge His hand in all things!

The 23 Most Popular Personality Tests In Ranking Order, As Of 2024

Compiled by Heather Harper, *Heather Harper Personal Trainer, https://www.workstyle.io/best-personality-test*

Here are the most popular personality tests:

1. Truity

Established in 2012, Truity is a popular test that has developed a library of scientifically validated personality tests to help people understand themselves and those around them.

Through their website, users can take a range of tests including;

- **Enneagram** (9 personality types)
- **Typefinder** (16 personality types)
- **Big Five Assessment**
- **Career Profiler**
- **Workplace DISC Test**

2. HIGH5 Test

HIGH5 is a free strengths test (somewhat like StrengthsFinder 2.0) that helps people find out what they are naturally good at.

3. DiSC

The DiSC personality profile was designed to measure dominance, influence, steadiness, and conscientiousness. The DiSC assessment contains 28 questions, where the participant picks a word that is most like them, and a word that is least like them for each question.

4. Personality Factor Questionnaire

The questionnaire is designed to measure normal behaviors and can be used for career development, employees selection, marital help, and counseling; but it does have some clinical reference.

5. HEXACO Model of Personality Structure Personality Inventory

The model measures six major personality dimensions, namely: honesty-humility, emotionality, extraversion, agreeableness, conscientiousness, openness to experience. It consists of 200 questions for the full-length assessment or 100 questions for the half-length assessment.

6. Revised NEO Personality Inventory

Designed to measure and test the Big-5 personality traits that are outlined in the five-factor model - namely: openness to experience, conscientiousness, extraversion, agreeableness, and neuroticism.

7. Myers-Briggs Type Indicator

The Myers-Briggs test is based upon a theory that was introduced by Carl Jung - a theory that humans experience the world using four psychological functions: sensation, intuition, feeling and thinking. These functions affect many things, such as one's work style, mode of rejuvenation, strengths, weaknesses, individual differences, and so on.

8. Eysenck Personality Inventory

The Eysenck Personality Inventory measures personality on two independent dimensions: extroversion versus introversion and neuroticism versus stability.

9. Eysenck Personality Questionnaire

Not to be confused with the Eysenck Personality Inventory, the Eysenck Personality Questionnaire was later introduced by Hans and Sybil Eysenck to measure personality across three dimensions of temperament: extroversion versus introversion, neuroticism versus stability and psychoticism versus socialization.

10. Minnesota Multiphasic Personality Inventory (MMPI)

MMPI can be used to assess adult personality and psychopathology across 10 scales: hysteria, depression, paranoia, hypochondriasis, psychopathic deviate, masculinity/femininity, psychasthenia, schizophrenia, hypomania, and social introversion. It has a high clinical reference and is often used to diagnose and assist treatment plans for mental illnesses.

11. The Birkman Method

The Birkman method is an online assessment that measures personality, social perception and occupational interests. The assessment is designed to provide insight into what specifically drives a person's behaviors in an occupational setting and social context.

12. Values and Motives Inventory

The Values and Motives Inventory is designed to identify what drives and energizes a person and where they are most likely to gain satisfaction from work. The inventory measures interpersonal, intrinsic and extrinsic values as well as summarizing possible motivating and demotivating factors to an individual at work.

13. Motives, Values and Preference Inventory (MPVI)

MPVI evaluates a person's core goals, values, drivers and interests. The results from this inventory can, in return, predict job success and satisfaction. The MPVI assesses personality on 10 scales: Recognition, Power, Hedonism, Altruistism, Affiliation, Tradition, Security, Commerce, Aesthetics and Science.

14. Hogan Personality Inventory (HPI)

HPI is based on the five-factor model and the socio-analytic theory. The HPI measures personality across key behavioral tendencies: adjustment, ambition, sociability, interpersonal sensitivity, prudence, inquisitiveness and learning approach.

15. Hogan Development Survey

The survey is designed to measure dark personality in an occupational setting across 11 traits: excitable, skeptical, cautious, reserved, leisurely, bold, mischievous, colorful, imaginative, diligent and dutiful. The traits measured are all qualities believed to emerge in employees at times of strain and are traits that can disrupt employee relationships, damage company reputation and derail people's chances of success.

16. California Psychological Inventory (CPI)

CPI is designed to describe "everyday behavior" across 18 scales. The inventory can be used for employee selection, individual development, succession planning, employee selection, employee retention, executive coaching and can outline performance improvements and motivation of individuals.

17. Personality Assessment Inventory (PAI)

PAI is designed to assess personality and psychopathology across four scales: clinical scales, treatment consideration scales, interpersonal scales, and validity scales.

18. Personality and Preference Inventory

The Personality and Preference Inventory is designed to comprehensively cover aspects of personality that are relevant to the workplace and is designed to elicit behaviors and preferences that are appropriate to vacant positions in the workplace. The inventory has ten 'role scales', which measure our perception of our behavior in a work situation; and ten 'needs scales', which measure an individual's preference for behaving in a particular way.

19. Keirsey Temperament Sorter

The Sorter utilizes a questionnaire which measures personality across four temperaments: artisan, guardian, idealist and rational.

20. True Colors

The True Colors test was designed to measure four basic learning styles: independent thinkers, pragmatic planners, action-oriented, people-oriented.

21. Caliper Profile

The Caliper Profile is an employee and applicant assessment instrument that measures an individual's job performance potential and discovers which person is best suited for a given job based on their intrinsic motivation.The results from these profiles are often used for hiring, employee development, team improvement, talent alignment, succession planning, employee engagement, and to increase productivity.

22. Rorschach Inkblot Test

The inkblot test is one of the most unique and quirky personality tests.The inkblot test is an assessment where an examiner presents the participant with an inkblot, and the participant tells the examiner what they see. Participant perception of the inkblot is then analyzed and interpreted by a psychologist using complex algorithms, exposing insights about the participant's personality.

23. Szondi Test

The Szondi test is based on the systematic drive theory and the dimensional model of personality. During the test, participants are shown a series of facial photographs which represent people who have been classified as homosexual, sadist, epileptic, hysteric, catatonic, paranoid, depressive, and maniac. Participants then pick the most appealing and most repulsive pictures.

StrengthsFinder 2.0 Feedback for Richard Tyson

The key premises of StrengthsFinder are:

1. That you have inherent gifts, talents, strengths, or attributes that motivate your life.
2. That your greatest potential for growth and fulfillment is in your areas of greatest personal strength.
3. That you should seek to discover your strengths, and upon discovering them, set high intrinsic goals (and purpose) related to those strengths, and then–*play to your strengths.*

Your unique strengths will fall into any of four major categories, defined as follows:

- **EXECUTING:** People with dominant Executing themes make things happen.
- **INFLUENCING:** People with dominant Influencing themes take charge, speak up, and make sure others are heard.
- **RELATIONSHIP BUILDING:** People with dominant Relationship Building themes build strong relationships that hold a theme together and make it greater than the sum of its parts.

- **STRATEGIC THINKING:** People with dominant Strategic Thinking themes absorb and analyze information that informs better decisions.

Having come to understand these categories and the fundamental premises undergirding this assessment , I was anxious to try StrengthsFinder for myself. **Here are the themes that emerged for me. The details for each of these were provided by reports generated by Gallup based on my responses to the StrengthsFinder assessment. I have added relevant excerpts from the book,** *StrengthsFinder 2.0 from Gallup: Discover Your Clifton Strengths,* **noted in footnote references.**

1. STRATEGIC THINKING: Learner

You have a great desire to learn and want to continuously improve. The process of learning, rather than the outcome, excites you. *Discover Your CliftonStrengths* notes that "You are energized by the steady and deliberate journey from ignorance to competence."[163]

Instinctively, you are drawn to the process of gaining knowledge and skills. You yearn to improve on what you can already do. When you meet people who value education as much as you do, you are eager to hear about their personal or professional ambitions, intentions, or goals. Understanding what others aim to accomplish in the coming weeks, months, or years can be the beginning of a practical partnership or an enduring friendship.

You thirst for new ideas and knowledge. Often you lose yourself in a book. You pore over the ideas contained on its pages for long stretches of time. You want to absorb as much information as possible.

---

[163] *Discover Your CliftonStrengths,* Don Clifton, page 121.

By nature, you appreciate opportunities to acquire knowledge, gain skills, or experience new things. You refuse to let your mind grow dull by being complacent–that is, smug or self-satisfied.

You love to learn, and you intuitively know how you learn best. Your natural ability to pick up and absorb information quickly and to challenge yourself to continually learn more keeps you on the cutting edge.

"The Learner Theme does not necessarily mean that you seek to become the subject matter expert, or that you are striving for the respect that accompanies a professional or academic credential. The outcome of the learning is less significant than the 'getting there.'"[164]

To take action to maximize your potential (to play to your Strengths):

○   Respect your gift; discipline yourself to continually and consistently learn. Seek and find opportunities to expand your knowledge.

○   "Refine how you learn. For example, you might learn best by teaching; if so, seek out opportunities to present to others. You might learn best through quiet reflection; if so, find this quiet time."[165]

○   Liberally share what you are learning with others who will be able to grow and develop from your knowledge.

○   Be a catalyst for change. Based on what you have learned, help others to overcome their fears and resistance to change.

○   "Because you are not threatened by unfamiliar information, you might excel in a consulting role (either internal or

---

[164] Ibid, page 121.
[165] Ibid, page 122.

external) in which you are paid to go into new situations and quickly pick up new competencies."[166]

○ Keep track of your learning process and progress. "Look for ways to measure the degree to which you and others feel that your learning needs are being met, to create individualized learning milestones and to reward achievements in learning."[167]

Watch out for blind spots:

○ Be cautious about imposing the value of learning too strongly with others; respect their motivations, and resist pushing them toward learning for learning's sake.

○ Recognize that you may love learning so much that the outcome stops mattering to you. Be careful not to let the process of knowledge acquisition get in the way of your results and productivity.

2. *STRATEGIC THINKING:* Context

"You look back. You look back because that is where the answers lie. You look back to understand the present....It was a time of blueprints. As you look back , you begin to see these blueprints emerge. You become wiser about the future because you saw its seeds being sown in the past."[168]

You enjoy thinking about the past. You look to history to understand the present. Your distinctive ability to see the link between where you have been and where you are going is extremely valuable for planning and decision-making.

You understand the present by researching its history. By nature, you gravitate to people who love to think about the past. Your taste in books and other written materials often leads you to

---

[166] Ibid, page 123
[167] Ibid, page 123
[168] Ibid, page 69.

the history sections of bookstores, libraries, and internet sites. Your passion for reading about humankind's ever-unfolding story allows you to feel quite comfortable in the presence of knowledgeable historians.

You enjoy animated exchanges of ideas between people who recognize the relevance of history in their everyday lives. You are intrigued by experts who can enlighten you about past events or historic people.

You are particularly interested in history's contribution to the current state of affairs. Information about global conflicts, past and present, holds your attention. Because of this strength, you may believe that history is likely to repeat itself. In that regard, you may discover that current events are reflections of past occurrences, foreshadowing the future.

To take action to maximize your potential (to play to your Strengths):

- o "Use your understanding of the past to help others map the future."[169] Because you recognize that the best predictor of future behavior is past behavior, you have the ability to couple your sense of history to likely future scenarios.

- o Study your own history. What actions or behaviors have contributed to your successes or failures. Share these with others to help them succeed.

- o Seek opportunities to learn from the successes and failures of others, especially those who may serve as a mentor, coach, or advisor to you.

- o Become an agent for positive change. Having strong Context talents does not mean that you live in the past. It means that you can clearly identify which aspects of the

---

[169] Ibid, page 70.

past to discard and which to keep to build a better, more sustainable future.

o   In working with organizations, help them strengthen their cultures with their stories of past successes and challenges overcome. Teach them the power of stories and folklore.

o   Empower others to make more informed decisions. Use your Context skills to pose questions that reveal valuable insights such as: When did we face a similar situation? What did we do? What happened? What did we learn? When a problem occurs, ask them to identify the factors that led to it. Guide their learning from the past to better decisions in the future.

o   "Partner with others who have strong Futuristic talents."[170]

Watch out for blind spots:

o   Some people might think that you live in the past and are resistant to change. Consider explaining the value of understanding history and what has–and has not–worked in the past, but keep an open mind when new situations arise.

o   Recognize that while you are fascinated by history and the lessons it reveals, others may find this information boring or overwhelming. Keep this in mind as you share your perspectives, and look for signs that you've lost the attention or interest of others.

3. *STRATEGIC THINKING:* Strategist

Strategists are those who have a distinct ability to see through the clutter and ambiguity of situations to find the best route to the achievement of desired outcomes. "This perspective allows you to see patterns where others simply see complexity.

---

[170] Ibid, page 71.

Mindful of these patterns, you play out alternative scenarios, always asking, 'What if this happened? Okay, well what if this happened? This recurring question helps you see around the next corner."[171]

You create alternative ways to proceed. Faced with any given scenario, you can quickly spot the relevant patterns and issues. You analyze the lessons of the past to find clues for handling future situations. Piecing together the causes and effects of historical events allows you to discover alternate routes to your goal. You are seldom taken by surprise because you routinely study your options, using them to craft innovative solutions. Your natural ability to anticipate, play our different scenarios and plan ahead make you an agile decision-maker.

You notice new as well as unusual configurations in facts, evidence, or data where others see only separate, unrelated bits of information. You are fascinated by problems that puzzle, confound, or frustrate most people.

By nature, you can reconfigure factual information or data in ways that reveal trends, raise issues, identify opportunities, or offer solutions. You bring an added dimension to discussions. You make sense out of seemingly unrelated information.

Instinctively, you select the right combination of words to convey your ideas or feelings. Your vocabulary provides you with precise phrases and terminology. You are likely to have an ease with language, expressing yourself with ease and grace. You effortlessly verbalize your thoughts. You relish the opportunity to share your insights. You derive pleasure from actively participating in conversations within which others propose ideas, seek solutions, or debate issues.

To take action to maximize your potential (to play to your Strengths):

---

[171] Ibid, page 153.

○ Take time to observe what is going on around you, both in your immediate work environment, in your community and marketplace, and in the world at large. Seek deep understanding and discernment regarding underlying trends, situations, and challenges. Think deeply about root causes and potential solutions to problems that may strengthen the value you deliver to others with whom you associate. Remember that your "musing time" is an essential component of your strategic thinking.

○ Strengthen the groups with whom you work by using your talent to discover and facilitate the best path to success.

○ Schedule regular time to think about your own goals and strategies. "Your strategic thinking will be necessary to keep a vivid vision from deteriorating into an ordinary pipe dream."[172]Time alone in this regard may prove to be highly valuable for both your long and near-term decisions.

○ Trust your insights. Because you consider options so naturally and easily, you may not realize how you arrived at a strategy. Even so, your exceptional talents as a strategist significantly increase that likelihood of success.

○ Seek out groups that do important work, and engage with them, contributing your strategic thinking. Your ideas and expert planning skills can make you a strong leader in any group. Your insights are especially valuable in the front end of new initiatives or enterprises.

○ "Make yourself known as a resource for consultation with those who are stumped by a particular problem or hindered by a particular obstacle or barrier,"[173]

○ Seek to partner with others who have strong Activator talents. Their drive to move into action will complement and strengthen your Strategist skills and talents.

---

[172] Ibid, page 155.
[173] Ibid, page 155.

Watch out for blind spots:

- ○ "You are likely to anticipate potential issues more easily than others."[174] This might be viewed as pessimism or negativity by others. They may misinterpret your Strategic talents as criticisms of their ideas. Be prepared to explain your thought processes. Help them understand that you are striving to consider all options, drawing both on what is already working well, what others have already done, and what needs improvement.

- ○ Because you have a natural gift for strategizing, it may appear to others that you are "winging it." It is therefore important to communicate the basis for your contributions, sharing the underlying premises that lead to your suggestions and decisions. This often requires extra effort in explanation, articulation and patient interchange with others.

4. *EXECUTING:* Achiever

You have a continuous need for achievement. "You feel that every day starts at zero. By the end of the day you must achieve something tangible in order to feel good about yourself. And by 'every day' you mean every single day–workdays, weekends, vacations. No matter how much you may feel you deserve a day of rest, if the day passes without some form of achievement, no matter how small, you will feel dissatisfied."[175]

You work hard and possess a great deal of stamina. You take immense satisfaction in being busy and productive. It is very likely that you possess the physical and mental endurance to withstand obstacles and stress. By nature, you possess a tremendous capacity for working long hours. Chances are good that you exhibit the physical and mental endurance needed to continuously toil after others have stopped working.

---

[174] Ibid, page 155.
[175] Ibid, page 25.

Your tireless efforts are typically directed toward your goals for the coming months, years, or decades. You are hardwired to pursue goals until they are reached. When obstacles arise, you become even more determined to succeed.

Driven by your talents, you welcome opportunities to methodically examine details in data. You notice when a series of numbers repeats itself. Your hours of mental labor enable you to spot important pieces of information that most people overlook.

Because of your strengths, you normally strive to do things right. Taking shortcuts strikes you as unprincipled, thoughtless, and careless. You likely refuse to produce sloppy work or engage in unethical practices.

You love to complete tasks, and your accomplishments fulfill you. You have a strong inner drive–an innate source of intensity, energy, and power that motivates you to work hard and get things done.

To take action to maximize your potential (to play to your Strengths):

○   Continuously set challenging goals. Take advantage of your self-motivation. Develop meaningful scoring systems that allow you to track your daily progress toward your goals.

○   Launch new initiatives and projects, but limit your commitments to projects that align with your highest goals and priorities.

○   "Select jobs that allow you to have the leeway to work as hard as you want and in which you are encouraged to measure your own productivity."[176]

○   Partner with other hard workers.

---

[176] Ibid, page 26.

- ○ Take time to celebrate each success before moving on to your next goal, item, or task, even if it's just for a few minutes.
- ○ Be sure to take regular breaks. Even though you are naturally equipped to work harder than others, you too, have your limits. Recognize the danger in burnout.
- ○ Make sure your to-do lists include activities and relationships beyond work.

Watch out for blind spots:

- ○ "As an Achiever, you relish the feeling of being busy, yet you also need to know when you are 'done.' To help with this, "attach timelines and measurement to goals so that effort leads to defined progress and tangible outcomes."[177]
- ○ "Your drive for action might cause you to find meetings a bit boring."[178] When faced with this, make sure that you understand the objective of the meeting–and take notes to stay engaged.
- ○ You may have a tendency to get frustrated when others don't work as hard as you do, and they may see you as too demanding. Remember, not everyone has the same drive and high expectations that you do. Be grateful for what others do, while continually encouraging and inspiring their efforts on your common endeavors.
- ○ Your natural drive may lead you to take on too many projects or to agree to deadlines that do not contribute to the achievement of what is most important. Make sure that you commit only to those activities that align with what you deem to be essential–and make sure that you have the time and resources to do the job right.

---

[177] Ibid, pages 26-27.
[178] Ibid, page 27.

○   "Make sure that in your eagerness to do more… that you do not skimp on quality."[179]

5. *RELATIONSHIP BUILDER:* Individualization

You are intrigued with the unique qualities of each person. You have the gift for figuring out how different people can work together productively. You bring people together. You form a bond with each individual as you come to understand his or her circumstances. You naturally identify and relate to each person's situation, gifts, talents, skills, and behaviors. You have the gift of helping people discover what they have in common, helping them get beyond their differences to shared purpose. You facilitate their ability to communicate and cooperate.

Instinctively, you are able to mix and match the talents, skills, knowledge, and experience of people. You seek insights about how diverse individuals respond to one another when facing challenges, disagreements, or problems. You use those insights to promote cohesive, efficient, and productive workgroups.

You are able to identify the unique qualities, motivations, strengths, limitations, preferences, or attitudes of many with whom you associate. You tend to look for one or two good things in each person, with which you use to set up opportunities for each to cooperate in pursuit of a common purpose. You readily compliment those who freely share their knowledge, skills, or talents to the projects you pursue.

You have a deep respect for diversity of ideas and opinions, and often mix and match the various styles of others regarding how they prefer to work, think, and problem solve. You notice and appreciate each person's unique characteristics. With this recognition, you don't treat everyone the same, seeking instead to respectfully bring out the best in each individual. You facilitate the development of cohesive, successful teams through

[179] Ibid, page 28.

collaborative approaches to setting and progressing toward the achievement of shared goals. "You know instinctively that the secret to great teams is casting by individual strengths so that everyone can do a lot of what they do well."[180]

By nature, you continually seek information regarding how people interact, work, overcome challenges, and thrive in their relationships. You have a restless, investigative mind that drives you to collect lots of research about the factors that produce strong productive teams. This extends beyond your work into your personal life, leading you to study broadly and deeply in history, religion, science, politics, entertainment, sports, art, and law. You have a strong ability to make connections between the things you study and the people with whom you interact.

To take action to maximize your potential (to play to your Strengths):

- o "Select a vocation in which your Individualization talents can be both used and appreciated, such as counseling, supervising, (or) teaching…"[181]

- o You intuitively personalize your interactions with those around you. This contributes to your comfort working within a broad range of styles, cultures, and people. Continue to play to this strength.

- o Your Individualization talents will often help you take a different approach to interpreting what you observe in both human behavior and in data. Where others may see only similarities or differences, you have the innate ability to see and interpret both. Use this skill as you work to facilitate team effectiveness.

---

[180] Ibid, page 109.
[181] Ibid, page 110.

o   Encourage those around you to follow their dreams, to have great purpose in their lives and in their work, and to maximize the power of their gifts and talents.

o   Figure out what every person on your team does best. Continue to discern and appreciate the uniqueness in each person with which you interact. Then help them capitalize on their talents, skills, and knowledge. Be ready to explain your rationale and your philosophy so people understand that you have their best interests in mind.

o   Continue to study successful people, thereby increasing your understanding of what contributed to their success.

o   Extend your study of strengths and style to yourself. Become an expert in describing your own attributes, how you learn, build relationships, and facilitate progress. Share those insights with others, using your example to help others to become more aware of the value of their own unique strengths, perspectives, talents, and viewpoints–and those of others with whom they interact.

o   Ask open-ended questions to those with whom you work. Seek to discover what works best for them, what they have learned about building strong, enduring relationships, how they most effectively learn and grow.

o   When making presentations or speaking,"use your Individualization talents to gather and share real-life stories that will make your points much better than generic information or theories would (be)."[182]

Watch out for blind spots:

o   Your strength in Individualization contributes a deeper knowledge and understanding of others than they have

---

[182] Ibid, page 111.

of you. You must take care not to assume that they are as acutely aware of your preferences, motivations, and needs as you are of theirs. Recognize that your responsibility is not only to understand others, but to help them understand you. It is therefore important that you articulate who you are. Don't expect people to instinctively know you.

- ○ Those who are strong in Individualization care deeply about each person and their needs and goals. While this is commendable, it also can lead you to put individuals ahead of the common purpose of the group, leading to a sense of favoritism and bias. This may prove to fatally undermine the success of teams and enterprises. For the greater good of the group, you must be ready to adjust your natural empathy and connection with individuals.

6. *EXECUTING:* **Arranger**

"You are a conductor. When faced with a complex situation involving many factors, you enjoy managing all of the variables, aligning and realigning them until you are sure you have arranged them in the most productive configuration possible. In your mind there is nothing special about what you are doing. You are simply trying to figure out the best way to get things done. But others, lacking this theme, will be in awe of your ability. 'How can you keep so many things in your head at once?' they will ask."[183]

You are a natural organizer, but you also have a flexibility that complements this ability, allowing you to move flexibly to new strategies and tactics that optimize both effectiveness and efficiency.

---

[183] Ibid, page 41.

To take action to maximize your potential (to play to your Strengths):

o   Take time to learn the goals of coworkers, clients, and friends. Offer your Arranger talents to help them organize for success.

o   "Help others see your far-reaching expertise by sharing your 'what if' thinking with them."[184] When they realize that you've identified and carefully considered many options and arrangements–and have engaged their best thinking as well, they'll feel increasing confidence in your leadership.

o   "You intuitively sense how very different people can work together."[185] Focus your skill on getting the right people in place to build highly competent and engaged teams to execute plans and meet goals.

o   "Seek complex, dynamic environments in which there are few routines."[186] Recognize that you have an exceptional ability to be involved with and manage multiple projects– and to be bored with activities and environments that are static or routine in nature.

o   "Be sure to keep track of ongoing deadlines for your many tasks, projects, and obligations."[187]

Watch out for blind spots:

o   Recognize that your Arranger talent may attract you to too many projects to manage successfully. Beware of your natural inclination to multitask.

o   "Although you enjoy the chance to juggle lots of activities, others with less powerful Arranger talents may become

---

[184] Ibid, page 44.
[185] Ibid, page 43.
[186] Ibid, page 43.
[187] Ibid, page 43.

anxious if they don't see you working on their projects frequently. Inform them of your progress to ease their fears."[188]

○ You need to "give people time to understand your way of doing things when you present (your ideas) to them. Your mental juggling is instinctive, but others might find it difficult to break with existing procedures. Take time to clearly explain why your way can be more effective."[189]

○ Your tendency to continually seek for improvement naturally leads to the reorganization of tasks, projects, and people. This may confuse others. Be sure to explain your ideas and entertain constructive dialogue with those who are stakeholders in these activities.

○ Recognize that others with whom you work may see your multiple tasks, projects, and obligations as evidence of ever-changing or unclear priorities. Welcome their engagement to assure that your priorities are clearly understood, and that they know their roles in helping you accomplish them.

○ Recognize that your Arranger talents may lead you to take responsibility and personal ownership of projects, processes, and people–without being asked to do so. Be aware that when you assume such authority without gaining the respect and trust of others, you may build unnecessary resistance to your ideas, even if they are inherently the right things to do.

7. *STRATEGIC THINKING:* Analytical

Your Analytical theme leads you to challenge others to produce hard data and evidence for the assumptions upon which they make their decisions. You rely heavily on "cause and effect" and you have a natural interest in discovering underlying patterns

---

[188] Ibid, page 43.
[189] Ibid, page 43.

and connections. You enjoy dissecting operating processes to determine what is most effective and efficient.

When faced with problems, you seek to discover the "root causes" that have led to–or will lead to–setbacks and obstacles. You enjoy peeling back the layers of problems until you arrive at their roots. You are a natural questioner, not with an inherent desire to destroy the ideas of others, but to establish the soundness of their assertions and arguments. You strive to be objective and dispassionate. Those with whom you enjoy long-term relationships see you as logical and rigorous.

To take action to maximize your potential (to play to your Strengths):

- o It is important that you continuously seek credible sources of information that you can rely on in order to remain objective and dispassionate in your questioning, discovery efforts, and your challenges. Seek out books, podcasts, articles, experts, and other resources that will provide you with a strong foundation for using your Analytical strengths. "You are at your best when you have well-researched sources of information and numbers to support your logic."[190]

- o "Look for patterns in data. See if you can discern a... precedent or relationship in (the) numbers. By connecting the dots in the data and inferring a causal link, you may be able to help others see these patterns."[191]

- o "Help others understand that your analytical approach will often require data and other information to logically back up new ideas that they might suggest."[192]

---

[190] Ibid, page 39.
[191] Ibid, page 40.
[192] Ibid, page 40.

○   Where possible, get involved with initiatives and projects in their inception so that you can evaluate their feasibility and direction before they are too far along.

Watch out for blind spots:

○   Your objectivity and fact-based approach to decision-making may seem skeptical or critical toward the ideas of others. Keep in mind that they will have emotional, subjective, and personal opinions. Although these may not be logical or rational to you, you need to give validation to their inputs. By consciously doing this, you will help assure that differences do not disintegrate into conflict.

○   Because you ask many questions, people may think that you doubt the validity of their ideas, or that you don't trust them. In this regard, you may unwittingly sow the seeds of poor working relationships. If, and when, you feel this is happening, take the time to step back from your analytical approach to assure them that your questions are intended to be helpful and to support the collective best judgment of the team.

○   Strive to understand how each person prefers to receive your ideas and challenges. Some may prefer one-to-one conversations, while others are more comfortable in a group discussion or in written interchanges on email or texting. Recognize the importance of courteous communication and dialogue.

○   Wherever possible, make your questions and challenges an invitation for creating the foundation for strong, viable decisions. Suggest that the resources for logically establishing that foundation can, and should, come from every stakeholder in those decisions. By inviting their participation, you increase the likelihood that your Analytical approach will be accepted and appreciated.

o   Recognize that your Analytical tendencies may seem to be "foot-dragging." While you are naturally deliberative, you must not lose sight of the need to move forward. Your challenge is to exert appropriate pressure on the brake, while also pressing on the accelerator. You must make sure that your fellow stakeholders know that you are aware of and are managing this dichotomy.

8. *RELATIONSHIP BUILDING:* Connectedness

You see a strong connection between people, circumstances, and events. You inherently believe that there are few coincidences in life and that almost every event has meaning. You believe we are all connected as brothers and sisters in the family of humanity. Certain of that unity, you are a bridge builder between people and cultures. You help others find meaning by looking at the bigger picture of the world around them, and you give them a sense of comfort and stability in the face of uncertainty. You are naturally considerate, caring, and accepting.

While you recognize the differences between people and their opinions, attitudes, and behaviors, you often exercise your skill to facilitate discussion about the "common ground" we all share.

"The exact articles of your faith will depend on your upbringing and your culture, but your faith is strong. It sustains you and your close friends…"

To take action to maximize your potential (to play to your Strengths):

o   "Consider roles in which you listen and counsel. You can become adept at helping other people see connection and purpose in everyday occurrences."[193]

o   Explore ways to expand and enliven your connections. Consider joining an organization that   facilitates Connectedness among its members.

---

[193] Ibid, page 62.

- o "Within your organization, help your colleagues understand how their efforts fit into the larger picture."[194] Seek opportunities to facilitate their focus and enthusiasm for the vision of the enterprise, including its purpose, mission, and values.

- o "Help people see the connections among their talents, their actions, their mission, and their successes. When people believe in what they are doing and feel like they are part of something bigger, their commitment to achievement is enhanced."[195]

- o "Your philosophy of life compels you to move beyond your own self-interests and the interests of your immediate constituency and sphere of influence. As such, you see the broader implications for your community and the world. Explore ways to communicate these insights to others."[196]

- o "Seek out global or cross-cultural responsibilities that capitalize on your understanding of the commonalities inherent in humanity. Build universal capability, and change the mindset of those who think in terms of 'us' and 'them.'"[197]

Watch out for blind spots:

- o "Don't spend too much time attempting to persuade others to see the world as a linked web. Be aware that your sense of connection is intuitive. If others don't share your intuition, rational argument will not persuade them."[198]

- o Use your Connectedness to look past societal labels, and focus on their essential needs. "Connectedness talents can help you look past someone's outer shell to embrace their humanity. Be particularly aware of this when you work

---

[194] Ibid, page 63.
[195] Ibid, page 63.
[196] Ibid, page 63.
[197] Ibid, page 63-64.
[198] Ibid, page 63.

with somebody whose background is very different from yours."[199]

○   You may react more calmly and passively to the bad news, negative situations, frustrations, or concerns of others. While you care, your tendency is to move toward a calm place where solutions can be discovered. Be aware that people sometimes need to vent and will want you to validate their feelings more than they want an immediate solution or philosophical response.

○   Some may perceive you as naive or idealistic because of your natural tendency to seek common ground and avoid conflict. They may not share your connected view of humanity, and therefore will likely be dismissive of your peacemaking tendencies. While you should keep your resolve to remain calm, you need to allow such people the opportunity to vent.

9. *STRATEGIC THINKING:* Input

You are, by nature, inquisitive; almost everything interests you! And, you are also a collector of the things that interest you. This includes tangible objects that may, or may not, have value for others. You also collect intangibles like information–words, facts, books, philosophies and doctrines–and even quotations. "And yours is the kind of mind that finds so many things interesting. The world is exciting precisely because of its infinite variety and complexity. If you read a great deal, it is not necessarily to refine your theories but, rather, to add more information to your archives. If you like to travel, it is because each new location offers novel artifacts and facts."[200]

You not only collect the things that interest you, you store them! You are uncomfortable throwing things away. Why? It is because you have the sense that you may need them at a

---

[199] Ibid, page 64.
[200] Ibid, page 113.

later time when they will be useful or bring value to yourself or others. You tend to continue collecting, compiling, and filing things away. And because of your intuitive sense of connecting and inter-relating ideas, concepts, and even tangible objects, you often find ways to create value and personal enjoyment out of your collections.

To take action to maximize your potential (to play to your Strengths):

- ○ Keep exploring, nourish your joy in discovering new experiences and learning new things.
- ○ Schedule time to read books and articles that motivate you. Stay current on the latest news.
- ○ Deliberately increase your vocabulary by collecting new words and learning their meaning.
- ○ Seek opportunities where you can acquire and share information every day, such as teaching, writing, or research work.
- ○ Identify your areas of specialization, and actively seek more information about them.
- ○ By virtue of your inquisitive nature, over the course of your life your mind becomes an exceptional repository of facts, data, and ideas. As that knowledge grows, "don't be afraid to position yourself as an expert. By simply following your Input talents, you could become known as the authority in your field."[201]
- ○ Devise a system to store and easily locate information so that you can access it quickly.

Watch out for blind spots:

- ○ Recognize that your broad interests may sometimes lead you into tangents from your core purpose and most

---

[201] Ibid, page 115.

important uses of your time. To help you with this, partner with others who are more singularly focused to "help you stay on track when your inquisitiveness leads you down intriguing but distracting avenues."[202]

o   "Your mind is open and absorbent. You naturally soak up information in the same way that a sponge soaks up water. But just as the primary purpose of the sponge is not to permanently contain what it absorbs, neither should your mind simply store more information. Input without output can lead to stagnation. As you gather and absorb information, be aware of the individuals and groups that can most benefit from your knowledge, and be intentional about sharing with them."[203]

o   Recognize that unrestrained input can lead to intellectual or physical clutter. Consider occasionally taking inventory and purging what you don't need so that your surroundings–and your mind–don't become overloaded.

o   You might have a tendency to give people so much information or so many resources that they become overwhelmed. Before you share your discoveries with others, consider sorting out what is most important and meaningful so they don't lose interest.

10. INFLUENCING: Maximizer

"Excellence, not average, is your measure. Taking something from below average to slightly above average takes a great deal of effort, and in your opinion, is not very rewarding. Transforming something strong into something superb takes just as much effort, but is much more thrilling."[204]

Strengths fascinate you. You are observant of the strengths of great leaders and people of success in all walks of life. You often

---

[202] Ibid, page 114.
[203] Ibid, page 115.
[204] Ibid, page 125.

focus your reading and study on such individuals. You recognize that excellence is rarely a random occurrence; rather it is a function of specific attitudes, behaviors, actions, and processes. You make it your quest to discern these, document them, and share them with others to improve performance.

Your focus on strengths–your own and those of others–as a way to stimulate personal and group excellence. You focus on quality, and you prefer working with and for those who demand the best. By seeing what each person naturally does best and empowering them to do it, you provide the fertile ground for excellence.

To take action to maximize your potential (to play to your Strengths):

o "Study success. Deliberately spend time with people who have discovered their strengths. The more you understand how marshaling strengths leads to success, the more likely you will be able to create success in your life."[205]

o Stay focused on your own strengths. Choose one talent you want to maximize each month, and invest in building on it. Refine your skills. Acquire new knowledge. Practice. Keep working toward mastery.

o Make your weaknesses irrelevant by developing working relationships with people who will help offset and compensate for your weaknesses.

o "Seek roles in which you are helping people to succeed. In coaching, managing, mentoring, or teaching roles, your focus on strengths will prove particularly beneficial to others."[206]

o Use your powers of observation, questioning, and discernment to help others recognize their own strengths– and how to best employ them.

---

[205] Ibid, page 127.
[206] Ibid, page 126.

○ "Devise ways to measure your performance and the performance of others. These measures will help you spot strengths, because the best way to identify a strength is to look for sustained levels of excellent performance."[207]

○ "Keep your focus on long-term relationships and goals. Many make a career out of short-term success, but your Maximizer talents will be most energized and effective as you turn top potential into true and lasting greatness."[208]

○ "Develop a plan to use your most powerful strengths outside of work. In doing so, consider how your talents relate to (your) mission in life, and how they might benefit your family or the community."[209]

Watch out for blind spots:

○ Your desire to exhaust all possible outcomes can frustrate those who want to come to a suitable conclusion and move forward. Sometimes, you will need to accept that "good enough" is adequate and appropriate.

○ You might be disappointed when a project or initiative falls short of excellence. Try not to get discouraged when you have to work on or sign off on something that is acceptable, but not ideal in your eyes.

○ Your focus on strengths may be misperceived by others as complacency regarding weaknesses. Be sure to explain why you spend more time building on (strengths) rather than fixing weaknesses. Challenge conventional wisdom which demands that you should find what is broken and fix it. Instead, share your commitment to identifying and investing in the parts of the organization or community that are working. You want most of your resources to be invested in the creation of pockets of sustainable excellence.

---

[207] Ibid, page 127.
[208] Ibid, page 128.
[209] Ibid, page 127.

CORE VALUES OF NOTABLE WORLD LEADERS

Jesus of Nazareth	Mahatma Gandhi	George Washington	Abraham Lincoln
Unconditional Love	Non-violence (Ahimsa)	Integrity	Integrity
Compassion	Truth (Satya)	Resilience	Perseverance
Forgiveness & Mercy	Self-discipline (Swa-dharma)	Perseverance	Resilience
Peacemaking	Simplicity	Courage	Justice
Humility	Self-sufficiency (Swaraj)	Patriotism	Equality
Selflessness	Equality	Sacrifice	Humility
Sacrifice	Social Justice	Humility	Unity
Integrity, moral uprightness	Service to Others (Seva)	Selflessness	Forgiveness & Reconciliation
Honesty	Humility	Ethical Leadership	Democracy
Faith & Trust in God		Unity	Open to diverse opinions
Justice		Civic Responsibility	Learning & knowledge
Courage		Democratic Ideals	Sense of humor
		Republicanism	Faith & Trust in God
		Faith & Trust in God	

Nelson Mandela	Florence Nightingale	Winston Churchill	Martin Luther King
Courage	Compassion	Courage	Equality
Perseverance	Empathy	Determination	Justice
Reconciliation	Service	Resilience	Nonviolent Resistance
Forgiveness	Sacrifice	Perseverance	Dignity
Equality	Innovation	Patriotism	Respect
Justice	Education	Unity	Courage
Servant Leadership	Advocacy	Adaptability	Integrity
Dignity & Respect for all People	Professional Care Standards	Power of the Spoken Word	Service
Freedom	Nursing Reform	Strategic Vision	Empathy
Democracy	Public Health Reform	Open to diverse opinions	Inclusion
		Diplomacy	Unity
			Faith & Trust in God

Benjamin Franklin	Ronald Reagan
Hard Work & Industry	Individual Liberty
Frugality	Patriotism
Lifelong Learning	Economic Opportunity
Innovation	Optimism
Community Service	National Security
Integrity	Anti-Communism
Pragmatism	Traditional Family Values
Common Sense	Power of the Spoken Word
Continuous Improvement	Faith & Trust in God

CORE VALUES OF NOTABLE BUSINESS LEADERS

Jeff Bezos, Amazon	Warren Buffett, Berkshire Hathaway	Andrew Carnegie, Carnegie Steel	Yvon Chouinard, Patagonia
Customer Centricity	Integrity & Ethics	Hard Work & Industry	Environmental Stewardship
Risk-Taking	Humility	Ambition	Quality
Innovation	Long-term Investing	Wealth	Durability
Long-range Thinking	Simplicity	Philanthropy	Work-life balance
Adaptability	Financial Prudence	Lifelong Learning	Corporate activism
Flexibility	Risk Management	Innovation	Ethical eco-friendly sourcing
Data-driven Decision Making	Lifelong Learning	Entrepreneurship	Employee well-being
Quality & High Standards	Generosity	Social Responsibility, Global Peace	Transparency, Accountability. Responsibility
Accountability	Philanthropy	Diplomacy	Innovation

Tim Cook, Apple	Henry Ford, Ford Motors	Andy Grove, Intel	Steve Jobs, Apple
Diversity & Inclusion	Innovation	Innovation & adaptability	Innovation
Privacy & Security	Quality	Strategic leadership	Simplicity
Sustainability	Affordability	Decisiveness	Design excellence, attention to detail
Environmental Stewardship	Efficiency & productivity	Results-based performance standards	Focus on user experience
Innovation	Employee well-being	Operational excellence & efficiency	Perseverance
Product excellence	Simplicity	Perseverance in the face of adversity	Resilience
Social Responsibility	Practicality	Employee development & empowerment	Passion, vision
Community engagement	Patriotism & National Pride		Market disruption
Ethics			
Transparency			

Herb Kelleher, Southwest Airlines	Elon Musk, Tesla & SpaceX
People-centric	Innovation & entrepreneuring
Customer delight	Market disruption
Employee empowerment & engagement	Sustainability
Fun & humor	Environmental Stewardship
Innovation	Ambition
Efficiency	Risk-taking
Continuous Improvement	Long-range Thinking
Adaptability	Tenacity
Ethics	Transparency

www.ingramcontent.com/pod-product-compliance
Lightning Source LLC
Chambersburg PA
CBHW071702120626
46550CB00001B/73